IELTS
Practice
Tests ▶ Plus 2

Morgan Terry
Judith Wilson

Pearson Education Limited
Edinburgh Gate
Harlow
Essex
CM20 2JE
And Associated Companies throughout the World

www.longman.com

ISBN-13: 978-0-582-84645-6 (Book)
ISBN-10: 0-582-84645-5 (Book)
ISBN-13: 978-0-582-84646-3 (Book for pack)
ISBN-10: 0-582-84646-3 (Book for pack)
ISBN-13: 978-1-4058-3312-7 (Book and CD pack)
ISBN-10: 1-4058-3312-2 (Book and CD pack)

Set in 11 pt Humanist 777 BT Light and 11 pt Arial

Printed in Malaysia, KHL-CTP

Tenth impression 2013

Prepared for publication by Stenton Associates

Illustrations by Jackie Harland

Acknowledgements

We are grateful to the following for permission to reproduce copyright material:

The Archaeological Institute of America for an extract adapted from "Space: The Final (Archaeological) Frontier" by P.J. Capelotti published in *Archaeology Magazine*, Volume 57, Number 6; Ellen Bialystok, Ph.D., FRSC for material adapted from "Psychology and Aging" June 2004; The British Library for material adapted from "Visiting The British Library"; Cycle Training UK Ltd for information adapted from www.cycletraining.co.uk; Mark Cousins (author of *The Story of Film* published by Pavilion Books) for an extract from "The Asian Aesthetic" first published in *Prospect* magazine November 2004 www.prospect.magazine.co.uk; Derbyshire County Council – Adult Community Education Service for extracts adapted from the brochure *Derbyshire Adult Community Education 2001/2*; *The Economist* for extracts from "Freud, Finance & Folly" published on 24th January 2004 and "Inside the mind of the consumer" published on 12th June 2004; The Environment Agency for an extract from *Environmental Action* by Tom Harris published Summer 2002; *Geographical* for an extract from "Growing for gold" edited by Christian Amodeo published in *Geographical* Volume 76, No 6, June 2004; Guardian Newspapers Limited for an extract from "Green virtues of green sand" by Paul Brown published in *The Guardian* 23rd October 2003; Lisa Headen, Justin Martin, Kirsten Maser and Katie Barlow for extracts adapted from the report *The affects of weather on the moods of Miami students – Teaching packet final 1*; Independent Newspapers for an extract from "It's 35°C and bone dry" by Steve Connor published in *The Independent* 16th January 2002; Michael Lind for an extract from "Worldly wealth" published in *Prospect Magazine* July 2004; *Le Monde* for an extract from "Painter of time" by Emmanuel de Roux published in *Le Monde* 8th April 2004; *New Scientist* for extracts from "Oops I did it again" by Ben Shouse published 28th July 2001; "If the face fits a woman will know" by Kate Douglas published 26th May 2001; "Hush hour on the highway" by Max Glaskin published 21st February 2004; "Running on empty" by Rick Lovett published 20th March 2004; "Battle of the bag" by Caroline Williams published 11th September 2004 and "Accidental Rainforest" by Fred Pearce published 18th September 2004; New York Times Agency for an extract from "In Africa, Making Offices out of an Anthill" by Donald G McNeil Jr published in *The New York Times* 13th February 1997; Origin Publishing Ltd for extracts from "Why aren't there more tiger attacks?" by Stephen Mills published in *BBC Wildlife Magazine* July 2002 and "Natural Choice (Coffee & Chocolate)" by Simon Birch published in *BBC Wildlife Magazine* July 2004; Pearson Education Limited for an extract from *Global Challenge for A2* by Warn and Naish; Spiked Ltd for an extract from "Keep taking the tablets" by Helen Guldberg published on www.spiked-online.com; and *Which?* for an extract from The Community Legal Service Information Leaflet 2 *Employment: Your Rights at Work* by The Consumers' Association and Ian Hunter.

In some instances we have been unable to trace the owners of copyright material and we would appreciate any information that would enable us to do so.

CONTENTS

Vocabulary Development

As well as providing exam practice, these Practice Tests can help you to develop or consolidate the core language needed for understanding the passages and talks in these tests, and for doing the writing and speaking tasks. There are eight vocabulary sections in the back of the book on pages 159–166 and although the language comes from the specific tests in this book, all the words and structures are commonly found in IELTS. You may wish to work through the topic-related exercises after you have tried a test or before, but try to use these sections to build up your core language.

INTRODUCTION TO IELTS

IELTS stands for *International English Language Testing System*. It is a test of English language skills designed for students who want to study in the medium of English either at university, college or secondary school.

There are two versions of the test: the **Academic Module** and the **General Training (GT) Module**. Students wishing to study at postgraduate or undergraduate level should take the Academic Module. The General Training Module is designed for those candidates who plan to undertake training or secondary school education. The General Training Module is also used in Australia and New Zealand to assess the language skills of incoming migrants. Candidates must decide in advance which of the two modules they wish to sit as the results are not interchangeable.

Students sit the Listening, Reading and Writing papers in that order on one day. The Speaking Test may be held up to two days later, though normally it is taken on the same day, after the Writing Test.

A computerised version of the Listening, Reading and Writing Tests is available at some IELTS centres but the paper-based version of IELTS will always be offered and is the standard format.

Overview of the test

The test is in four parts reflecting the four basic language skills:

- **Listening** *taken by all candidates*
- **Reading** *Academic or General Training*
- **Writing** *Academic or General Training*
- **Speaking** *taken by all candidates*

Results

Performance is rated on a scale of 0–9. Candidates receive a Test Report Form which shows their overall performance reported as a single band score as well as the individual scores they received for each part of the test.

THE IELTS NINE-BAND SCALE

Band 9 – Expert User

Has fully operational command of the language: appropriate, accurate and fluent with complete understanding.

Band 8 – Very Good User

Has fully operational command of the language with only occasional unsystematic inaccuracies and inappropriacies. Misunderstandings may occur in unfamiliar situations. Handles complex detailed argumentation well.

Band 7 – Good User

Has operational command of the language, though with occasional inaccuracies, inappropriacies and misunderstandings in some situations. Generally handles complex language well and understands detailed reasoning.

Band 6 – Competent User

Has generally effective command of the language despite some inaccuracies, inappropriacies and misunderstandings. Can use and understand fairly complex language, particularly in familiar situations.

Band 5 – Modest User

Has partial command of the language, coping with overall meaning in most situations, though is likely to make many mistakes. Should be able to handle basic communication in own field.

Band 4 – Limited User

Basic competence is limited to familiar situations. Has frequent problems in understanding and expression. Is not able to use complex language.

Band 3 – Extremely Limited User

Conveys and understands only general meaning in very familiar situations. Frequent breakdowns in communication occur.

Band 2 – Intermittent User

No real communication is possible except for the most basic information using isolated words or short formulas in familiar situations and to meet immediate needs. Has great difficulty in understanding spoken and written English.

Band 1 – Non User

Essentially has no ability to use the language beyond possibly a few isolated words.

Band 0 – Did not attempt the test

No assessable information provided.

Overview of the IELTS Test

Listening – (played once only) approx 30 minutes + 10 minutes transfer time

	No. of items	Discourse types	No. of speakers	Question types	Target Listening Skills
Section 1	10	A transactional conversation – general context	2	• multiple choice • short answer questions • notes / table / form / flow chart / sentence completion • summary completion • diagram labelling • matching • classification	• listening for main ideas • listening for specific information • understanding speaker's opinion
Section 2	10	An informational talk – general context	1		
Section 3	10	A conversation – education / training context	2–4		
Section 4	10	A lecture – education / training context	1		
	Total 40			Up to 3 question types per passage	

Academic Reading – 60 minutes

	No. of items	Text types	Question types	Target Reading Skills
Passage 1	13–14	Academic texts – i.e. journals, newspapers, textbooks and magazines representative of reading requirements for undergraduate and postgraduate students General interest rather than discipline specific Graded in difficulty	• multiple choice • short answer questions • notes / table / form / flow chart / sentence / summary completion • diagram labelling • classification • paragraph headings • matching lists / phrases • locating information in paragraphs • True / False / Not Given • Yes / No / Not Given	• skimming and scanning • understanding main ideas • reading for detail • understanding opinion and attitude
Passage 2	13–14			
Passage 3	13–14			
	Total 40	Total of 2000–2750 words	Up to 4 question types per passage	

Academic Writing – 60 minutes

	No. of tasks	Text types	Task types	Target Writing Skills
Task 1 (20 mins)\n\nCarries one-third of marks	150 words	A summarising description of graphic or pictorial input	Information transfer exercise\n\n(No explanations of the information required)	• present, describe, interpret, compare data\n• describe a process or how something works\n• use appropriate and accurate language
Task 2 (40 mins)\n\nCarries two-thirds of marks	250 words	An extended piece of discursive writing	Candidates are presented with a given point of view or problem on which to base an organised, extended response	• argue, defend or attack a point of view using supporting evidence\n• identify causes and/or suggest a solution to a problem\n• compare and contrast opinions\n• evaluate the effects of a development
	Total 2	Minimum of 150 words (T1)\n\nMinimum of 250 words (T2)		Task requirements selected from the range above

General Training Reading – 60 minutes

	No. of items	Text types	Question types	Target Reading Skills
Section 1 Social Survival	13–14	Informational texts related to everyday situations	• multiple choice\n• short answer questions\n• notes / table / form / flow chart / sentence / summary completion\n• diagram labelling\n• classification\n• paragraph headings\n• matching statements to texts / sections\n• locating information in paragraphs	• skimming and scanning\n• understanding main ideas\n• reading for detail\n• understanding opinion and attitude
Section 2 Course Related	13–14	Texts from an educational or training context but related to the survival needs of students		
Section 3 General Reading	13–14	One descriptive or narrative text on a topic of general interest		
	Total 40	Total of 2000–2750 words	Up to 4 question types per part	

General Training Writing – 60 minutes

	No. of tasks	Text types	Task types	Target Writing Skills
Task 1 (20 mins) Carries one-third of marks	150 words	A short letter – informal, semi-formal or formal style	An input prompt poses a problem or describes a situation which requires a written response in letter format Three bullet points outline what should be included in the letter	• respond to task • show familiarity with letter writing style • include the information highlighted in the bullets • use appropriate and accurate language
Task 2 (40 mins) Carries two-thirds of marks	250 words	An extended piece of discursive writing	An extended, organised response to questions or issues raised in the task	• express and justify a point of view on the topic • compare and contrast opinions drawing on personal experience • evaluate a situation or development • consider the causes of a problem and suggest possible solutions
	Total 2	Minimum of 150 words (T1) Minimum of 250 words (T2)		Task requirements selected from the range above

Speaking – 11–14 minutes

	No. of parts	Format: Individual interview with an Examiner	Nature of interaction	Target Speaking Skills
Part 1	4–5 mins	Introduction and interview	Examiner asks set questions about familiar topics, using a fixed framework	• giving personal information • talking about everyday issues and habits • expressing opinions
Part 2	3–4 mins	Individual long turn	Candidate has to speak for about two minutes on a topic chosen by the Examiner. Candidate is given one minute to prepare and can make notes in that time	• showing an ability to keep going without interlocutor support • managing language: organisation and expression of ideas • using a range of language appropriately
Part 3	4–5 mins	Exploring the topic – developing a discussion	Examiner leads the candidate to consider more general issues related to the Part 2 topic. Candidate is encouraged to develop language of a more abstract nature	• expressing views and opinions • explaining • displaying understanding of the conversational rules of English

Listening module (approx 30 minutes + transfer time)

About the Listening module

The Listening module has four sections. Before each section, you will hear a short introduction telling you about the speaker/s and the situation. (This is not printed on the question paper.) You then have some time to look through the questions. In Sections 1–3 (but not Section 4) there is also a break in the middle giving you time to look at the questions in the second half. There will be a variety of tasks in the test, and there may be several different task types in one section. Each section is heard once only and the questions always follow the order of information in the recording.

All answers must be correctly spelt.

SECTION 1

Questions 1–10

Section 1 is always a conversation between two people. It is on a topic related to daily life, and often one of the speakers wants to find out information or get something done.

Strategy

Identifying the topic

1 Look at the task on page 9. What is the topic of this listening? What tells you?

Doing the tasks

Task: Note completion

Completing gapped notes is a common activity in IELTS listening. The headings and layout of the notes give you information about what the conversation is about and the type of information required.

2 Look at the notes on the opposite page and read the five headings written in **bold**. What do they tell you about the conversation you will hear?

3 Match these phrases from the recording to the appropriate headings: a) *the details of where you live* b) *They're both …* c) *But the second one's …* d) *the first bookcase is …*

4 Which question/s will need: a) a number b) a material c) a proper name?

Task: Multiple-choice questions

For one type of listening multiple-choice question, you have to choose one answer from a choice of three.

5 Look at Question 10. In this case, you have to choose the correct map. Look at the three maps. What do they all have in common? What are the differences? What key language should you listen for?

Questions 1–9

Complete the notes below.

*Write **NO MORE THAN THREE WORDS AND/OR A NUMBER** for each answer.*

Tip Strip

- When you read the instructions for tasks such as note-taking, <u>underline</u> the number of words you are allowed to write for each answer.
- **Questions 1, 3, 8:** For questions involving things like measurements or money you must write the unit of measurement (e.g. **cm, m, £**) if this is not already given on the question paper. You do not need to write the full form (e.g. **centimetres**) – the abbreviated form or the symbol is fine.
- At the end of each section, check your work. Notice that although the instructions say *write no more than three words*, your answers may all be shorter than this. For Questions 2, 4, 5, 6, 7 and 9 your answers should be just one word.

ENQUIRY ABOUT BOOKCASES

Example	*Answer*
Number of bookcases available:	........*two*........

Both bookcases

Width: **1** ....

Made of: **2** ....

First bookcase

Cost: **3** ....

Colour: **4** ....

Number of shelves: six (four are **5** ....)

Second bookcase

Colour: dark brown

Other features: – almost 80 years old

                              – has a **6** .... at the bottom

                              – has glass **7** ....

Cost: **8** ....

Details of seller

Name: Mrs **9** ....

Address: 41 Oak Rise, Stanton.

Question 10

*Choose the correct letter, **A**, **B** or **C**.*

Which map shows the correct location of the seller's house?

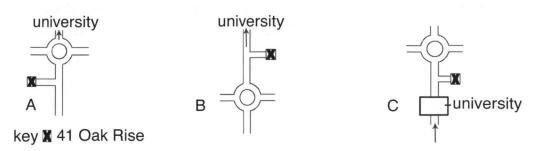

key ▣ 41 Oak Rise

Questions 11–20

In **Section 2** you will hear one main speaker giving information about a public event or about something that the listeners may be involved in or take part in.

Strategy

Identifying the topic

1 Look through Questions 11–20. What is the main topic of the talk? How many different task types are there? What are they?

Doing the tasks

Task: Summary completion

In summary completion tasks you have to fill in gaps in a short paragraph which summarises the main ideas of one part of the talk. The sentences will not be exactly the same as what you hear – you need to listen for parallel expressions. Use words from the recording to complete the gaps.

2 Look at Questions 11–13 below. Is the information given in note form or in complete sentences? Which question will need a) an adjective b) a number c) a place?

3 Where will the break in the recording probably come?

Task: Table completion

In table completion tasks you have to fill in gaps in a table which will have several columns. Each column will have a heading. The information is usually in note form, so you do not generally need to include words like articles or verbs.

4 Look at the table on page 11. What three general types of information will be given in this part of the talk? What tells you?

5 Match these phrases from the recording to the appropriate headings: a) *His paintings depict* b) *who came here from* c) *was born in* d) *her paintings use* e) *when she arrived in New Zealand* (the extracts are in order).

6 Look at the numbered gaps in the table. Do they go a) across the rows b) up and down the columns?

7 Look carefully at the gaps in the table. How many will probably require a noun? Which of the gapped words will definitely be plural forms? How do you know? Which may be either singular or plural?

Questions 11–13

Complete the summary below.

*Write **NO MORE THAN THREE WORDS AND/OR A NUMBER** for each answer.*

Charity Art Sale

The paintings will be displayed in the Star Gallery and in a nearby

11 .... The sale of pictures will begin at **12** .... on

Thursday, and there will be refreshments beforehand. The money raised

will all be used to help **13** .... children in New Zealand and other

countries.

Questions 14–20

Complete the table below.

Write **NO MORE THAN THREE WORDS AND/OR A NUMBER** *for each answer.*

Tip Strip
• Remember to check your work, especially plural endings. When you have finished, check that you have written five plural nouns in your answers to this section.

Artist	Personal information	Type of painting
Don Studley	• daughter is recovering from a problem with her back • self-taught artist	• pictures of the 14 .... of New Zealand
James Chang	• originally from Taiwan • had a number of 15 .... there	• 16 .... paintings • strong colours
Natalie Stevens	• has shown pictures in many countries • is an artist and a website 17	• soft colours, various media • mainly does 18 ....
Christine Shin	• lived in New Zealand for 19 .... • Korean	• paintings are based on 20 .... • watercolours of New Zealand landscapes

Questions 21–30

Section 3 is a conversation about an academic topic such as a course, project, assignment or piece of research. It usually involves two or three speakers, who may be students and/or tutors.

> ### Strategy
>
> **Identifying the topic**
> 1 Look at the first task below. Is this discussion going to be about a course, a project or a piece of research? How do you know?
>
> **Doing the tasks**
> **Task: Classification**
> In a classification task you have to match points from the listening to a set of groups or classes. As with all IELTS listening tasks, the numbered points will be heard in order.
> 2 What general idea are the three choices for the classification task below all related to?
> 3 To do the task, you need to listen for expressions related to this general idea. Match each extract from the recording to one of the options A–C in the task.
> a) *We can't just choose anyone.*
> b) *'I guess it's OK if … .' 'No, it's got to be … .'*
> c) *it's up to us*
>
> **Task: Note completion**
> 4 Look at Questions 26–29 on page 13. Are they on the same topic as the first task or a completely different topic? How do you know?

Questions 21–25

What instructions were the students given about their project?

A they must do this
B they can do this if they want to
C they can't do this

*Write the correct letter, **A**, **B** or **C** next to Questions 21–25.*

21 Choose a writer from a list provided.   ......

22 Get biographical information from the Internet.   ......

23 Study a collection of poems.   ......

24 Make a one-hour video.   ......

25 Refer to key facts in the writer's life.   ......

Tip Strip
• In a conversation, one person may know more about the topic than the other. Listen carefully to what both people say before deciding on your answer.

Complete the notes below.

*Write **NO MORE THAN THREE WORDS** for each answer.*

Other requirements for the project

- extract chosen from the author's work must reflect the **26** .... and .... of the author.

- students must find sound effects and **27** .... to match the texts they choose.

- students must use a **28** .... of computer software programs to make the video.

- students must include information about the **29** .... of all material

Criteria for assessment

- completion of all components – 25%

- **30** .... (must represent essence of author's work) – 50%

- artistic and technical design of video – 25%

Questions 31–40

Section 4 is a talk or lecture on an academic topic. There is only one speaker. There is no break in the middle, so you must look through all the questions in the time given at the beginning.

Strategy

Identifying the topic

1 At the beginning, the lecturer tells you this talk is about ecology. Look through the questions and decide how the talk is structured. Is it a) a problem and its solution b) a discovery and its explanation c) an event and its result?

Doing the tasks

Task: Multiple choice

2 Look at multiple-choice Questions 31–33 below and underline key words in the sentence opening.

3 Key ideas may be expressed differently in the recording and the questions. Find phrases in Question 31 which match these expressions from the recording a) *remoter regions* b) *environment is harsh*.

Identifying topic shift

As there is no break in Section 4, it is especially important to listen for words signalling a change from one part of the lecture to another.

4 Which of the following expressions could be used to introduce the second half of the lecture: a) *Now the research I want to tell you about was …* b) *So, the big question is: how can these colonies survive there?* c) *All of this might have great significance for …* ?

Task: Sentence completion

In sentence completion tasks, the sentences summarise the main ideas, so this is similar to a summary completion task. The sentences will have the same meaning as the information in the recording but will use parallel expressions. The completed sentences must be grammatically correct.

5 Underline key words and phrases in Sentences 34–40.

6 Which gap in Sentences 34–40 needs a) the name of a process b) the name of a place c) an adjective?

Questions 31–33

*Choose the correct answer, **A**, **B** or **C**.*

31 'Extremophiles' are life forms that can live in

    A isolated areas.

    B hostile conditions.

    C new habitats.

32 The researchers think that some of the organisms they found in Antarctica are

    A new species.

    B ancient colonies.

    C types of insects.

33 The researchers were the first people to find life forms in Antarctica

    A in the soil.

    B under the rock surface.

    C on the rocks.

Questions 34–40

Complete the sentences below.

*Write **ONE WORD** for each answer.*

How the extremophiles survive

34 Access to the sun's heat can create a .... for some organisms.

35 The deeper the soil, the higher the .... of salt.

36 Salt can protect organisms against the effects of .... , even at very low temperatures.

37 All living things must have access to .... water.

38 Salt plays a part in the process of .... , which prevents freezing.

39 The environment of .... is similar to the dry valleys of Antarctica.

40 This research may provide evidence of the existence of extraterrestrial life forms and their possible .... on other planets.

Tip Strip
Questions 34–40:

• In questions where you have to write words, the word you need for the answer will always be in the recording.

• You should write the word exactly as you hear it, without changing the form in any way (e.g. from plural to singular).

• If the word you choose is not grammatically correct, you have chosen the wrong answer.

• **Question 37:** You only need to write an adjective here. If you add an extra noun from the recording (e.g. *form*) your answer will be grammatically incorrect.

Tip Strip
Questions 1–40:

• When you have finished all the sections, practise transferring your answers to the answer sheet (page 208).

• You should only copy what you have written yourself. Do not copy anything printed on the question paper.

• As you copy your answers, check that the words you have written make sense in the context, are grammatically correct and are correctly spelt.

• Notice how long it takes you to transfer your answers. (In the exam you will have ten minutes.)

Reading module (1 hour)

About the Reading module
The Reading module has three reading passages on academic topics of general interest. There are forty questions, and a variety of task types. Each question is worth one mark, so you should aim to spend about the same amount of time on each part.

READING PASSAGE 1

*You should spend about 20 minutes on **Questions 1–13**, which are based on Reading Passage 1 on pages 18–19.*

Strategy

Finding out what the text is about
In order to locate the answers to the questions, and also to follow the writer's main argument, it is useful to spend a short time getting an overview of the text.

1 Read the title and subtitle of Reading Passage 1 on page 18 and look quickly through Paragraph 1. Which phrase has a similar meaning to *snow-maker*? Why is this device needed?

Strategy

Task: Matching paragraph headings
Often it is useful to skim quickly through the entire text to get a better idea of the content. However, here the first task (matching headings to paragraphs) will help you to do this. You have to choose the heading which best summarises the paragraph.

1 Read the first paragraph carefully, then look through the list of headings. The answer (v) has been given as an example. In Paragraph A, underline the part of the text that refers to a) the problem and b) the solution.
2 Why is heading iii not the correct heading for Paragraph A?
3 Read Paragraph B and look at the example heading (x). Why is this a better answer than heading ix?

Now do Questions 1–5. Look down the list of headings and choose the one that you think matches best. You need to find a heading that summarises or paraphrases the overall meaning of the paragraph.

Questions 1–5

Reading Passage 1 has seven paragraphs A–G.

Choose the correct heading for each paragraph from the list of headings below.

Write the correct number (i–x) in boxes 1–5 on your answer sheet.

List of headings
List of headings
i Considering ecological costs
ii Modifications to the design of the snow gun
iii The need for different varieties of snow
iv Local concern over environmental issues
v A problem and a solution
vi Applications beyond the ski slopes
vii Converting wet snow to dry snow
viii New method for calculating modifications
ix Artificial process, natural product
x Snow formation in nature

Example	*Answer*
Paragraph **A**	*v*
Paragraph **B**	*x*

1 Paragraph **C**

2 Paragraph **D**

3 Paragraph **E**

4 Paragraph **F**

5 Paragraph **G**

Snow-makers

Skiing is big business nowadays. But what can ski resort owners do if the snow doesn't come?

A In the early to mid twentieth century, with the growing popularity of skiing, ski slopes became extremely profitable businesses. But ski resort owners were completely dependent on the weather; if it didn't snow, or didn't snow enough, they had to close everything down. Fortunately, a device called the snow gun can now provide snow whenever it is needed. These days such machines are standard equipment in the vast majority of ski resorts around the world, making it possible for many resorts to stay open four months or more a year.

B Snow formed by natural weather systems comes from water vapour in the atmosphere. The water vapour condenses into droplets, forming clouds. If the temperature is sufficiently low, the water droplets freeze into tiny ice crystals. More water particles then condense onto the crystal and join with it to form a snowflake. As the snowflake grows heavier, it falls towards the Earth.

C The snow gun works very differently from a natural weather system, but it accomplishes exactly the same thing. The device basically works by combining water and air. Two different hoses are attached to the gun, one leading from a water pumping station which pumps water up from a lake or reservoir, and the other leading from an air compressor. When the compressed air passes through the hose into the gun, it atomises the water – that is, it disrupts the stream so that the water splits up into tiny droplets. The droplets are then blown out of the gun and if the outside temperature is below 0ºC, ice crystals will form, and will then make snowflakes in the same way as natural snow.

D Snow-makers often talk about dry snow and wet snow. Dry snow has a relatively low amount of water, so it is very light and powdery. This type of snow is excellent for skiing because skis glide over it easily without getting stuck in wet slush. One of the advantages of using a snow-maker is that this powdery snow can be produced to give the ski slopes a level surface. However, on slopes which receive heavy use, resort owners also use denser, wet snow underneath the dry snow. Many resorts build up the snow depth this way once or twice a year, and then regularly coat the trails with a layer of dry snow throughout the winter.

E The wetness of snow is dependent on the temperature and humidity outside, as well as the size of the water droplets launched by the gun. Snow-makers have to adjust the proportions of water and air in their snow guns to get the perfect snow consistency for the outdoor weather conditions. Many ski slopes now do this with a central computer system that is connected to weather-reading stations all over the slope.

F But man-made snow makes heavy demands on the environment. It takes about 275,000 litres of water to create a blanket of snow covering a 60 x 60 metre area. Most resorts pump water from one or more reservoirs located in low-lying areas. The run-off water from the slopes feeds back into these reservoirs, so the resort can actually use the same water over and over again. However, considerable amounts of energy are needed to run the large air-compressing pumps, and the diesel engines which run them also cause air pollution.

G Because of the expense of making snow, ski resorts have to balance the cost of running the machines with the benefits of extending the ski season, making sure they only make snow when it is really needed, and when it will bring the maximum amount of profit in return for the investment. But man-made snow has a number of other uses as well. A layer of snow keeps a lot of the Earth's heat from escaping into the atmosphere, so farmers often use man-made snow to provide insulation for winter crops. Snow-making machines have played a big part in many movie productions. Movie producers often take several months to shoot scenes that cover just a few days. If the movie takes place in a snowy setting, the set decorators have to get the right amount of snow for each day of shooting either by adding man-made snow or melting natural snow. And another important application of man-made snow is its use in the tests that aircraft must undergo in order to ensure that they can function safely in extreme conditions.

Task: Diagram labelling

Passages which describe mechanical devices or processes may include a diagram labelling task.

1 Look at the diagram below. What does it illustrate? How do you know?
2 Which paragraph in the passage explains how this device works? (Use the heading matching task to help you).

Read the paragraph carefully and study the diagram at the same time. Some labels are already given. Use these to help you.

3 On which side of the diagram does the process begin – left or right?
4 How many words can you write for each answer?

Now do Questions 6–8. Be careful to copy the words you need accurately from the passage.

Questions 6–8

Label the diagram below.

Choose **NO MORE THAN TWO WORDS** *from the passage for each answer.*

Write your answers in boxes 6–8 on your answer sheet.

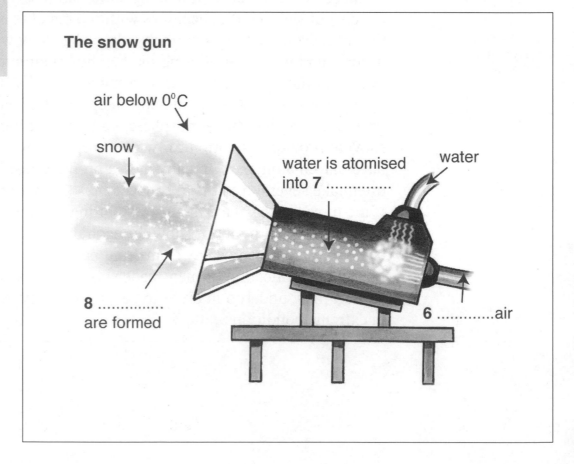

The snow gun

air below 0°C

snow

water is atomised into 7 ....

water

8 ....
are formed

6 ....air

Questions 9–13

Complete the sentences below.

Choose **NO MORE THAN THREE WORDS** from the passage for each answer.

Write your answers in boxes 9–13 on your answer sheet.

9 Dry snow is used to give slopes a level surface, while wet snow is used to increase the .... on busy slopes.

10 To calculate the required snow consistency, the .... and .... of the atmosphere must first be measured.

11 The machinery used in the process of making the snow consumes a lot of .... , which is damaging to the environment.

12 Artificial snow is used in agriculture as a type of .... for plants in cold conditions.

13 Artificial snow may also be used in carrying out safety checks on ....

Questions 14–26

You should spend about 20 minutes on Questions 14–26, which are based on Reading Passage 2 below.

Strategy

Finding out what the text is about
1 The title of this text asks a question. In which paragraph, the first or the last, would you expect to find a) the answer to the question b) an expansion of the question? Look at Paragraphs A and G to check your answer.
2 Is this text a) mainly about tigers b) about animals in general? Scan quickly through the text, looking for animal names, to find the answer.

Why are so few tigers man-eaters?

A As you leave the Bandhavgarh National Park in central India, there is a notice which shows a huge, placid tiger. The notice says, 'You may not have seen me, but I have seen you.' There are more than a billion people in India and Indian tigers probably see humans every single day of their lives. Tigers can and do kill almost anything they meet in the jungle – they will even attack elephants and rhino. Surely, then, it is a little strange that attacks on humans are not more frequent.

B Some people might argue that these attacks were in fact common in the past. British writers of adventure stories, such as Jim Corbett, gave the impression that village life in India in the early years of the twentieth century involved a state of constant siege by man-eating tigers. But they may have overstated the terror spread by tigers. There were also far more tigers around in those days (probably 60,000 in the subcontinent, compared to just 3000 today). So in proportion, attacks appear to have been as rare then as they are today.

C It is widely assumed that the constraint is fear; but what exactly are tigers afraid of? Can they really know that we may be even better armed than they are? Surely not. Has the species programmed the experiences of all tigers with humans into its genes to be inherited as instinct? Perhaps. But I think the explanation may be more simple and, in a way, more intriguing.

D Since the growth of ethology[1] in the 1950s, we have tried to understand animal behaviour from the animal's point of view. Until the first elegant experiments by pioneers in the field, such as Konrad Lorenz, naturalists wrote about animals as if they were slightly less intelligent humans. Jim Corbett's breathless accounts of his duels with man-eaters in truth tell us more about Jim Corbett than they do about the animals. The principle of ethology, on the other hand, requires us to attempt to think in the same way as the animal we are studying thinks, and to observe every tiny detail of its behaviour without imposing our own human significances on its actions.

E I suspect that a tiger's fear of humans lies not in some preprogrammed ancestral logic but in the way he actually perceives us visually. If you try to think like a tiger, a human in a car might appear just to be part of the car, and because tigers don't eat cars the human is safe – unless the car is menacing the tiger or its cubs, in which case a brave or enraged tiger may charge. A human on foot is a different sort of puzzle. Imagine a tiger sees a man who is 1.8m tall. A tiger is less than 1m tall but he may be up to 3m long from head to tail. So when a tiger sees the man face on, it might not be unreasonable for him to assume that the man is 6m long. If he met a deer of this size, he might attack the animal by leaping on its back, but when he looks behind the man, he can't see a back. From the front the man is huge, but looked at from the side he all but disappears. This must be very disconcerting. A hunter has to be confident that it can tackle its prey, and no one is confident when they are disconcerted. This is especially true of a solitary hunter such as the tiger and

may explain why lions – particularly young lionesses who tend to encourage one another to take risks – are more dangerous than tigers.

F If the theory that a tiger is disconcerted to find that a standing human is both very big and yet somehow invisible is correct, the opposite should be true of a squatting human. A squatting human is half the size and presents twice the spread of back, and more closely resembles a medium-sized deer. If tigers were simply frightened of all humans, then a squatting person would be no more attractive as a target than a standing one. This, however, appears not to be the case. Many incidents of attacks on people involve villagers squatting or bending over to cut grass for fodder or building material.

G The fact that humans stand upright may therefore not just be something that distinguishes them from nearly all other species, but also a factor that helped them to survive in a dangerous and unpredictable environment.

---

[1] **ethology** – the branch of zoology that studies the behaviour of animals in their natural habitats

Task: Locating information in paragraphs

In Reading Passage 1, you matched headings to paragraphs in order to reflect the main idea of each paragraph. In the task below you have to look in more detail at the different types of information given in paragraphs – e.g. explanations, reasons, examples or problems.

1 Read through Paragraph A. Which sentence has a parallel meaning to *tiger attacks on humans might be expected to happen more often than they do* in Question 15?

2 Question 15 asks you to find a *reason*. Does Paragraph A give a reason for expecting tiger attacks on humans to be frequent? If so, what is it?

3 Now look through the rest of the text and answer Questions 14–18. Remember to check that you have the right type of information in each case. Mark the question numbers in the text.

Questions 14–18

*Reading Passage 2 has seven paragraphs labelled **A–G**.*

Which paragraph contains the following information?

*Write the correct letter **A–G** in boxes 14–18 on your answer sheet.*

14 a rejected explanation of why tiger attacks on humans are rare

15 a reason why tiger attacks on humans might be expected to happen more often than they do

16 examples of situations in which humans are more likely to be attacked by tigers

17 a claim about the relative frequency of tiger attacks on humans

18 an explanation of tiger behaviour based on the principles of ethology

Tip Strip

• Read the text one paragraph at a time, thinking about the main types of information it contains and looking through the items for any that match the information in the paragraph. (Some paragraphs may have no matching information.)

True / False / Not Given

These questions focus on factual information. The questions follow the order of information in the passage and may cover one section of the passage, or the whole passage.

1 Look at Question 19 and underline the key words. (Proper nouns such as those referring to people and places are often useful key words as these will be the same in the text.)

2 Scan quickly from the beginning of the text to locate the section you need. Read this section of the text carefully and decide if the statement is **True** (there is information in the text to tell you that these tigers *are* a protected species), **False** (there is information that they *are not* a protected species) or **Not Given** (there is no information about their status as a protected species).

Mark the section of the text where you found the answer, then continue with the other questions. If you can't find the answer to one question, leave it and come back to it later.

Questions 19–23

Do the following statements agree with the information given in Reading Passage 2?

In boxes 19–23 on your answer sheet write

TRUE　　　　*if the statement agrees with the information*
FALSE　　　　*if the statement contradicts the information*
NOT GIVEN　*if there is no information on this*

19 Tigers in the Bandhavgarh National Park are a protected species.

20 Some writers of fiction have exaggerated the danger of tigers to man.

21 The fear of humans may be passed down in a tiger's genes.

22 Konrad Lorenz claimed that some animals are more intelligent than humans.

23 Ethology involves applying principles of human behaviour to animals.

Questions 24–26

*Choose the correct answer, **A**, **B**, **C** or **D**.*

Write your answers in boxes 24–26 on your answer sheet.

24 Why do tigers rarely attack people in cars?

   A They have learned that cars are not dangerous.

   B They realise that people in cars cannot be harmed.

   C They do not think people in cars are living creatures.

   D They do not want to put their cubs at risk.

25 The writer says that tigers rarely attack a man who is standing up because

   A they are afraid of the man's height.

   B they are confused by the man's shape.

   C they are puzzled by the man's lack of movement.

   D they are unable to look at the man directly.

26 A human is more vulnerable to tiger attack when squatting because

   A he may be unaware of the tiger's approach.

   B he cannot easily move his head to see behind him.

   C his head becomes a better target for the tiger.

   D his back appears longer in relation to his height.

*You should spend about 20 minutes on **Questions 27–40**, which are based on Reading Passage 3 below.*

Strategy

Finding out what the text is about

1 The title of the text below does not give you the main topic, but does suggest that it is to do with medicine. Look at the subtitle and underline a phrase which gives you the main topic of the text.

2 How do you expect this text to be organised: a) a problem and a solution b) a chronological account c) good points and bad points? Skim quickly through the text, looking at the opening to each paragraph only, to check.

Keep taking the tablets

The history of aspirin is a product of a rollercoaster ride through time, of accidental discoveries, intuitive reasoning and intense corporate rivalry

In the opening pages of *Aspirin: The Remarkable Story of a Wonder Drug*, Diarmuid Jeffreys describes this little white pill as 'one of the most amazing creations in medical history, a drug so astonishingly versatile that it can relieve headache, ease your aching limbs, lower your temperature and treat some of the deadliest human diseases'.

Its properties have been known for thousands of years. Ancient Egyptian physicians used extracts from the willow tree as an analgesic, or pain killer. Centuries later the Greek physician Hippocrates recommended the bark of the willow tree as a remedy for the pains of childbirth and as a fever reducer. But it wasn't until the eighteenth and nineteenth centuries that salicylates – the chemical found in the willow tree – became the subject of serious scientific investigation. The race was on to identify the active ingredient and to replicate it synthetically. At the end of the nineteenth century a German company, Friedrich Bayer & Co, succeeded in creating a relatively safe and very effective chemical compound, acetylsalicylic acid, which was renamed aspirin.

The late nineteenth century was a fertile period for experimentation, partly because of the hunger among scientists to answer some of the great scientific questions, but also because those questions were within their means to answer. One scientist in a laboratory with some chemicals and a test tube could make significant breakthroughs – whereas today, in order to map the human genome for instance, one needs 'an army of researchers, a bank of computers and millions and millions of dollars'.

But an understanding of the nature of science and scientific inquiry is not enough on its own to explain how society innovates. In the nineteenth century, scientific advance was closely linked to the industrial revolution. This was a period when people frequently had the means, motive and determination to take an idea and turn it into reality. In the case of aspirin that happened piecemeal – a series of minor, often unrelated advances, fertilised by the century's broader economic, medical and scientific developments, that led to one big final breakthrough.

The link between big money and pharmaceutical innovation is also a significant one. Aspirin's continued shelf life was ensured because for the first 70 years of its life, huge amounts of money were put into promoting it as an ordinary everyday analgesic. In the 1970s other analgesics, such as ibuprofen and paracetamol, were entering the market, and the pharmaceutical companies then focused on publicising these new drugs. But just at the same time, discoveries were made regarding the beneficial role of aspirin in preventing heart attacks, strokes and other afflictions. Had it not been for these findings, this pharmaceutical marvel may well have disappeared.

So the relationship between big money and drugs is an odd one. Commercial markets are necessary for developing new products and ensuring that they remain around long enough for scientists to carry out research on them. But the commercial markets are just as likely to kill off certain products when something more attractive comes along. In the case of aspirin, a potential 'wonder drug' was around for over 70 years without anybody investigating the way in which it achieved its effects, because they were making more than enough money out of it as it was. If ibuprofen or paracetamol had entered the market just a decade earlier, aspirin might then not be here today. It would be just another forgotten drug that people hadn't bothered to explore.

None of the recent discoveries of aspirin's benefits were made by the big pharmaceutical companies; they were made by scientists working in the public sector. 'The reason for that is very simple and straightforward,' Jeffreys says in his book. 'Drug companies will only pursue research that is going to deliver financial benefits. There's no profit in aspirin any more. It is incredibly inexpensive with tiny profit margins and it has no patent any more, so anyone can produce it.' In fact, there's almost a disincentive for drug companies to further boost the drug, he argues, as it could possibly put them out of business by stopping them from selling their more expensive brands.

So what is the solution to a lack of commercial interest in further exploring the therapeutic benefits of aspirin? More public money going into clinical trials, says Jeffreys. 'If I were the

"Try to find something that works like aspirin but costs much more."

Department of Health, I would say "this is a very inexpensive drug. There may be a lot of other things we could do with it." We should put a lot more money into trying to find out.'

Jeffreys' book – which not only tells the tale of a 'wonder drug' but also explores the nature of innovation and the role of big business, public money and regulation – reminds us why such research is so important.

Tip Strip
• The first set of questions will probably refer to the first part of the text.

Questions 27–32

*Complete each sentence with the correct ending **A–H** from the box below.*

*Write the correct letter **A–H** in boxes 27–32 on your answer sheet.*

27 Ancient Egyptian and Greek doctors were aware of

28 Frederick Bayer & Co were able to reproduce

29 The development of aspirin was partly due to the effects of

30 The creation of a market for aspirin as a painkiller was achieved through

31 Aspirin might have become unavailable without

32 The way in which aspirin actually worked was not investigated by

---

A the discovery of new medical applications.

B the negative effects of publicity.

C the large pharmaceutical companies.

D the industrial revolution.

E the medical uses of a particular tree.

F the limited availability of new drugs.

G the chemical found in the willow tree.

H commercial advertising campaigns.

Yes / No / Not Given

This task is similar to True / False / Not Given except that the questions focus on opinions rather than facts.

1 Look at Question 33. Which three paragraphs in the text describe events in the nineteenth century?
2 Read the second of these paragraphs. Which phrase reflects the idea of 'small-scale research'? Which phrase means 'important discoveries'?
3 Does Question 33 exactly reflect the views of the writer?
Now continue with Questions 34–37 in the same way.

Questions 33–37

Do the following statements agree with the views of the writer in Reading Passage 3?

In boxes 33–37 on your answer sheet write

YES   *if the statement agrees with the views of the writer*
NO   *if the statement contradicts the views of the writer*
NOT GIVEN *if it is impossible to say what the writer thinks about this*

33 For nineteenth-century scientists, small-scale research was enough to make important discoveries.

34 The nineteenth-century industrial revolution caused a change in the focus of scientific research.

35 The development of aspirin in the nineteenth century followed a structured pattern of development.

36 In the 1970s sales of new analgesic drugs overtook sales of asprin.

37 Commercial companies may have both good and bad effects on the availability of pharmaceutical products.

Questions 38–40

Complete the summary below using the list of words A–I below.

Write the correct letter A–I in boxes 38–40 on your answer sheet.

Research into aspirin

Jeffreys argues that the reason why **30** .... did not find out about new uses of aspirin is that aspirin is no longer a **39** .... drug. He therefore suggests that there should be **40** .... support for further research into the possible applications of the drug.

A useful	**B** cheap	**C** state	**D** international
E major drug companies		**F** profitable	**G** commercial
H public sector scientists		**I** health officials	

Writing module (1 hour)

About Writing Task 1

In Academic Writing Task 1 you must describe the information shown in a diagram. You must write at least 150 words in your description and you should spend no more than 20 minutes on this task as it represents only one-third of the writing marks.

STRATEGY

Before you write make sure you understand the information the diagram is showing. Allow yourself two or three minutes to read the task carefully and look at the diagram.

---

1 Understanding the information

Look at the task opposite and answer the questions below.
1 Which country is the data about?
2 What two main periods of time does the horizontal axis show?
3 What do the two lines represent?
4 What measurement is used in the vertical axis?
5 What does the gap between the lines represent?

2 Identifying the main topic

Different types of diagram show different information. Graphs show changes. What is the main topic of the graph opposite?
1 changes in per capita energy consumption
2 changes in type of energy used
3 changes in the gap between energy production and consumption
4 changes in modes of production

3 Writing the introduction

Choose expressions below to paraphrase the introduction.

The graph **1** *compares figures for / gives figures for / shows changes in* **2** *US energy / the consumption and production of energy in the US / the gap between US energy consumption and production* **3** *from 1950 to 2000 / between 1950 and 2000 / since 1950.* It also **4** *shows figures / predicts figures / estimates trends* **5** *up to 2025 / for 2025 / by 2025.*

4 Using the right language for the right information

a Look at the types of information typically shown in graphs and identify three things you need to describe in the task on page 33.
1 changes over time
2 a comparison of different things
3 contrasting trends
4 a contrast across age groups
5 a prediction of future trends
6 changing proportions over time

b To practise using the right kind of language look at vocabulary page 159.

5 Selecting and organising information

Focus on the main trends. Do not simply list all the information.

a Look at the openings to five pieces of information and put them in a logical order.
1 However, production grew only gradually over the next …
2 Projections up to 2025 suggest that this trend …
3 Between 1950 and 1970 both the production and consumption of energy increased …
4 In contrast, growth in consumption …
5 Energy imports needed to bridge this gap therefore increased …

b Group the information into three paragraphs.

6 Summarising statement

It is important to summarise the key information. You can do this at the beginning or at the end of your description. Do NOT try to explain the information.

a Choose the best summarising statement for this Task 1.

1 Both consumption and production of energy in the US will continue to rise.

2 Energy consumption in the US is rising faster than production.

3 Energy production in the US is not keeping up with consumption, so imports will continue to increase.

b Write three signals you can use to indicate that this is your summary.
*For example: **Overall, the graph indicates that ...***

7 Timed writing

You have already thought carefully about this task. Now write your own answer in **15 minutes**.

Look at the sample answer only AFTER you have written your own.

WRITING TASK 1

You should spend about 20 minutes on this task.

The graph below compares figures for the production and consumption of energy in the US from 1950 to 2000. It also predicts figures for 2025.

Summarise the information by selecting and reporting the main features, and make comparisons where relevant.

Write at least 150 words.

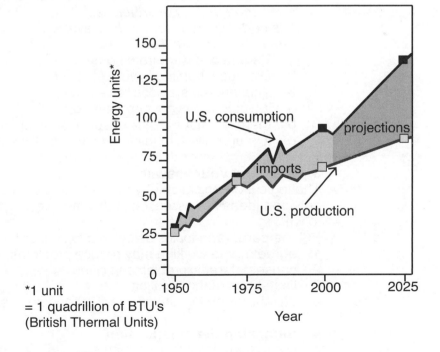

*1 unit
= 1 quadrillion of BTU's
(British Thermal Units)

8 Assessing your writing

a Remember to edit your writing for any common mistakes.

b Use the Task 1 list on page 156 for checking your written answer.

About Writing Task 2

This task usually consists of a background statement that raises issues about a topic of general interest. This is followed by a question or instruction to the candidate.

Strategy

Before you start to write
• identify the issues.
• be clear about what you have to do.
• plan your answer.

1   Identifying the issues

These are not always stated explicitly so you need to read the question carefully. Tick three ideas below that are implied in the Task 2 question opposite.
1   Traffic in cities today is a problem.
2   There are too many people living in cities so some should move out.
3   There is not enough transport for everyone to use.
4   Traffic problems are mainly due to individuals travelling for work, study or shopping purposes.
5   There are not enough jobs in the economy today.
6   Today people can work, study or shop from home.

2   Being clear about what you need to do

This question type asks you to agree or disagree with the statement.
a   Do you agree or disagree with the three ideas you identified in Exercise 1? Do you agree that this is the ONLY way to reduce traffic problems?
It is likely that you will agree with some ideas but probably not all of them. Use signals to indicate this.
b   Combine 1–3 and a–c below using each of the expressions given.
   Even though … , nevertheless, …
   It is certainly true that … . However, …
   It may be the case that … , but …
   1   People can work from home
   2   Distance learning is very efficient
   3   This presents a possible solution
   a   it would be a very unpopular one.
   b   there would be a lack of social contact for students.
   c   it is unrealistic to think they would all want to.

3   Planning your answer

The logical organisation of your ideas and the way you signal the relationships between ideas are assessed in this module, so plan your answer before you start to write.
Put the paragraph topics below in a logical order.
1   agree: home working may reduce problems, but not the only solution.
2   causes of traffic problems in cities
3   limitations of this solution
4   distance working, studying and shopping possibilities

4   Signalling the organisation

a   Look at the following opening expressions. Put them in a logical order to reflect your argument.
   a   It is also true that today …
   b   In terms of other solutions, we need to …
   c   Probably these are mainly due to …
   d   So, in conclusion, I think that …
   e   However, even if …
   f   It is certainly true that today …

5 Supporting your ideas

It is not enough to state your point of view. You have to justify your ideas by supporting them with evidence.

a Look at the supporting ideas below and match them to the three ideas in Exercise 1.

   a the options IT gives us today.

   b the number of vehicles on our roads and the amount of pollution they cause.

   c the rush hours we experience every morning and evening.

b Write supporting sentences for the ideas in Exercise 1. Begin with each of the following in turn:

   1 *This is obvious from …*

   2 *This is evident in …*

   3 *We can see this in …*

6 Using academic language

a Giving your opinion does not mean that you always write *I think*. Use impersonal expressions for a more academic style.

e.g. *It is obvious that …*

Skim the exercises above and add other expressions to the list.

b For help with vocabulary, look at the Language of the Urban Environment section on page 165.

7 Speed writing

Write your own answer to Task 2 below. Spend no more than 35 minutes writing it.

WRITING TASK 2

You should spend about 40 minutes on this task.

Write about the following topic.

The only way to reduce the amount of traffic in cities today is by reducing the need for people to travel from home for work, education or shopping.

To what extent do you agree or disagree?

Give reasons for your answer and include any relevant examples from your own knowledge or experience.

Write at least 250 words.

8 Assessing your response

a Check your writing for the most common grammatical and vocabulary mistakes you make.

b Use the list for Task 2 on pages 157–158 for checking your answer.

Speaking module (11–14 minutes)

About the Speaking module
In the three parts of this module you are assessed on how clearly and fluently you can express ideas and information, the range of vocabulary and grammar you can use and how clear your pronunciation is.

Strategy

Listen carefully. Before each set of questions the examiner will tell you which topic you need to think about.

PART 1

1 Giving relevant answers
Look at answers 1–6 below and identify which ones directly answer the question.
Q: How often do you use computers?
1 It's very important to use computers.
2 I don't know.
3 Only about twice a week.
4 All the time.
5 I love using the computer.
6 Not much compared with some people.

2 Extending your answers
Possible ways of extending your answers are by giving: a) a reason b) contrasting information c) an example.
a Are the following answer extensions type a, b or c above?
  i But that's always for using email. I hardly ever use it for websites and stuff.
  ii … for things like writing work reports, or checking my email.
  iii … because I haven't got one myself. I have to use the ones at college.
b Extend the correct answers in Exercise 1 with i–iii above.
c Now answer the questions in Part 1 opposite.

PART 2

3 Reading the prompts carefully
Which prompts from Part 2 on page 37 may need:
  a) a present perfect tense b) a conditional structure c) a present tense?

4 Using your minute to make notes
Make notes for Part 2 on page 37 in one minute.

5 Using signals to organise your talk
Put the signals below in a logical order for the Part 2 task on page 37.
1 Well, my busiest time is usually in the mornings, because that's when I …
2 If I could change my schedule, I think I'd like to have more time for …

3 I suppose my routine's been pretty much the same for the last …
4 I'd better start by telling you that I'm currently …

6 Using idiomatic language
Choose the best responses to the questions at the end of Part 2 on page 37.
1 Yes. / More or less. / My friends have similar routines.
2 No, I don't generally like routines. / No, I don't. / No, I wouldn't go that far.

PART 3

7 Listening to the questions
Pay attention to the time period you are being asked about. This may vary a lot in Part 3.
1 Which Part 3 question opposite is asking you to predict the future?
2 Which is asking you about things that have changed since the past?
3 Which is asking you to compare two present-day opinions?

8 Using generalisations
Part 3 is testing how well you can discuss general issues, rather than talking about yourself.
Choose appropriate Part 3 openers to the question:
What are the benefits and drawbacks of having a daily routine?
1 For me, I find that my work is …
2 Generally, I think most people …
3 It depends on the person, but …
4 I like change, so I …
5 In my country, attitudes to …

9 Using signals
You are assessed not on the content of your ideas, but on how logically and clearly you can express them. Use signals to
a sequence your ideas.
b relate ideas and information.
c indicate how you feel about the idea.
Put the signals below into group a, b or c.
1 unfortunately
2 two main issues, firstly …
3 inevitably
4 on the other hand …
5 it depends largely on …
6 as a result
7 another potential problem
8 in the near future … in the long term

10 Now try Part 3 of the test opposite.
Try to record yourself and listen carefully to your pronunciation.

PART 1

The examiner will ask you some questions about yourself or your own experience. You will then be asked some questions about other familiar topics.

Tip Strip

- Listen to the questions carefully and answer on topic.

- It is not enough to give short answers. Extend your responses by giving the examiner more, but relevant, details.

- Remember to let the examiner speak too. Turn-taking is important.

Can you tell me your name, please?
What nationality are you?
What part of your country are you from?
Tell me about your region.

Now let's talk about computers and the Internet.

How often do you use the computer? What for?
Do you like using the Internet? Why / Why not?
How did you learn to use a computer?
Do you think it is important to know how to use a computer? Why / Why not?

PART 2

You will talk about a given topic for two minutes. You will be able to read the topic and some prompts and you will have one minute to prepare your talk and make notes.

Tip Strip

- The examiner will stop you after you have been talking for two minutes.

- The topic may be about the past, the present or something you would like to happen in the future – or a mix of different times. Make sure you know which tense you should use.

- If you note ideas for each of the prompts you will be able to talk on topic for the full two minutes.

Describe a typical day at work, school or college.

You should say:
what you do
when you do it
how long you've had this routine

Explain what you would like to change in your work or study routine.

At the end of your Part 2 talk the examiner may ask you one or two questions to close the topic. These are usually *Yes / No* questions that do NOT need extended answers.

Do your friends have similar routines?
Do you generally like routines?

PART 3

The examiner will ask you some questions that relate to your topic, but on a more general or abstract level. You should give extended responses and the language you need is the language of discussion, which is more formal.

Tip Strip

- If you don't understand a question in Part 3, ask the examiner what he / she means.

- Avoid giving answers about yourself.

Let's think about how people feel about routines.

Do young people and old people have different attitudes to routines where you live?
What are the benefits and drawbacks of having a daily routine?

Let's consider choice in routines.

What factors influence most people's daily routines?
Do you think people get enough choice in their daily routines? Why / Why not?

What about changes in routines?

How are work or study schedules today different from those in the past? Why?
Is this a positive or negative development? Why?
How do you think people's routines and schedules will change in the future?

Listening module (approx 30 minutes + transfer time)

Questions 1–10

> ### Strategy
>
> **Identifying the topic**
>
> 1 Look at Questions 1–10. What is the topic of this section? What tells you?
>
> **Doing the tasks**
>
> 2 How many different task types are there in this section?
>
> **Task: Multiple choice**
>
> 3 Look at the three multiple-choice questions and match these phrases from the recording to the appropriate questions: a) *any particular area?* b) *what about employment?* c) *I suppose you'll be looking for somewhere with …?*
>
> **Task: Table completion**
>
> 4 Look at the table. What is the meaning of the symbols ✓ and ✗ in column 3?
>
> 5 Which question/s from the table will probably need a) a number b) a place c) a type of room d) a description of a problem?

Questions 1–3

*Choose the correct letter, **A**, **B** or **C**.*

> *Example:*
>
> Martin wants to
>
> **A** sell a flat.
>
> (**B**) rent a flat.
>
> **C** buy a flat.

1 What is Martin's occupation?

   A He works in a car factory.

   B He works in a bank.

   C He is a college student.

2 The friends would prefer somewhere with

   A four bedrooms.

   B three bedrooms.

   C two bathrooms.

Tip Strip
• **Question 3:** Notice that this question is about *Phil* – not Martin.

3 Phil would rather live in

   A the east suburbs.

   B the city centre.

   C the west suburbs.

Questions 4–10

Complete the table below.

Write **NO MORE THAN THREE WORDS AND/OR A NUMBER** *for each answer.*

Tip Strip

• In table completion tasks, always read across the rows from left to right following the order of the item numbers, and NOT up and down the columns.

• When you transfer your answer to Question 5 to the answer sheet, you do not need to copy the £ sign as this is already written on the question paper.

Details of flats available		
Location	**Features**	**Good (✓) and bad (✗) points**
Bridge Street, near the **4**	• 3 bedrooms • very big living room	✓ **5** £ .... a month ✓ transport links ✗ no shower ✗ could be **6** ....
7	• 4 bedrooms • living room • **8**	✓ **9** .... and well equipped ✓ shower ✓ will be **10** .... ✗ £800 a month

Strategy

Identifying the topic

1 Look at the task below, which is about the British Library. Who do you expect the speaker to be: a) an official b) a member of the public?

2 Do you expect to hear information about a) how to join the library b) the library building?

Doing the tasks

Task: Diagram labelling

Diagram labelling activities are often based on a plan or map of a place. You may have to write words in the gaps on the diagram, or choose the correct word from a list.

3 Look at the plan of the British Library opposite. How many floors are shown on the plan? Which word on the plan refers to the outside of the library?

4 Look at this extract from the recording and complete it using words from the plan: *Right, well, here we are, standing at the .... on the lower ground floor just to the right of the Main Entrance.*

5 What key words should you listen for to help you find the answer to Question 16? What about Question 17?

Questions 11–15

Complete the sentences below.

*Write **NO MORE THAN THREE WORDS** for each answer.*

The British Library

11 The reading rooms are only open for group visits on ....

12 The library was officially opened in ....

13 All the library rooms together cover .... m^2.

14 The library is financed by the ....

15 The main function of the library is to provide resources for people doing

....

Tip Strip
- Look carefully at the item numbers as you listen. As in all IELTS listening tasks, the item numbers in labelling activities follow the order of information in the recording.
- You do not need to write the articles (e.g. *a / the*) in diagram labelling tasks.

Label the plan below.

Write **NO MORE THAN THREE WORDS** for each answer.

Plan of the British Library

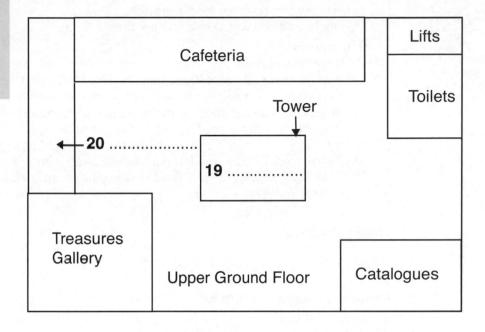

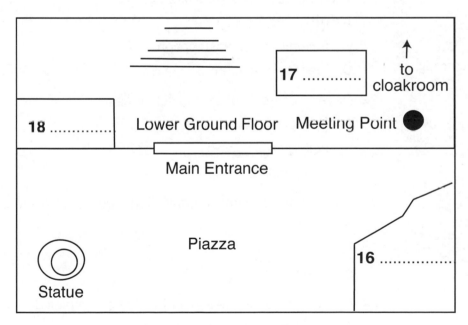

Questions 21–30

Tip Strip

• If the topic of the listening (e.g. 'work placement') appears unfamiliar, don't worry. The recording will often give you information about the general topic at the beginning. You should listen to this carefully, even if it is not tested, as it will help you to understand the rest of the talk.

Strategy

Identifying the topic

1 Look at the tasks for Section 3. What is this section about? How do you know?

2 Which two of the following are the main topics? a) What Dave has to do next to improve his project b) How Dave's project will be marked c) How Dave carried out the research for his project.
In which order do you expect to hear them?

Doing the tasks

Task: Note completion

3 Look at the gapped notes (Questions 26–30). Match each of the following phrases from the tapescript to one section of the notes (Introduction or Findings) and number them in the order in which you expect to hear them.

a) *What did you think of my second set of findings … ?*

b) *First of all, I think you need to make some slight changes to …*

c) *Right, now I think the last part, which deals with …*

d) *Anyway, moving on … I like the way you've grouped your findings into three main topic areas.*

Questions 21–25

Choose the correct answer, *A*, *B* or *C*.

Project on work placement

Tip Strip

• **Question 21:** Look at the tapescript extract below. Listen for the missing words to find the correct answer.

But I felt everyone just kind of .... and I guess I wanted to find out if that's the case.

Notice that the information that relates to the stem (the main aim of Dave's project) comes *after* the information that gives you the answer.

21 The main aim of Dave's project is to

   A describe a policy.

   B investigate an assumption.

   C identify a problem.

22 Dave's project is based on schemes in

   A schools.

   B colleges.

   C universities.

23 How many academic organisations returned Dave's questionnaire?

   A 15

   B 50

   C 150

24 Dave wanted his questionnaires to be completed by company

   A Human Resources Managers.

   B Line Managers.

   C owners.

25 Dr Green wants Dave to provide a full list of

   A respondents.

   B appendices.

   C companies.

Questions 26–30

Complete the notes below.

*Write **NO MORE THAN TWO WORDS** for each answer.*

Notes on project

Introduction

– improve the **26** .... of ideas

– include a **27** .... of 'Work Placement'

– have separate sections for literature survey and research
  28 .... and methods

Findings

Preparation stage – add summary

29 .... development – good

Constraints on learning – provide better links to the **30** ....
from research

> ## Strategy
>
> **Identifying the topic**
> 1 Section 4 is an extract from a lecture. What is the general topic? How do you know?
> 2 In which part of the lecture (the first or the second) do you expect to hear
>   a) what the word 'bilingualism' means b) an account of an experiment related to bilingualism c) a summary of early research into bilingualism?
>
> **Doing the tasks**
> **Task: Sentence completion** (See Test 1 Listening Section 4)
> 3 Underline words or phrases in Questions 31–35 with parallel meanings to the following extracts from the recording (the extracts are in order) a) *we can say* b) *at least two* c) *interfered in some way with* d) *is now regarded as unsound* e) *it didn't take into account* f) *we believe now* g) *provides some evidence that*

Questions 31–35

Complete the sentences below.

*Write **NO MORE THAN THREE WORDS** for each answer.*

Tip Strip
• There is no pause in Section 4, so look through all the questions carefully in the time you are given at the beginning.

31 Bilingualism can be defined as having an equal level of communicative .... in two or more languages.

32 Early research suggested that bilingualism caused problems with .... and mental development.

33 Early research into bilingualism is now rejected because it did not consider the .... and .... backgrounds of the children.

34 It is now thought that there is a .... relationship between bilingualism and cognitive skills in children.

35 Research done by Ellen Bialystok in Canada now suggests that the effects of bilingualism also apply to ....

Task: Multiple-choice questions
Use key words in the question or sentence beginning to locate the information in the text. Check each possible answer carefully.

Questions 36–40

*Choose the correct letter, **A**, **B** or **C**.*

Tip Strip
- **Question 36:**
  Sometimes speakers will leave out a verb if it has already been used once in the sentence, e.g. *they didn't have to react at all to … , just to …* . Here *just to* means *people just had to react to …* .
- **Question 37:** Listen for information about the 'Simon effect' in general, and the experiment (*this case*) in particular.

36 In Dr Bialystok's experiment, the subjects had to react according to

  A the colour of the square on the screen.

  B the location of the square on the screen.

  C the location of the shift key on the keyboard.

37 The experiment demonstrated the 'Simon effect' because it involved a conflict between

  A seeing something and reacting to it.

  B producing fast and slow reactions.

  C demonstrating awareness of shape and colour.

38 The experiment shows that, compared with the monolingual subjects, the bilingual subjects

  A were more intelligent.

  B had faster reaction times overall.

  C had more problems with the 'Simon effect'.

39 The results of the experiment indicate that bilingual people may be better at

  A doing different types of tasks at the same time.

  B thinking about several things at once.

  C focusing only on what is needed to do a task.

40 Dr Bialystok's first and second experiments both suggest that bilingualism may

  A slow down the effects of old age on the brain.

  B lead to mental confusion among old people.

  C help old people to stay in better physical condition.

Reading module (1 hour)

*You should spend about 20 minutes on **Questions 1–13**, which are based on Reading Passage 1 opposite.*

Strategy

Finding out what the text is about

It will help you to understand an academic text if you can get a very general overview of how it is organised. This information can be found very quickly by looking at the title, subtitle and paragraph openings.

1   Look at the title and subtitle of the reading passage on page 47. Choose **one** word that gives you the main topic of the article.
2   Look very quickly at the first line in each paragraph. Does this article mainly focus on a) describing a problem b) suggesting a solution?

Task: Matching paragraph headings

3   Look at the first example done for you. In Paragraph A, which two verbs are related to the idea of 'assessment'? Which adjective has a similar meaning to 'more effective'? Why is there a need for a more effective means of risk assessment, according to this paragraph?
4   Now read Paragraph 2. What subject was Daniel Kahneman qualified in? What did he become interested in? Are his ideas accepted now? Now read through the paragraph headings and choose the one which reflects these ideas.

Questions 1–6

*Reading Passage 1 has nine paragraphs **A–I**.*

*Choose the correct heading for Paragraphs B and D–H from the list of headings below. Write the correct number (**i–xi**) in boxes 1–6 on your answer sheet.*

Tip Strip

- Check through **all** the headings for each paragraph. You may find a heading that you have already used fits a later paragraph better.

List of headings
i   Not identifying the correct priorities
ii   A solution for the long term
iii   The difficulty of changing your mind
iv   Why looking back is unhelpful
v   Strengthening inner resources
vi   A successful approach to the study of decision-making
vii   The danger of trusting a global market
viii Reluctance to go beyond the familiar
ix   The power of the first number
x   The need for more effective risk assessment
xi   Underestimating the difficulties ahead

Example	Answer
Paragraph A	x
1 Paragraph B	
Paragraph C	xi
2 Paragraph D	
3 Paragraph E	
4 Paragraph F	
5 Paragraph G	
6 Paragraph H	

Why risks can go wrong

Human intuition is a bad guide to handling risk

A People make terrible decisions about the future. The evidence is all around, from their investments in the stock markets to the way they run their businesses. In fact, people are consistently bad at dealing with uncertainty, underestimating some kinds of risk and overestimating others. Surely there must be a better way than using intuition?

B In the 1960s a young American research psychologist, Daniel Kahneman, became interested in people's inability to make logical decisions. That launched him on a career to show just how irrationally people behave in practice. When Kahneman and his colleagues first started work, the idea of applying psychological insights to economics and business decisions was seen as rather bizarre. But in the past decade the fields of behavioural finance and behavioural economics have blossomed, and in 2002 Kahneman shared a Nobel Prize in economics for his work. Today he is in demand by business organisations and international banking companies. But, he says, there are plenty of institutions that still fail to understand the roots of their poor decisions. He claims that, far from being random, these mistakes are systematic and predictable.

C One common cause of problems in decision-making is over-optimism. Ask most people about the future, and they will see too much blue sky ahead, even if past experience suggests otherwise. Surveys have shown that people's forecasts of future stock market movements are far more optimistic than past long-term returns would justify. The same goes for their hopes of ever-rising prices for their homes or doing well in games of chance. Such optimism can be useful for managers or sportsmen, and sometimes turns into a self-fulfilling prophecy. But most of the time it results in wasted effort and dashed hopes. Kahneman's work points to three types of over-confidence. First, people tend to exaggerate their own skill and prowess; in polls, far fewer than half the respondents admit to having below-average skills in, say, driving. Second, they overestimate the amount of control they have over the future, forgetting about luck and chalking up success solely to skill. And third, in competitive pursuits such as dealing on shares, they forget that they have to judge their skills against those of the competition.

D Another source of wrong decisions is related to the decisive effect of the initial meeting,

James never left his bed, seeing nothing but danger in the financial world.

particularly in negotiations over money. This is referred to as the 'anchor effect'. Once a figure has been mentioned, it takes a strange hold over the human mind. The asking price quoted in a house sale, for example, tends to become accepted by all parties as the 'anchor' around which negotiations take place. Much the same goes for salary negotiations or mergers and acquisitions. If nobody has much information to go on, a figure can provide comfort – even though it may lead to a terrible mistake.

E   In addition, mistakes may arise due to stubbornness. No one likes to abandon a cherished belief, and the earlier a decision has been taken, the harder it is to abandon it. Drug companies must decide early to cancel a failing research project to avoid wasting money, but may find it difficult to admit they have made a mistake. In the same way, analysts may have become wedded early to a single explanation that coloured their perception. A fresh eye always helps.

F   People also tend to put a lot of emphasis on things they have seen and experienced themselves, which may not be the best guide to decision-making. For example, somebody may buy an overvalued share because a relative has made thousands on it, only to get his fingers burned. In finance, too much emphasis on information close at hand helps to explain the tendency by most investors to invest only within the country they live in. Even though they know that diversification is good for their portfolio, a large majority of both Americans and Europeans invest far too heavily in the shares of their home countries. They would be much better off spreading their risks more widely.

G   More information is helpful in making any decision but, says Kahneman, people spend proportionally too much time on small decisions and not enough on big ones. They need to adjust the balance. During the boom years, some companies put as much effort into planning their office party as into considering strategic mergers.

H   Finally, crying over spilled milk is not just a waste of time; it also often colours people's perceptions of the future. Some stock market investors trade far too frequently because they are chasing the returns on shares they wish they had bought earlier.

I   Kahneman reckons that some types of businesses are much better than others at dealing with risk. Pharmaceutical companies, which are accustomed to many failures and a few big successes in their drug-discovery programmes, are fairly rational about their risk-taking. But banks, he says, have a long way to go. They may take big risks on a few huge loans, but are extremely cautious about their much more numerous loans to small businesses, many of which may be less risky than the big ones. And the research has implications for governments too. They face a whole range of sometimes conflicting political pressures, which means they are even more likely to take irrational decisions.

Questions 7–10

*Choose the correct answer, **A**, **B**, **C** or **D**.*

Write your answers in boxes 7–10 on your answer sheet.

7   People initially found Kahneman's work unusual because he

   A   saw mistakes as following predictable patterns.

   B   was unaware of behavioural approaches.

   C   dealt with irrational types of practice.

   D   applied psychology to finance and economics.

8   The writer mentions house-owners' attitudes towards the value of their homes to illustrate that

   A   past failures may destroy an optimistic attitude.

   B   people tend to exaggerate their chances of success.

   C   optimism may be justified in certain circumstances.

   D   people are influenced by the success of others.

9   Stubbornness and inflexibility can cause problems when people

   A   think their financial difficulties are just due to bad luck.

   B   avoid seeking advice from experts and analysts.

   C   refuse to invest in the early stages of a project.

   D   are unwilling to give up unsuccessful activities or beliefs.

10   Why do many Americans and Europeans fail to spread their financial risks when investing?

   A   They feel safer dealing in a context which is close to home.

   B   They do not understand the benefits of diversification.

   C   They are over-influenced by the successes of their relatives.

   D   They do not have sufficient knowledge of one another's countries.

Task: Short answer questions

Short answer questions usually concentrate on factual information. The questions reflect the order of information in the text, but the answers may be widely spaced in the text, so you need to use key words in the questions to help you scan the text quickly. Your answer does NOT need to be a complete sentence, and you do not usually need to include words like articles.

1 Read Question 11. Scan the paragraph openings quickly to find one about problems related to being over-optimistic.

2 Look through this paragraph to find the names of two occupations, and read this sentence carefully to see if it answers the question.

Questions 11–13

Answer the questions below, using **NO MORE THAN THREE WORDS** *for each answer.*

Write your answers in boxes 11–13 on your answer sheet.

11 Which two occupations may benefit from being over-optimistic?

12 Which practical skill are many people over-confident about?

13 Which type of business has a generally good attitude to dealing with uncertainty?

You should spend about 20 minutes on **Questions 14–26**, which are based on Reading Passage 2 below.

Strategy

Finding out what the text is about

Occasionally the text may not have a heading or a subheading. In this case, it is still important to get a quick overview of the text before answering the questions.

1 Scan the first line of each paragraph and choose one word which gives you the general topic of this passage.

It may also be useful to use the tasks to help you to get an overview of the topic.

2 Look at Questions 14–18. Do these relate to a) the past b) the present c) the future?

3 Look at Questions 19–25. What do these tell you about the content of Reading Passage 2?

4 Look at Question 26. Why do you think this reading passage did not have a title?

There has always been a sense in which America and Europe owned film. They invented it at the end of the nineteenth century in unfashionable places like New Jersey, Leeds and the suburbs of Lyons. At first, they saw their clumsy new camera-projectors merely as more profitable versions of Victorian lantern shows, mechanical curiosities which might have a use as a sideshow at a funfair. Then the best of the pioneers looked beyond the fairground properties of their invention. A few directors, now mostly forgotten, saw that the flickering new medium was more than just a diversion. This crass commercial invention gradually began to evolve as an art. D W Griffith in California glimpsed its grace, German directors used it as an analogue to the human mind and the modernising city, Soviets emphasised its agitational and intellectual properties, and the Italians reconfigured it on an operatic scale.

So heady were these first decades of cinema that America and Europe can be forgiven for assuming that they were the only game in town. In less than twenty years western cinema had grown out of all recognition; its unknowns became the most famous people in the world; it made millions. It never occurred to its financial backers that another continent might borrow their magic box and make it its own. But film industries were emerging in Shanghai, Bombay and Tokyo, some of which would outgrow those in the west.

Between 1930 and 1935, China produced more than 500 films, mostly conventionally made in studios in Shanghai, without soundtracks. China's best directors – Bu Wancang and Yuan Muzhi – introduced elements of realism to their stories.

The Peach Girl (1931) and *Street Angel* (1937) are regularly voted among the best ever made in the country.

India followed a different course. In the west, the arrival of talkies gave birth to a new genre – the musical – but in India, every one of the 5000 films made between 1931 and the mid-1950s had musical interludes. The films were stylistically more wide-ranging than the western musical, encompassing realism and escapist dance within individual sequences, and they were often three hours long rather than Hollywood's 90 minutes. The cost of such productions resulted in a distinctive national style of cinema. They were often made in Bombay, the centre of what is now known as 'Bollywood'. Performed in Hindi (rather than any of the numerous regional languages), they addressed social and peasant themes in an optimistic and romantic way and found markets in the Middle East, Africa and the Soviet Union.

In Japan, the film industry did not rival India's in size but was unusual in other ways. Whereas in Hollywood the producer was the central figure, in Tokyo the director chose the stories and hired the producer and actors. The model was that of an artist and his studio of apprentices. Employed by a studio as an assistant, a future director worked with senior figures, learned his craft, gained authority, until promoted to director with the power to select screenplays and performers. In the 1930s and 40s, this freedom of the director led to the production of some of Asia's finest films.

The films of Kenji Mizoguchi were among the greatest of these. Mizoguchi's films were usually set in the nineteenth century and analysed the way in which the lives of the female characters whom he chose as his focus were constrained by the society of the time. From *Osaka Elegy* (1936) to *Ugetsu Monogatari* (1953) and beyond, he evolved a sinuous way of moving his camera in and around a scene, advancing towards significant details but often retreating at moments of confrontation or strong feeling. No one had used the camera with such finesse before.

Even more important for film history, however, is the work of the great Ozu. Where Hollywood cranked up drama, Ozu avoided it. His camera seldom moved. It nestled at seated height, framing people square on, listening quietly to their words. Ozu rejected the conventions of editing, cutting not on action, as is usually done in the west, but for visual balance. Even more strikingly, Ozu regularly cut away from his action to a shot of a tree or a kettle or clouds, not to establish a new location but as a moment of repose. Many historians now compare such 'pillow shots' to the Buddhist idea that *mu* – empty space or nothing – is itself an element of composition.

As the art form most swayed by money and market, cinema would appear to be too busy to bother with questions of philosophy. The Asian nations proved and are still proving that this is not the case. Just as deep ideas about individual freedom have led to the aspirational cinema of Hollywood, so it is the beliefs which underlie cultures such as those of China and Japan that explain the distinctiveness of Asian cinema at its best. Yes, these films are visually striking, but it is their different sense of what a person is, and what space and action are, which makes them new to western eyes.

Task: True / False / Not Given

1 Look through Questions 14–18. Do you think they relate to a) one part of the reading passage b) the whole of the reading passage? (The last strategy activity, 'Finding out what the text is about', should help you here.)

2 Look at the statement in Question 14. Use the first part of the statement to help you to locate the paragraph which contains the information.

3 Find a phrase in this paragraph which has a parallel meaning to *a minor attraction*.

4 Is the rest of the statement also reflected in the text?

Questions 14–18

Do the following statements agree with the information given in Reading Passage 2?

In boxes 1–5 on your answer sheet write

TRUE　　　　*if the statement agrees with the information*
FALSE　　　*if the statement contradicts the information*
NOT GIVEN　*if there is no information on this*

14 The inventors of cinema regarded it as a minor attraction.

15 Some directors were aware of cinema's artistic possibilities from the very beginning.

16 The development of cinema's artistic potential depended on technology.

17 Cinema's possibilities were developed in varied ways in different western countries.

18 Western businessmen were concerned about the emergence of film industries in other parts of the world.

Questions 19–25

*Complete the notes below using the list of words (**A–K**) from the box below.*

Write the correct letters in boxes 19–25 on your answer sheet.

Chinese cinema

• large number of **19** .... films produced in 1930s

• some early films still generally regarded as **20** ....

Indian cinema

• films included musical interludes

• films avoided **21** .... topics

Japanese cinema

• unusual because film director was very **22** ....

• two important directors:

        Mizoguchi – focused on the **23** .... restrictions faced by women

                 – camera movement related to **24** .... content of film

        Ozu   – **25** .... camera movement

A emotional	**B** negative	**C** expensive	**D** silent	**E** social
F outstanding	**G** little	**H** powerful	**I** realistic	**J** stylistic
K economic				

Task: Multiple choice – main idea of passage

This type of multiple-choice question focuses on the main idea of the reading passage. You may have to choose a title or subtitle, or the phrase which is the best summary of the passage, or of the writer's purpose. All the options may contain true information, but only one will reflect the main idea.

1 Which two paragraphs of the reading passage may help you to identify the main idea? Which one of these paragraphs is probably the most important?

2 Is the main part of this reading passage mainly about a) western cinema b) Asian cinema?

3 Is the passage mainly about a) the similarities between western and Asian cinema b) the special qualities of Asian cinema?

Question 26

Tip Strip

- In this type of question, be careful that your own opinions don't interfere with your choice of answer. Remember you are looking for the *writer's* idea, not your own.

26 Which of the following is the most suitable title for Reading Passage 2?

A Blind to change: how is it that the west has ignored Asian cinema for so long?

B A different basis: how has the cinema of Asian countries been shaped by their cultures and beliefs?

C Outside Asia: how did the origins of cinema affect its development worldwide?

D Two cultures: how has western cinema tried to come to terms with the challenge of the Asian market?

Strategy

Finding out what the text is about

1 Look at the title and subtitle of Reading Passage 3. Which two of these topics is it most likely to be related to a) tourism b) transport c) history d) technology?
2 Now look at the first lines of Paragraphs A–J and check your answer. What is the main topic: vehicles or roads?
3 What is the general organisation of this passage: a) a problem and its causes b) a problem and one solution c) a problem and several possible solutions?

Quiet roads ahead

The roar of passing vehicles could soon be a thing of the past

A The noise produced by busy roads is a growing problem. While vehicle designers have worked hard to quieten engines, they have been less successful elsewhere. The sound created by the tyres on the surface of the road now accounts for more than half the noise that vehicles create, and as road building and car sales continue to boom – particularly in Asia and the US – this is turning into a global issue.

B According to the World Health Organization, exposure to noise from road traffic over long periods can lead to stress-related health problems. And where traffic noise exceeds a certain threshold, road builders have to spend money erecting sound barriers and installing double glazing in blighted homes. Houses become harder to sell where environmental noise is high, and people are not as efficient or productive at work.

C Already, researchers in the Netherlands – one of the most densely populated countries in the world – are working to develop techniques for silencing the roads. In the next five years the Dutch government aims to have reduced noise levels from the country's road surfaces by six decibels overall. Dutch mechanical engineer Ard Kuijpers has come up with one of the most promising, and radical, ideas. He set out to tackle the three most important factors: surface texture, hardness and ability to absorb sound.

D The rougher the surface, the more likely it is that a tyre will vibrate and create noise. Road

builders usually eliminate bumps on freshly laid asphalt with heavy rollers, but Kuijpers has developed a method of road building that he thinks can create the ultimate quiet road. His secret is a special mould 3 metres wide and 50 metres long. Hot asphalt, mixed with small stones, is spread into the mould by a rail-mounted machine which flattens the asphalt mix with a roller. When it sets, the 10-millimetre-thick sheet has a surface smoother than anything that can be achieved by conventional methods.

E To optimise the performance of his road surface – to make it hard wearing yet soft enough to snuff out vibrations – he then adds another layer below the asphalt. This consists of a 30-millimetre-thick layer of rubber, mixed with stones which are larger than those in the layer above. 'It's like a giant mouse mat, making the road softer,' says Kuijpers.

F The size of the stones used in the two layers is important, since they create pores of a specific size in the road surface. Those used in the top layer are just 4 or 5 millimetres across, while the ones below are approximately twice that size – about 9 millimetres. Kuijpers says the surface can absorb any air that is passing through a tyre's tread[1], damping oscillations that would otherwise create noise. And in addition they make it easier for the water to drain away, which can make the road safer in wet weather.

G Compared with the complex manufacturing process, laying the surface is quite simple. It emerges from the factory rolled, like a carpet, onto a drum 1.5 metres in diameter. On site, it is unrolled and stuck onto its foundation with bitumen. Even the white lines are applied in the factory.

H The foundation itself uses an even more sophisticated technique to reduce noise further. It consists of a sound-absorbing concrete base containing flask-shaped slots up to 10 millimetres wide and 30 millimetres deep that are open at the top and sealed at the lower end. These cavities act like Helmholtz resonators – when sound waves of specific frequencies enter the top of a flask, they set up resonances inside and the energy of the sound dissipates into the concrete as heat. The cavities play another important role: they help to drain water that seeps through from the upper surface. This flow will help flush out waste material and keep the pores in the outer layers clear.

I Kuijpers can even control the sounds that his resonators absorb, simply by altering their dimensions. This could prove especially useful since different vehicles produce noise at different frequencies. Car tyres peak at around

1000 hertz, for example, but trucks generate lower-frequency noise at around 600 hertz. By varying the size of the Kuijpers resonators, it is possible to control which frequencies the concrete absorbs. On large highways, trucks tend to use the inside lane, so resonators here could be tuned to absorb sounds at around 600 hertz while those in other lanes could deal with higher frequency noise from cars.

J Kuijpers believes he can cut noise by five decibels compared to the quietest of today's roads. He has already tested a 100-metre-long section of his road on a motorway near Apeldoorn, and Dutch construction company Heijmans is discussing the location of the next roll-out road with the country's government. The success of Kuijpers' design will depend on how much it eventually costs. But for those affected by traffic noise there is hope of quieter times ahead.

---

[1] the tyre's tread – the indentations or ridges on the surface of a tyre

Strategy

Task: Locating information in paragraphs

1 Read through Paragraph A and underline the topic sentence. Then look at Question 30. Is this related to the topic sentence? Does Paragraph A describe *various economic reasons*?

2 Now read through Paragraph B. Is this about road noise? Does it describe *various economic reasons* for reducing road noise?

Questions 27–32

*Reading Passage 3 has ten paragraphs labelled **A–J**.*

Which paragraph contains the following information?

*Write the correct letter **A–J** in boxes 27–32 on your answer sheet.*

27 a description of the form in which Kuijpers' road surface is taken to its destination

28 an explanation of how Kuijpers makes a smooth road surface

29 something that has to be considered when evaluating Kuijpers' proposal

30 various economic reasons for reducing road noise

31 a generalisation about the patterns of use of vehicles on major roads

32 a summary of the different things affecting levels of noise on roads

Tip Strip

• Questions which ask you to locate information in paragraphs concentrate on details within a text, whereas paragraph heading questions tend to focus on main ideas.

• Remember that some paragraphs may not contain any of the required information.

Task: Diagram labelling

1 Look at the diagram below and make sure you understand it. What is a *cross section*? What is the name given to the top part of the road? What is the name given to the lowest part?
2 Use the title of the diagram to help you to locate the place where the information may be given. Which paragraph/s give information about:
   a) the upper layer?
   b) the lower layer?
   c) the foundation?

Questions 33–35

Label the diagram below.

*Choose **NO MORE THAN ONE WORD AND/OR A NUMBER** from the passage for each answer.*

Write your answers in boxes 33–35 on your answer sheet.

Tip Strip

• A diagram-labelling task may relate to one section of the text, or to several paragraphs.

Cross section of Kuijpers' proposed noise-reducing road

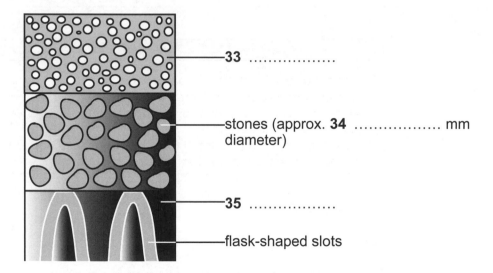

33 ....

stones (approx. **34** .... mm diameter)

35 ....

flask-shaped slots

Task: Table completion

This is similar to a note-taking task except that the information is given in columns. You may have to choose words from a box, or from the reading passage.

1 Look carefully at the headings to the table. What type of information are the missing words all related to?

2 Look at Paragraph F. This gives information about the structure and function of the upper and lower layers. Which of these types of information comes first?

3 Which paragraph gives information about the structure and function of the foundation? In what order is this information given?

Tip Strip

• Sometimes two different task types may focus on the same part of the text. However, they will not be testing exactly the same information.

Questions 36–40

*Complete the table below using the list of words (**A–K**) from the box below.*

Write the correct letters in boxes 36–40 on your answer sheet.

Kuijpers' noise-reducing road: components and function

Layer	Component	Function
upper and lower	stones	• reduce oscillations caused by **36** .... • create pores which help **37** ....
foundation	slots	• convert **38** .... to heat. • help to remove **39** .... • can be adapted to absorb different **40** ....

A frequencies	**B** the engine	**C** rubbish	**D** resonators
E air flow	**F** dissipation	**G** sound energy	**H** pores	**I** lanes
J drainage	**K** sources		

Writing module (1 hour)

Strategy

Before you write, use the task prompt, any headings and/or labels in the diagram to help you to understand the information. With tables, remember to read from left to right across the columns and from top to bottom down the rows.

1 Understanding the information

Look at the diagram and answer the questions.
1   The diagram is about: a) the services the sports club offers b) what members like and dislike about the club c) reasons why members joined the club.
2   What aspects of the sports club are considered?
3   What do the percentages represent?

2 Identifying the main topic

Tables can show changing information and/or contrasting information. What does this table show?

3 Writing the Introduction

Remember to paraphrase the introduction and show you have understood the main topic. Write an appropriate introduction from the options below.

1 *This table / The table below* 2 *shows / compares* 3 *the opinions of male and female club members about / what members think about* 4 *the activities, facilities and opening hours / the services* in a 5 *particular / city* sports club.

4 Selecting and organising information

It is very important to group, compare or contrast the information rather than simply listing it. You need to focus on main trends or differences, so it is not necessary to report all the details. Look at the task opposite.
1   Which two columns could you group together?
2   Who is happier about the range of activities?
3   How does this compare with their counterparts?
4   Which aspect are they most in agreement about?
5   Which aspect are women most happy about?
6   How does this compare with the men?
7   What link words could you use for these contrasts?

5 Using the right language

1   Do the exercises in the Language of Comparison and Contrast on page 161.
2   Look at the questions in 4 above and identify examples of comparative structures.
3   Remember to avoid repeating the same expressions. What other expressions can you use instead of a) *male and female members* b) *satisfied with* c) *not satisfied with*?

6 Summarising statement

1 What word/s can you use to signal this summary of the information?
2 From the club's point of view, what is the most useful information in the survey?
3 Contrast the men's and women's views on this.

7 Timed writing

You have already thought carefully about this task. Now write your own answer in 15 minutes.

WRITING TASK 1

You should spend about 20 minutes on this task.

The table below shows the results of a survey to find out what members of a city sports club think about the club's activities, facilities and opening hours.

Summarise the information by selecting and reporting the main features, and make any comparisons where relevant.

Write at least 150 words.

Tip Strip
• Use the figures selectively to illustrate the main trends.

Range of activities	Very satisfied	Satisfied	Not satisfied
Female members	35%	35%	30%
Male members	55%	40%	5%
Club facilities			
Female members	64%	22%	14%
Male members	63%	27%	10%
Opening hours			
Female members	72%	25%	3%
Male members	44%	19%	37%

8 Assessing your writing

1 Remember to edit your writing for any common mistakes.
2 Use the checklist on page 156 to assess your writing.
3 Now look at the sample Band 9 answer on page 174.

> ## Strategy
>
> This task carries twice as many marks as Writing Task 1, so you should spend twice as much time on it. Remember to write at least 250 words in your answer.
> For useful vocabulary look at General Academic Language on page 166 and The Language of Education and Research on page 162.

1   Identifying the issues

Read the task prompt on page 63 carefully and think about the following.
1   What problem is implied in the statement?
2   What possible measure is suggested?
3   What would be the advantages of this measure?
4   What would be the disadvantages of this measure?

2   Being clear about what you need to do

With this type of question it is not sufficient to simply write about as many advantages and disadvantages as you can think of.
1   What kind of argument do you need to write for this task?
2   Is there only one answer?

3   Planning your answer

How you organise your answer will depend on what you think about the topic. It is often better to begin with the ideas you are not so certain about and lead up to your conclusion. Both plans below are possible. Choose which plan would suit your answer:
a)   Introduction: problem
      Suggested measures: advantages
      Disadvantages
      Conclusion
b)   Introduction: problem
      Suggested measures: disadvantages
      Advantages
      Conclusion

4   Signalling organisation

You need to guide your reader through your argument with clear signals.
a)   Put the sentence openings below in a logical order.
     1   Another benefit would be …
     2   As a result, governments may need to take measures to encourage …
     3   Furthermore, it would lead to long-term problems in …
     4   However, the disadvantages of such a policy …
     5   In conclusion, …
     6   In many countries today, university students tend to choose …
     7   One way would be for governments to …
     8   This would have the advantage of …
b)   Identify which opening introduces:
     a) a contrast   e) the need for a solution
     b) an introduction to the topic   f) an example of a solution
     c) an advantage   g) the writer's overall opinion on the proposed
                                                    policy
     d) an additional advantage   h) an additional disadvantage

5 Supporting your ideas

You need to support your ideas by providing clarifications, reasons, consequences or examples. Look at the statement below and add supporting ideas by answering the questions.

1   This kind of policy would be unfair. (Why?)
2   It could attract people who are unsuited to that particular field. (How?)
3   Students may drop out more often or choose not to get jobs in the target subjects. (So?)

6 Using academic language

This kind of question is discussing a hypothetical solution. This is common in academic discourse. It means that you need to use hypothetical and/or tentative language in your answer. Look at Sentences 1–3 in Exercise 5 above and underline any examples of this kind of language.

7 Speed writing

You have already thought about the Task 2 topic. Use no more than 35 minutes for writing and checking your answer.

WRITING TASK 2

You should spend about 40 minutes on this task.

Write about the following topic.

Modern societies need specialists in certain fields, but not in others.

Some people therefore think that governments should pay university fees for students who study subjects that are needed by society. Those who choose to study less relevant subjects should not receive government funding.

Would the advantages of such an educational policy outweigh the disadvantages?

Give reasons for your answer and include any relevant examples from your own knowledge or experience.

Write at least 250 words.

8 Assessing your writing

1   Check your writing for mistakes.
2   Use the checklist on pages 157–158 to assess your response.
3   Now read the sample answer.

Speaking module (11–14 minutes)

PART 1

1 Giving relevant answers

The first few questions will usually be about very familiar information. But listen carefully – don't guess or your answer may be off topic.

Look at the first set of Part 1 questions on the opposite page and identify which one asks you to talk about a) the past b) what abilities you need for something c) your hopes.

2 Extending your answers

Remember to add to your answer by giving a reason, an example or a contrast. Answer the second set of Part 1 questions opposite, using 1–3 below to extend your answers.

1   *because I always seem to have some work I still need to do.*
2   *like visiting friends for a chat, or going to see a movie, for instance.*
3   *I think we need to really make it count. Otherwise we just waste it – watching TV and stuff.*

PART 2

3 Reading the prompts carefully

Look at the Part 2 task opposite and answer the questions.

1   Which prompt/s are hypothetical?
2   Where might you need the past tense?
3   Can you talk about somewhere you know well?

4 Using your one minute preparation time to make notes

This will help you to organise what you are going to say so that you can keep going for two minutes, but don't run out of time before you have covered the main points. Make sure you write notes only. You do NOT have time to write out whole sentences.

5 Using signals to organise your talk

Order these signals according to the Task prompts in Part 2 opposite.

1   I first heard about it when …
2   I'm not sure where it is exactly, but I think it's …
3   The region I'd really love to get the chance to visit is …

4   I don't know that much about it, but it's supposed to have …
5   I suppose the main reason I'd like to go there is …
6   If I manage to go there, I'd really like to explore … and perhaps I could …

PART 3

6 Listening to the questions and paying attention to the time period

Look at the Part 3 questions opposite. Which one requires you to:
a   describe the features of something
b   make a prediction
c   give reasons for a change in something
d   identify problems?

7 Using more formal and less subjective language

Which of the openers below would be appropriate for Part 3?
1   The majority of tourists …
2   Personally, I prefer …
3   There's plenty of evidence to suggest that …
4   In India attitudes have changed a lot …

8 Using signals

Part 3 is the most abstract, discursive part of the test. Remember to use signals to organise and link your ideas.

Which of the signals below a) contrast information b) sequence information c) evaluate information?
1   In the first place, I think …
2   in some cases … but there are other examples where …
3   One problem is that …
4   The biggest drawback is …

The examiner will ask you some questions about yourself, such as:

Can you tell me your name?
And what do you do?
Why did you choose this job / this subject?
What job would you like to do in the future? Why?
What skills do you need for that job?

Let's talk about free time now.

What do you enjoy doing in your free time?
Do you think you get enough free time? Why / Why not?
How important is it to use your free time usefully?

PART 2

The topic for your talk will be written on a card which the examiner will hand you. Read it carefully and then make some brief notes.

Describe a part of the world you would like to visit.

You should say:
        where it is
        how and what you know about it
        what you would like to do there

Explain why you would like to visit this part of the world.

The examiner may ask you one or two questions to close the topic. You do NOT need to give extended answers to these. For example, he or she might ask you:

Do you think you will visit this part of the world some day?
Have you travelled abroad very much?

PART 3

Once your talk in Part 2 is over, your examiner will ask further questions related to the topic in Part 2. The examiner may ask you to speak about these points:

Let's talk about international tourism.

Why do you think people want to visit other countries?
What makes some places very attractive to tourists?
Do people travel abroad more or less than they did in the past? Why / Why not?
Will international tourism increase or decrease in the future? Why?

Let's consider the effects of tourism.

How can tourism benefit local people and places?
Are there any drawbacks of tourism?
Does tourism help to promote international understanding? Why / Why not?
How reliable is tourism as an industry?

TEST 3

Listening module (approx 30 minutes + transfer time)

SECTION 1 **Questions 1–10**

Tip Strip

- Listen carefully to the introduction and also to the first part of the recording to find out who the people are and why they are having the conversation.
- **Question 8:** Don't repeat the word *money* in your answer as this is already given on the question paper (on the left).

Strategy

Task: Form completion

Form completion tasks are very similar to note completion. However, in a form completion task, the information will be used to complete a printed form and so the topic is often more official. As with gapped notes, some of the information is already given.

1 Look at the form below. What is its purpose?
2 How many main sections are there in the form?
3 Who is involved in this particular project? What type of project is it?

Questions 1–10

Complete the form below.

Write **NO MORE THAN THREE WORDS AND/OR A NUMBER** for each answer.

<table>
<tr><td colspan="2" align="center">Council Youth Scheme
Application for Funding for Group Project</td></tr>
<tr><td>Example</td><td>Answer</td></tr>
<tr><td>Name</td><td>Ralph Pearson</td></tr>
<tr><td>Contact address</td><td>1 .... , Drayton DR6 8AB</td></tr>
<tr><td>Telephone number</td><td>01453 586098</td></tr>
<tr><td>Name of group</td><td>Community Youth Theatre Group</td></tr>
<tr><td>Description of group</td><td>amateur theatre group (2 .... members)
involved in drama 3 .... and ....</td></tr>
<tr><td>Amount of money requested</td><td>4 £ ....</td></tr>
<tr><td>Description of project</td><td>to produce a short 5 .... play for young children</td></tr>
<tr><td>Money needed for</td><td>• 6 .... for scenery
• costumes
• cost of 7 ....
• 8 ....
• sundries</td></tr>
<tr><td colspan="2">How source of funding will be credited
    acknowledged in the 9 .... given to audience</td></tr>
<tr><td colspan="2">Other organisations approached for funding (and outcome)
    National Youth Services – money was 10 ....</td></tr>
</table>

Questions 11–20

> ## Strategy
>
> **Task: Multiple-choice questions**
> Read the sentence opening or question and underline key words. Listen for similar words or parallel expressions.
> **Task: Matching**
> In matching tasks you have to match two sets of information: a list in a box, and numbered items below.
> 1 Look at the task for Questions 16–20. Will the order of information in the recording follow the order of a) the list in the box, or b) the numbered items below?
> 2 Do you have to use all the things in the list?
> 3 Do you have to write words or letters for your answers?

Questions 11–15

*Choose the correct answer, **A**, **B** or **C**.*

Tip Strip

- All three options (A, B and C) will probably be mentioned, but they may not be in the same order as they are written on the question paper. However, the questions (11, 12, 13, etc.) will be in the same order.

- **Question 11:** Your answer must be something that *surprises* visitors to Darwin when they arrive, not just something true about the city.

11 Joanne says that visitors to Darwin are often surprised by

    A the number of young people.

    B the casual atmosphere.

    C the range of cultures.

12 To enjoy cultural activities, the people of Darwin tend to

    A travel to southern Australia.

    B bring in artists from other areas.

    C involve themselves in production.

13 The Chinese temple in Darwin

    A is no longer used for its original purpose.

    B was rebuilt after its destruction in a storm.

    C was demolished to make room for new buildings.

14 The main problem with travelling by bicycle is

    A the climate.

    B the traffic.

    C the hills.

15 What does Joanne say about swimming in the sea?

    A It is essential to wear a protective suit.

    B Swimming is only safe during the winter.

    C You should stay in certain restricted areas.

Questions 16–20

What can you find at each of the places below?

Choose your answers from the box and write the correct letter A–H next to Questions 16–20.

A	a flower market
B	a chance to feed the fish
C	good nightlife
D	international arts and crafts
E	good cheap international food
F	a trip to catch fish
G	shops and seafood restaurants
H	a wide range of different plants

Tip Strip
• **Question 19:** Joanne describes the main attraction of this place *before* she says what the name of the place is.

16 'Aquascene'   ......

17 Smith Street Mall   ......

18 Cullen Bay Marina   ......

19 Fannie Bay   ......

20 Mitchell Street   ......

Questions 21–30

Strategy

Task: Sentence completion

Listen for main ideas. Remember that the sentence may use parallel expressions, but the words you need to fill the gap will be in the recording. Check that your answers make sense in the sentence and are grammatically correct.

Task: Matching

Remember that you will hear information about the numbered items in order. Look at the box as you listen and consider each of the items A–F.

Task: Multiple choice with multiple answers.

For this task, you have to choose several answers from a list. Look carefully at the question to see how many answers you have to choose. You can write your answers on the answer sheet in any order. As with other multiple-choice questions, underline key words and listen for parallel phrases.

1 Look at Questions 28–30. How many answers do you have to choose?

2 Do you have to listen for things which have already been decided, or things which haven't been decided yet?

3 Which of these phrases from the recording might signal the information you need? a) *we've already made …* b) *We can't specify … yet* c) *We decided on …* d) *we might …* e) *we'll do that …* f) *we're still thinking about …*

Tip Strip

- In completion tasks such as sentence and note completion, the missing information is often an important word in the speech or conversation. It may therefore be stressed by the speaker.

- In conversations, people may change their opinions as they discuss the topic. Be prepared to change your answers as the speakers discuss these two topics.

Questions 21–23

Complete the sentences below.

*Write **NO MORE THAN THREE WORDS** for each answer.*

Effects of weather on mood

21 Phil and Stella's goal is to ……………… the hypothesis that weather has an effect on a person's mood.

22 They expect to find that 'good' weather (weather which is ……………… and ………………) has a positive effect on a person's mood.

23 Stella defines 'effect on mood' as a ……………… in the way a person feels.

Questions 24–27

Tip Strip
- For matching tasks, read the information in the box carefully in the preparation time at the beginning and underline key words if you have time. You need to think about *all* the options as you listen.

What information was given by each writer?

*Choose your answers from the box and write the letters **A–F** next to Questions 24–27.*

A the benefits of moving to a warmer environment

B the type of weather with the worst effect on mood

C how past events affect attitudes to weather

D the important effect of stress on mood

E the important effect of hours of sunshine on mood

F psychological problems due to having to cope with bad weather

---

24 Vickers   ......

25 Whitebourne   ......

26 Haverton   ......

27 Stanfield   ......

Questions 28–30

*Choose **THREE** letters **A–H**.*

Which **THREE** things do Phil and Stella still have to decide on?

    A   how to analyse their results

    B   their methods of presentation

    C   the design of their questionnaire

    D   the location of their survey

    E   weather variables to be measured

    F   the dates of their survey

    G   the size of their survey

    H   the source of data on weather variables

Questions 31–40

> ### Strategy
> **Task: Multiple choice with multiple answers**
> Read the question carefully and underline key words. All the options will probably be mentioned, but they will not all be correct answers to the question.
> **Task: Table completion**
> Use the title and column headings to help you understand the context. Remember to read along the rows from left to right.

Tip Strip

• Lecturers often use signposting words to make the relationship between ideas clear. They may also ask a question, and then go on to answer it in the following part of the talk.

Questions 31–32

*Choose **TWO** letters A–F.*

Which two of the following problems are causing concern to educational authorities in the USA?

- **A** differences between rich and poor students
- **B** high numbers dropping out of education
- **C** falling standards of students
- **D** poor results compared with other nationalities
- **E** low scores of overseas students
- **F** differences between rural and urban students

Questions 33–34

*Choose **TWO** letters A–F.*

According to the speaker, what are two advantages of reducing class sizes?

- **A** more employment for teachers
- **B** improvement in general health of the population
- **C** reduction in number of days taken off sick by teachers
- **D** better use of existing buildings and resources
- **E** better level of education of workforce
- **F** availability of better qualified teachers

Questions 35–40

Complete the table below.

Write **NO MORE THAN THREE WORDS AND/OR A NUMBER** *for each answer.*

USA RESEARCH PROJECTS INTO CLASS SIZES

State	Schools involved	Number of students participating	Key findings	Problems
Tennessee	about 70 schools	in total **35**	significant benefit especially for **36** .... pupils	• lack of agreement on implications of data
California	**37** .... schools	1.8 million	very little benefit	• shortage of **38** .... , especially in poorer areas • no proper method for **39** .... of project
Wisconsin	14 schools (with pupils from **40** .... families)		similar results to Tennessee project	

*You should spend about 20 minutes on **Questions 1–13**, which are based on Reading Passage 1 below.*

A song on the brain

Some songs just won't leave you alone. But this may give us clues about how our brain works

A Everyone knows the situation where you can't get a song out of your head. You hear a pop song on the radio – or even just read the song's title – and it haunts you for hours, playing over and over in your mind until you're heartily sick of it. The condition now even has a medical name – 'song-in-head syndrome'.

B But why does the mind annoy us like this? No one knows for sure, but it's probably because the brain is better at holding onto information than it is at knowing what information is important. Roger Chaffin, a psychologist at the University of Connecticut says, 'It's a manifestation of an aspect of memory which is normally an asset to us, but in this instance it can be a nuisance.'

C This eager acquisitiveness of the brain may have helped our ancestors remember important information in the past. Today, students use it to learn new material, and musicians rely on it to memorise complicated pieces. But when this useful function goes awry it can get you stuck on a tune. Unfortunately, superficial, repetitive pop tunes are, by their very nature, more likely to stick than something more inventive.

D The annoying playback probably originates in the auditory cortex. Located at the front of the brain, this region handles both listening and playback of music and other sounds. Neuroscientist Robert Zatorre of McGill University in Montreal proved this some years ago when he asked volunteers to replay the theme from the TV show *Dallas* in their heads. Brain imaging studies showed that this activated the same region of the auditory cortex as when the people actually heard the song.

E Not every stored musical memory emerges into consciousness, however. The frontal lobe of the brain gets to decide which thoughts become conscious and which ones are simply stored away. But it can become fatigued or depressed, which is when people most commonly suffer from song-in-head syndrome and other intrusive thoughts, says Susan Ball, a clinical psychologist at Indiana University School of Medicine in Indianapolis. And once the unwanted song surfaces, it's hard to stuff it back down into the subconscious. 'The more you try to suppress a thought, the more you get it,' says Ball. 'We call this the pink elephant phenomenon. Tell the brain not to think about pink elephants, and it's guaranteed to do so,' she says.

F For those not severely afflicted, simply avoiding certain kinds of music can help. 'I know certain pieces that are kind of "sticky" to me, so I will not play them in the early morning for fear that they will run around in my head all day,' says Steven Brown, who trained as a classical pianist but is now a neuroscientist at the University of Texas Health Science Center at San Antonio. He says he always has a song in his head and, even more annoying, his mind never seems to make it all the way through. 'It tends to involve short fragments between, say, 5 or 15 seconds. They seem to get looped, for hours sometimes,' he says.

G Brown's experience of repeated musical loops may represent a phenomenon called 'chunking', in which people remember musical phrases as a single unit of memory, says Caroline Palmer, a psychologist at Ohio State University in Columbus. Most listeners have little choice about what chunks they remember. Particular chunks may be especially 'sticky' if you hear them often or if they follow certain predictable patterns, such as the chord progression of rock 'n' roll music. Palmer's research shows that the more a piece of music conforms to these patterns, the easier it is to remember. That's why you're more likely to be haunted by the tunes of pop music than by those of a classical composer such as J. S. Bach.

H But this ability can be used for good as well as annoyance. Teachers can tap into memory reinforcement by setting their lessons to music.

For example, in one experiment students who heard a history text set as the lyrics to a catchy song remembered the words better than those who simply read them, says Sandra Calvert, a psychologist at Georgetown University in Washington DC.

I   This sort of memory enhancement may even explain the origin of music. Before the written word could be used to record history, people memorised it in songs, says Leon James, a psychologist at the University of Hawaii. And music may have had an even more important role. 'All music has a message,' he says. 'This message functions to unite society and to standardise the thought processes of people in society.'

Tip Strip
- In multiple-choice questions, use key words in the question or sentence beginning to locate the information in the text.
- Check each possible answer carefully.

Questions 1–3

*Choose the correct answer, **A**, **B**, **C** or **D**.*

Write your answers in boxes 1–3 on your answer sheet.

1   The writer says that 'song-in-head syndrome' may occur because the brain
   A   confuses two different types of memory.
   B   cannot decide what information it needs to retain.
   C   has been damaged by harmful input.
   D   cannot hold onto all the information it processes.

2   A tune is more likely to stay in your head if
   A   it is simple and unoriginal.
   B   you have musical training.
   C   it is part of your culture.
   D   you have a good memory.

3   Robert Zatorre found that a part of the auditory cortex was activated when volunteers
   A   listened to certain types of music.
   B   learned to play a tune on an instrument.
   C   replayed a piece of music after several years.
   D   remembered a tune they had heard previously.

Tip Strip

- In academic texts, names are often given in full the first time the person is mentioned, and the person is referred to by their surname after that. Pronouns (e.g. *he / she*) may also be used instead of proper names.

- Opinions and theories may be reported indirectly as well as in direct speech.

Strategy

Task: Matching

In matching tasks you have to match two sets of information. One set may be proper names (e.g. of people, places or institutions) and the other set may be statements, opinions, discoveries or theories.

1 Look at the list of people in the box. Scan the text and underline the places where each one is mentioned. What do you notice about the order in which the names are listed?

2 Look at Questions 4–7. Do these sentences describe *discoveries* or *theories*? How do you know?

3 Read the information in the passage about Roger Chaffin. Then look through Questions 4–7. Do any of these sentences have a parallel meaning to this information? If not, move on to the next name.

Questions 4–7

Look at the following theories (Questions 4–7) and the list of people below.

Match each theory with the person it is credited to.

Write the correct letter A–F in boxes 4–7 on your answer sheet.

Tip Strip

- There are more people than theories, so you do not need to use them all.

4 The memorable nature of some tunes can help other learning processes.

5 Music may not always be stored in the memory in the form of separate notes.

6 People may have started to make music because of their need to remember things.

7 Having a song going round your head may happen to you more often when one part of the brain is tired.

List of people

A   Roger Chaffin

B   Susan Ball

C   Steven Brown

D   Caroline Palmer

E   Sandra Calvert

F   Leon James

Task: Locating information in paragraphs
Read each paragraph of the text and look through the questions to see if there is one that matches information given in the paragraph. Look for the *type* of information given at the beginning of each question prompt (e.g. a description / two reasons) and for parallel expressions which reflect the content.

Questions 8–13

*Reading Passage 1 has nine paragraphs labelled **A–I**.*

Which paragraph contains the following information?

*Write the correct letter **A–I** in boxes 8–13 on your answer sheet.*

NB You may use any letter more than once.

8 a claim that music strengthens social bonds

9 two reasons why some bits of music tend to stick in your mind more than others

10 an example of how the brain may respond in opposition to your wishes

11 the name of the part of the brain where song-in-head syndrome begins

12 examples of two everyday events that can set off song-in-head syndrome

13 a description of what one person does to prevent song-in-head syndrome

READING PASSAGE 2

You should spend about 20 minutes on **Questions 14–27**, which are based on Reading Passage 2 below.

Worldly Wealth

Can the future population of the world enjoy a comfortable lifestyle, with possessions, space and mobility, without crippling the environment?

The world's population is expected to stabilize at around nine billion. Will it be possible for nine billion people to have the lifestyle enjoyed today only by the wealthy? One school of thought says no: not only should the majority of the world's people resign themselves to poverty forever, but rich nations must also revert to simpler lifestyles in order to save the planet.

Admittedly, there may be political or social barriers to achieving a rich world. But in fact there seems to be no insuperable physical or ecological reason why nine billion people should not achieve a comfortable lifestyle, using technology only slightly more advanced than that which we now possess. In thinking about the future of civilization, we ought to start by asking what people want. The evidence demonstrates that as people get richer they want a greater range of personal technology, they want lots of room (preferably near or in natural surroundings) and they want greater speed in travel. More possessions, more space, more mobility.

In the developed world, the personal technologies of the wealthy, including telephones, washing machines and cars, have become necessities within a generation or two. Increasing productivity that results in decreasing costs for such goods has been responsible for the greatest gains in the standard of living, and there is every reason to believe that this will continue.

As affluence grows, the amount of energy and raw materials used for production of machinery will therefore escalate. But this need not mean an end to the machine age. Rather than being thrown away, materials from old machinery can be recycled by manufacturers. And long before all fossil fuels are exhausted, their rising prices may compel industrial society not only to become more energy efficient but also to find alternative energy sources sufficient for the demands of an advanced technological civilization – nuclear fission, nuclear fusion, solar energy, chemical photosynthesis, geothermal, biomass or some yet unknown source of energy.

The growth of cities and suburbs is often seen as a threat to the environment. However, in fact the increasing amount of land consumed by agriculture is a far greater danger than urban sprawl. Stopping the growth of farms is the best way to preserve many of the world's remaining wild areas. But is a dramatic downsizing of farmland possible? Thanks to the growth of agricultural productivity, reforestation and 're-wilding' has been under way in the industrial countries for generations. Since 1950 more land in the US has been set aside in parks than has been occupied by urban and suburban growth. And much of what was farmland in the nineteenth century is now forest again. Taking the best Iowa maize growers as the norm for world food productivity, it has been calculated that less than a tenth of present cropland could support a population of 10 billion.

In *The Environment Game*, a vision of a utopia that would be at once high-tech and environmentalist, Nigel Calder suggested that 'nourishing but unpalatable primary food produced by industrial techniques – like yeast from petroleum – may be fed to animals, so that we can continue to eat our customary meat, eggs, milk, butter, and cheese – and so that people in underdeveloped countries can have adequate supplies of animal protein for the first time.'

In the long run, tissue-cloning techniques could be used to grow desired portions of meat by themselves. Once their DNA has been extracted to create cowless steaks and chickenless drumsticks, domesticated species of livestock, bred for millennia to be stupid or to have grotesquely enhanced traits, should be allowed to become extinct, except for a few specimens in zoos. However, game such as wild deer, rabbits and wild ducks will be ever more abundant as farms revert to wilderness, so this could supplement the laboratory-grown meat in the diets of tomorrow's affluent.

With rising personal incomes come rising expectations of mobility. This is another luxury of today's rich that could become a necessity of tomorrow's global population – particularly if its members choose to live widely dispersed in a post-agrarian wilderness. In his recent book *Free Flight*, James Fallows, a pilot as well as a writer, describes serious attempts by both state and private entrepreneurs in the USA to promote an 'air taxi' system within the price range of today's middle class – and perhaps tomorrow's global population.

Two of the chief obstacles to the science fiction fantasy of the personal plane or hover car are price and danger. While technological improvements are driving prices down, piloting an aircraft in three dimensions is still more difficult than driving a car in two, and pilot error causes more fatalities than driver error. But before long our aircraft and cars will be piloted by computers which are never tired or stressed.

So perhaps there are some grounds for optimism when viewing the future of civilization. With the help of technology, and without putting serious strains on the global environment, possessions, space and mobility can be achieved for all the projected population of the world.

Questions 14–19

Tip Strip
- In this Yes / No / Not Given task, the statements focus on claims rather than facts.
- Even if a statement is 'Not Given' there will probably still be some related information in the passage. However, it will not be possible to find information about *all* parts of the statement, so the writer's opinion on this exact topic cannot be known.

Do the following statements reflect the claims of the writer in Reading Passage 2?

In boxes 14–19 on your answer sheet write

YES   if the statement reflects the writer's claims
NO   if the statement contradicts the writer's claims
NOT GIVEN   if it is impossible to say what the writer thinks about this

14 Today's wealthy people ignore the fact that millions are living in poverty.

15 There are reasons why the future population of the world may not enjoy a comfortable lifestyle.

16 The first thing to consider when planning for the future is environmental protection.

17 As manufactured goods get cheaper, people will benefit more from them.

18 It may be possible to find new types of raw materials for use in the production of machinery.

19 The rising prices of fossil fuels may bring some benefits.

Strategy

Task: Summary completion
In Test 1 Reading Passage 3 you completed a summary using words from a box. You may also have to do a similar task choosing words from the passage. In both cases, the information and items in the summary may be in a different order from the text.
1 Read the instructions on the following page for this task. How many words can you write for each answer?
2 Look at the title of the summary and at the subheading to the text. Which words appear in both places? In which part of the text – beginning, middle or end – will you find information about both these things? (If you have marked the parts of the text where you found Questions 14–19, this will also help you to locate the information for the summary.)

Complete the summary below.

Choose **ONE WORD ONLY** from the passage for each answer.

Write your answers in boxes 20–25 on your answer sheet.

Space for an increased population

According to the writer, the use of land for **20** ……………… is the most serious threat to the environment. However, in the US, there has already been an increase in the amount of land used for **21** ……………… and forests. Far less land would be required to feed the world's population if the **22** ……….……… of the land could be improved worldwide. It has also been claimed that the industrial production of animal foods could allow greater access to animal **23** ……………… by the entire world's population. Scientists could use **24** ……………… from domesticated animals to help produce meat by tissue cloning, and these species could then be allowed to die out. In addition to this type of meat, **25** ……………… will also be widely available.

Questions 26–27

Choose the correct answer, **A**, **B**, **C** or **D**.

Write your answers in boxes 26–27 on your answer sheet.

26 Greater mobility may be a feature of the future because of changes in
  A the location of housing.
  B patterns of employment.
  C centres of transport.
  D the distribution of wealth.

27 Air transport will be safe because of
  A new types of aircraft.
  B better training methods.
  C three-dimensional models.
  D improved technology.

Space: The Final Archaeological Frontier

Space travel may still have a long way to go, but the notion of archaeological research and heritage management in space is already concerning scientists and environmentalists.

In 1993, University of Hawaii's anthropologist Ben Finney, who for much of his career has studied the technology once used by Polynesians to colonize islands in the Pacific, suggested that it would not be premature to begin thinking about the archaeology of Russian and American aerospace sites on the Moon and Mars. Finney pointed out that just as today's scholars use archaeological records to investigate how Polynesians diverged culturally as they explored the Pacific, archaeologists will someday study off-Earth sites to trace the development of humans in space. He realized that it was unlikely anyone would be able to conduct fieldwork in the near future, but he was convinced that one day such work would be done.

There is a growing awareness, however, that it won't be long before both corporate adventurers and space tourists reach the Moon and Mars. There is a wealth of important archaeological sites from the history of space exploration on the Moon and Mars and measures need to be taken to protect these sites. In addition to the threat from profit-seeking corporations, scholars cite other potentially destructive forces such as souvenir hunting and unmonitored scientific sampling, as has already occurred in explorations of remote polar regions. Already in 1999 one company was proposing a robotic lunar rover mission beginning at the site of Tranquility Base and rumbling across the Moon from one archaeological site to another, from the wreck of the Ranger 8 probe to Apollo 17's landing site. The mission, which would leave vehicle tyre-marks all over some of the most famous sites on the Moon, was promoted as a form of theme-park entertainment.

According to the vaguely worded *United Nations Outer Space Treaty* of 1967, what it terms 'space junk' remains the property of the country that sent the craft or probe into space. But the treaty doesn't explicitly address protection of sites like Tranquility Base, and equating the remains of human exploration of the heavens with 'space junk' leaves them vulnerable to scavengers. Another problem arises through other international treaties proclaiming that land in space cannot be owned by any country or individual. This presents some interesting dilemmas for the aspiring manager of extraterrestrial cultural resources. Does the US own Neil Armstrong's famous first footprints on the Moon but not the lunar dust in which they were recorded? Surely those footprints are as important in the story of human development as those left by hominids at Laetoli, Tanzania. But unlike the Laetoli prints, which have survived for 3.5 million years encased in cement-like ash, those at Tranquility Base could be swept away with a casual brush of a space tourist's hand. To deal with problems like these, it may be time to look to innovative international administrative structures for the preservation of historic remains on the new frontier.

The Moon, with its wealth of sites, will surely be the first destination of archaeologists trained to work in space. But any young scholars hoping to claim the mantle of history's first lunar archaeologist will be disappointed. That distinction is already taken.

On November 19, 1969, astronauts Charles Conrad and Alan Bean made a difficult manual landing of the *Apollo 12* lunar module in the Moon's Ocean of Storms, just a few hundred feet from an unmanned probe, *Surveyor 3*, that had landed in a crater on April 19, 1967. Unrecognized at the time, this was an important moment in the history of science. Bean and Conrad were about to conduct the first archaeological studies on the Moon.

After the obligatory planting of the American flag and some geological sampling, Conrad and Bean made their way to *Surveyor 3*. They observed that the probe had bounced after touchdown and carefully photographed the impressions made by its footpads. The whole spacecraft was covered in dust, perhaps kicked up by the landing.

The astronaut-archaeologists carefully removed the probe's television camera, remote sampling arm, and pieces of tubing. They bagged and labelled these artefacts, and stowed them on board their lunar module. On their return to Earth, they passed them on to the Daveson Space Center in Houston,

Texas, and the Hughes Air and Space Corporation in El Segundo, California. There, scientists analyzed the changes in these aerospace artefacts.

One result of the analysis astonished them. A fragment of the television camera revealed evidence of the bacteria *Streptococcus mitis*. For a moment it was thought Conrad and Bean had discovered evidence for life on the Moon, but after further research the real explanation became apparent. While the camera was being installed in the probe prior to the launch, someone sneezed on it. The resulting bacteria had travelled to the Moon, remained in an alternating freezing/boiling vacuum for more than two years, and returned promptly to life upon reaching the safety of a laboratory back on Earth.

The finding that not even the vastness of space can stop humans from spreading a sore throat was an unexpected spin-off. But the artefacts brought back by Bean and Conrad have a broader significance. Simple as they may seem, they provide the first example of extraterrestrial archaeology and – perhaps more significant for the history of the discipline – formational archaeology, the study of environmental and cultural forces upon the life history of human artefacts in space.

Questions 28–33

Tip Strip

- When completing sentences using words from a box, remember that the sentences follow the order of information in the passage. Use key words and proper nouns in the sentence openings to help you to locate the information.

- Look carefully at the tenses used in the sentence openings and endings. Modal verbs such as *could* or *may* (e.g. in sentence endings B, D, G, H) can refer to different time periods.

*Complete each sentence with the correct ending **A–H** from the box below.*

*Write the correct letter **A–H** in boxes 28–33 on your answer sheet.*

28 Ben Finney's main academic work investigates the way that

29 Ben Finney thought that in the long term

30 Commercial pressures mean that in the immediate future

31 Academics are concerned by the fact that in isolated regions on Earth,

32 One problem with the 1967 UN treaty is that

33 The wording of legal agreements over ownership of land in space means that

---

A activities of tourists and scientists have harmed the environment.

B some sites in space could be important in the history of space exploration.

C vehicles used for tourism have polluted the environment.

D it may be unclear who has responsibility for historic human footprints.

E past explorers used technology in order to find new places to live.

F man-made objects left in space are regarded as rubbish.

G astronauts may need to work more closely with archaeologists.

H important sites on the Moon may be under threat.

Questions 34–38

Complete the flow chart below.

*Choose **NO MORE THAN ONE WORD** from the passage for each answer.*

During the assembly of the *Surveyor 3* probe, someone **34** ……………… on a TV camera.

The TV camera was carried to the Moon on *Surveyor 3*.

The TV camera remained on the Moon for over **35** ……………… years.

Apollo 12 astronauts **36** ……………… the TV camera.

The TV camera was returned to Earth for **37** ……………… .

The *Streptococcus mitis* bacteria were found.

The theory that this suggested there was **38** ……………… on the Moon was rejected.

Scientists concluded that the bacteria can survive lunar conditions.

*Choose **TWO** letters **A–E**.*

The **TWO** main purposes of the writer of this text are to explain

A the reasons why space archaeology is not possible.

B the dangers that could follow from contamination of objects from space.

C the need to set up careful controls over space tourism.

D the need to preserve historic sites and objects in space.

E the possible cultural effects of space travel.

Writing module (1 hour)

Strategy

When Task 1 consists of more than one diagram you do not have time to report all the information. Remember to focus on trends and try to link the information in the two diagrams and to refer to both diagrams in your summarising statement.

WRITING TASK 1

You should spend about 20 minutes on this task.

The charts below give information about the way in which water was used in different countries in 2000.

Summarise the information by selecting and reporting the main features, and make comparisons where relevant.

Write at least 150 words.

Tip Strip

- The trends in one country are very close to the world pattern of water use. You can make use of this to link the information across the two diagrams.
- For help with vocabulary look at the Language of Cause and Effect on page 160.

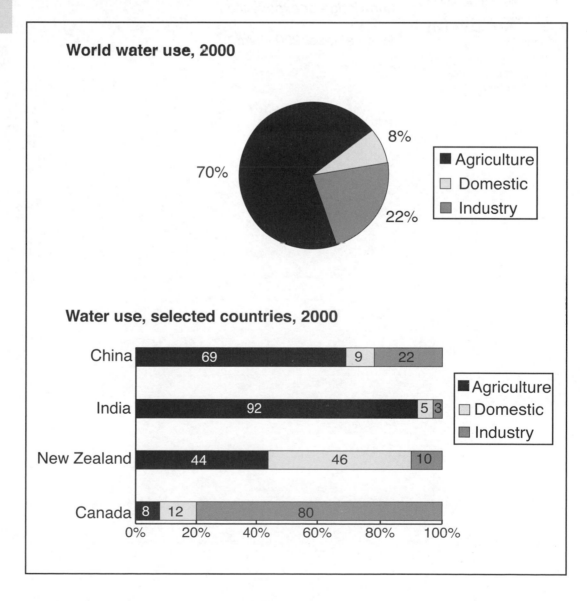

World water use, 2000

70% — 8% — 22%

- Agriculture
- Domestic
- Industry

Water use, selected countries, 2000

	Agriculture	Domestic	Industry
China	69	9	22
India	92	5	3
New Zealand	44	46	10
Canada	8	12	80

0% 20% 40% 60% 80% 100%

Strategy

In this type of Task 2 you have to write about more than one aspect of the topic. Make sure you answer both questions.

WRITING TASK 2

You should spend about 40 minutes on this task.

Write about the following topic.

Young people in the modern world seem to have more power and influence than any previous young generation.

Why is this the case?

What impact does this have on the relationship between old and young people?

Give reasons for your answer and include any relevant examples from your own knowledge or experience.

Write at least 250 words.

Tip Strip

- Remember to signal the different sections and to write an appropriate conclusion to your answer.
- In this particular task you need to write about the *causes* of the situation described and the *effects* it may have.
- For help with vocabulary look at the Language of Cause and Effect on page 160.
- When you have finished remember to assess your writing.

Speaking module (11–14 minutes)

PART 1

Answer the following examiner questions.

Tip Strip
• Remember to extend your answers.

What's your name?
Where do you come from?
Tell me about the place you grew up in.
What did young people do in their free time there?

Now let's talk about sport.

How popular is sport in your country?
Do most people play sport or watch it on TV? Why?
Did you do any sport when you were a child? Which?
Do you play any sport now? Why / Why not?
Is sport important for people today? Why / Why not?

PART 2

You have one minute to make notes on the following topic. Then talk about it for two minutes.

Tip Strip
• Read the task card carefully and make notes on all the prompts. This will help you to talk in an organised way for two minutes.

> Describe a person that you met recently and liked.
>
> You should say:
>   who this person is
>   what you were doing at the time
>   how you met him / her
>
> Explain why you liked this person.

Do you think you will see this person again?
Do you like meeting new people?

PART 3

Think about the issues and answer the questions.

Tip Strip
• Remember in Part 3 you are asked to discuss more general topics so you will need to speak generally and more formally. Give reasons or examples in your answers.

Let's think about friends and friendship generally.

How do people usually meet new friends where you live?
Is it easier for adults or children to make new friends? Why?
How are relationships with friends different from relationships at work / college?
Is it possible for people to be close friends with their boss or teacher? Why / Why not?

Now let's consider the importance of friends.

Some people think that friends can never be as important as family. Do you agree?
How are responsibilities towards friends and family different?
Will the relative importance of friends and family change in future societies?

Listening module (approx 30 minutes + transfer time)

Questions 1–10

> **Strategy**
>
> **Task: Table completion**
> Read the main heading, if there is one, and look at the column headings to get an idea of what to listen for. Check the number of words you are allowed to write. Think about what sort of information (e.g. a number, a noun, an adjective) is needed for each gap.
> **Task: Classification**
> In Questions 7–10, listen to the discussion of the numbered items and answer the question using options A, B or C.

Questions 1–6

Complete the table below.

*Write **NO MORE THAN THREE WORDS AND/OR A NUMBER** for each answer.*

Tip Strip
- IELTS is an international examination and in the Listening Module you may hear a variety of accents, e.g. Australian, American, Canadian, British or New Zealand.
- For table completion, notes are generally used, so articles, verbs, etc. can often be omitted.

Budget accommodation in Queenstown, New Zealand

Accommodation	Price (dormitory)	Comments
Travellers' Lodge		*Example* *fully booked*
Bingley's	**1** US$	• in town centre • café with regular **2** .... nights • sundeck
Chalet Lodge	US$ 18.00	• located in a **3** .... alpine setting • 10 mins from town centre • **4** .... are welcome
Globetrotters	US$ 18.50	• in town centre • **5** .... included • chance to win a **6** ....

Who wants to do each of the activities below?

A only Jacinta
B only Lewis
C both Jacinta and Lewis

*Write the correct letter, **A**, **B** or **C**, next to Questions 7–10.*

7 bungee jump ......

8 white-water rafting ......

9 jet-boat ride ......

10 trekking on wilderness trail ......

Tip Strip
• In classification tasks, you only need to write a letter (A, B or C) for each answer.
• In this task, you need to listen for the opinions of the speakers about each activity. Listen for language of opinion, agreement and disagreement.

Questions 11–20

Strategy

Task: Multiple-choice questions
Read the sentence opening or question and underline key words. Listen for similar words or parallel expressions.

Task: Completing a list
In this task you have to listen for several points, and write them in the form of a list. The task focuses on understanding main ideas, usually factual information. You should write your answers as briefly as possible.

1 Look at Questions 15–17. What type of information are you listening for?

2 Which of the following words from the tapescript could be possible answers to the question: a) *training activities* b) *schools* c) *employees and staff* d) *local councils* e) *East London* f) *companies* g) *green transport plans*?

Task: Note completion
Look at the information given in the notes to help you to identify the information you need.

Questions 11–14

*Choose the correct letter, **A**, **B** or **C**.*

Tip Strip

• **Question 11:** Listen to what is said about cycling in European countries. Does the speaker say that the situation in London is the same, or different?

11 Jack says that in London these days, many people

   A see cycling as a foolish activity.

   B have no experience of cycling.

   C take too many risks when cycling.

12 If people want to cycle to school or work, CitiCyclist helps them by

   A giving cycling lessons on the route they take.

   B advising them on the safest route to choose.

   C teaching them basic skills on quiet roads first.

13 Jack works with some advanced cyclists who want to develop

   A international competitive riding skills.

   B knowledge of advanced equipment.

   C confidence in complex road systems.

14 CitiCyclist supports the view that cyclists should

   A have separate sections of the road from motor traffic.

   B always wear protective clothing when cycling.

   C know how to ride confidently on busy roads.

Questions 15–17

List **THREE** types of organisations for which CitiCyclist provides services.

*Write **NO MORE THAN THREE WORDS** for each answer.*

15 ....

16 ....

17 ....

Questions 18–20

Complete the notes below.

Tip Strip
• Look at what is written after the gap as well as before the gap to make sure you identify the exact information you need.

*Write **NO MORE THAN THREE WORDS AND/OR A NUMBER** for each answer.*

website address:	citicyclist.co.uk
phone:	**18** ....
cost (single person):	**19** .... per lesson
usual length of course:	**20** .... (except complete beginners)

Questions 21–30

Strategy
Task: Short answer questions
In this task you have to answer questions, which usually focus on factual information. You should **not** write your answers in sentence form. Often the best answer will just be one or two words.
1 Look at Questions 21–23. What are the key words in each question?
2 What part of speech is probably needed for each answer – a noun, an adjective or a verb?
Task: Multiple-choice questions
Read the sentence opening or question and underline key words. Listen for similar words or parallel expressions.
Task: Sentence completion
Listen for main ideas. Remember that the sentence may use parallel expressions, but the words you need to fill the gap will be in the recording. Check your answers make sense in the sentence and are grammatically correct.

Questions 21–23

Answer the questions below.

*Write **NO MORE THAN THREE WORDS** for each answer.*

Tip Strip

- **Two** of your answers should be in the plural form. If you write the singular form, your answer will be marked wrong.

21 What do Sharon and Xiao Li agree was the strongest aspect of their presentation?

   ………………

22 Which part of their presentation was Xiao Li least happy with?

   ………………

23 Which section does Sharon feel they should have discussed in more depth?

   ………………

Questions 24–27

*Choose the correct letter, **A**, **B** or **C**.*

24 Sharon and Xiao Li were surprised when the class said

    A they spoke too quickly.

    B they included too much information.

    C their talk was not well organised.

25 The class gave Sharon and Xiao Li conflicting feedback on their

    A timing.

    B use of visuals.

    C use of eye contact.

26 The class thought that the presentation was different from the others because

    A the analysis was more detailed.

    B the data collection was more wide-ranging.

    C the background reading was more extensive.

Tip Strip

• IELTS Listening tasks may involve choosing or labelling different types of graphs and bar charts.

• To prepare for this question, look at the key and the label of the vertical axis. Think about which key numbers and expressions you need to listen for.

27 Which bar chart represents the marks given by the tutor?

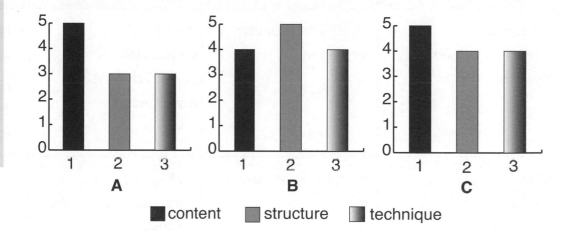

content   structure   technique

Questions 28–30

Complete the sentences below.

*Write **ONE WORD ONLY** for each answer.*

28 The tutor says that the .... of the presentation seemed rather sudden.

29 The tutor praises the students' discussion of the .... of their results.

30 The tutor suggests that they could extend the .... review in their report.

Questions 31–40

Questions 31–33

Complete the notes below.

Write **NO MORE THAN THREE WORDS** *for each answer.*

The World Health Organisation says a healthy city must

- have a **31** ……………. and ……………… environment.

- meet the **32** ……………… of all its inhabitants.

- provide easily accessible health services.

- encourage ordinary people to take part in **33** ……………… .

Questions 34–40

Complete the table below.

Write **NO MORE THAN THREE WORDS** *for each answer.*

Place / Project	Aim	Method	Achievement
Sri Lanka Community Contracts System	to upgrade squatter settlements	the **34** ……………… constructed infrastructure, e.g. drains, paths	• better housing and infrastructure • provided better **35** ……………… opportunities
Mali cooperative	to improve sanitation in city	• **36** ……………… graduates organising garbage collection • public education campaign via **37** ……………… and discussion groups	• greater environmental awareness • improved living conditions
Egypt (Mokattam) **38** ………………	to support disadvantaged women	women provided with the **39** ……………… and equipment for sewing and weaving	• rise in the **40** ……………… and quality of life of young women

You should spend about 20 minutes on **Questions 1–14**, *which are based on Reading Passage 1 below.*

Green virtues of green sand

Revolution in glass recycling could help keep water clean

A For the past 100 years special high grade white sand, dug from the ground at Leighton Buzzard in the UK, has been used to filter tap water to remove bacteria and impurities – but this may no longer be necessary. A new factory that turns used wine bottles into green sand could revolutionise the recycling industry and help to filter Britain's drinking water. Backed by $1.6m from the European Union and the Department for Environment, Food and Rural Affairs (Defra), a company based in Scotland is building the factory, which will turn beverage bottles back into the sand from which they were made in the first place. The green sand has already been successfully tested by water companies and is being used in 50 swimming pools in Scotland to keep the water clean.

B The idea is not only to avoid using up an increasingly scarce natural resource, sand, but also to solve a crisis in the recycling industry. Britain uses 5.5m tonnes of glass a year, but recycles only 750,000 tonnes of it. The problem is that half the green bottle glass in Britain is originally from imported wine and beer bottles. Because there is so much of it, and it is used less in domestic production than other types, green glass is worth only $25 a tonne. Clear glass, which is melted down and used for whisky bottles, mainly for export, is worth double that amount.

C Howard Dryden, a scientist and managing director of the company, Dryden Aqua, of Bonnyrigg, near Edinburgh, has spent six years working on the product he calls Active Filtration Media, or AFM. He concedes that he has given what is basically recycled glass a 'fancy name' to remove the stigma of what most people would regard as an inferior product. He says he needs bottles that have already contained drinkable liquids to be sure that drinking water filtered through the AFM would not be contaminated. Crushed down beverage glass has fewer impurities than real sand and it performed better in trials. 'The fact is that tests show that AFM does the job better than

sand, it is easier to clean and reuse and has all sorts of properties that make it ideal for other applications,' he claimed.

D The factory is designed to produce 100 tonnes of AFM a day, although Mr Dryden regards this as a large-scale pilot project rather than full production. Current estimates of the UK market for this glass for filtering drinking water, sewage, industrial water, swimming pools and fish farming are between 175,000 to 217,000 tonnes a year, which will use up most of the glass available near the factory. So he intends to build five or six factories in cities where there are large quantities of bottles, in order to cut down on transport costs.

E The current factory will be completed this month and is expected to go into full production on January 14th next year. Once it is providing a 'regular' product, the government's drinking water inspectorate will be asked to perform tests and approve it for widespread use by water companies. A Defra spokesman said it was hoped that AFM could meet approval within six months. The only problem that they could foresee was possible contamination if some glass came from sources other than beverage bottles.

F Among those who have tested the glass already is Caroline Fitzpatrick of the civil and environmental engineering department of University College London. 'We have looked at a number of batches and it appears to do the job,' she said. 'Basically, sand is made of glass and Mr Dryden is turning bottles back into sand. It seems a straightforward idea and there is no reason we can think of why it would not work. Since glass from wine bottles and other beverages has no impurities and clearly did not leach any substances into the contents of the bottles, there was no reason to believe there would be a problem,' Dr Fitzpatrick added.

G Mr Dryden has set up a network of agents round the world to sell AFM. It is already in use in central America to filter water on banana plantations where the fruit has to be washed before being despatched to European markets. It is also in use in sewage works to filter water before it is returned to rivers, something which is becoming legally necessary across the European Union because of tighter regulations on sewage works. So there are a great number of applications involving cleaning up water. Currently, however, AFM costs $670 a tonne, about four times as much as good quality sand. 'But that is because we haven't got large-scale production. Obviously, when we get going it will cost a lot less, and be competitive with sand in price as well,' Mr Dryden said. 'I believe it performs better and lasts longer than sand, so it is going to be better value too.'

H If AFM takes off as a product it will be a big boost for the government agency which is charged with finding a market for recycled products. Crushed glass is already being used in road surfacing and in making tiles and bricks. Similarly, AFM could prove to have a widespread use and give green glass a cash value.

Strategy

Task: Locating information in paragraphs

Read each paragraph of the text and look through Questions 1–10 to see if there is one that matches information given in the paragraph. Look for the type of information given at the beginning (e.g. *a description / two reasons*) and for parallel expressions which reflect the content.

Questions 1–10

*Reading Passage 1 has 8 paragraphs labelled **A–H**.*

Which paragraph contains the following information?

*Write the correct letter **A–H** in boxes 1–10 on your answer sheet.*

NB *You may use any letter more than once.*

1   a description of plans to expand production of AFM

2   the identification of a potential danger in the raw material for AFM

3   an example of AFM use in the export market

4   a comparison of the value of green glass and other types of glass

5   a list of potential applications of AFM in the domestic market

6   the conclusions drawn from laboratory checks on the process of AFM production

7   identification of current funding for the production of green sand

8   an explanation of the chosen brand name for crushed green glass

9   a description of plans for exporting AFM

10 a description of what has to happen before AFM is accepted for general use

Tip Strip

• For Questions 11 and 12 all the information you need comes in two paragraphs.

Strategy

Task: Summary completion

Read through the summary to get a general idea of the content. Use key words to locate the part of the text that contains the information you need.

Questions 11–14

Complete the summary below.

*Choose **NO MORE THAN TWO WORDS** from the passage for each answer.*

Write your answers in boxes 11–14 on your answer sheet.

Green sand

The use of crushed green glass (AFM) may have two significant impacts: it may help to save a diminishing **11** ……………… while at the same time solving a major problem for the **12** ……………… in the UK. However, according to Howard Dryden, only glass from bottles that have been used for **13** ……………… can be used in the production process. AFM is more effective than **14** ……………… as a water filter, and also has other uses.

NATURAL CHOICE
Coffee and chocolate

What's the connection between your morning coffee, wintering North American birds and the cool shade of a tree? Actually, quite a lot, says Simon Birch.

When scientists from London's Natural History Museum descended on the coffee farms of the tiny Central American republic of El Salvador, they were astonished to find such diversity of insect and plant species. During 18 months' work on 12 farms, they found a third more species of parasitic wasp than are known to exist in the whole country of Costa Rica. They described four new species and are aware of a fifth. On 24 farms they found nearly 300 species of tree – when they had expected to find about 100.

El Salvador has lost much of its natural forest, with coffee farms covering nearly 10% of the country. Most of them use the 'shade-grown' method of production, which utilises a semi-natural forest ecosystem. Alex Munro, the museum's botanist on the expedition, says: 'Our findings amazed our insect specialist. There's a very sophisticated food web present. The wasps, for instance, may depend on specific species of tree.'

It's the same the world over. Species diversity is much higher where coffee is grown in shade conditions. In addition, coffee (and chocolate) is usually grown in tropical rainforest regions that are biodiversity hotspots. 'These habitats support up to 70% of the planet's plant and animal species, and so the production methods of cocoa and coffee can have a hugely significant impact,' explains Dr Paul Donald of the Royal Society for the Protection of Birds.

So what does 'shade-grown' mean, and why is it good for wildlife? Most of the world's coffee is produced by poor farmers in the developing world. Traditionally they have grown coffee (and cocoa) under the shade of selectively thinned tracts of rain forest in a genuinely sustainable form of farming. Leaf fall from the canopy provides a supply of nutrients and acts as a mulch that suppresses weeds. The insects that live in the canopy pollinate the cocoa and coffee and prey on pests. The trees also provide farmers with fruit and wood for fuel.

'Bird diversity in shade-grown coffee plantations rivals that found in natural forests in the same region,' says Robert Rice from the Smithsonian Migratory Bird Center. In Ghana, West Africa, – one of the world's biggest producers of cocoa – 90% of the cocoa is grown under shade, and these forest plantations are a vital habitat for wintering European migrant birds. In the same way, the coffee forests of Central and South America are a refuge for wintering North American migrants.

More recently, a combination of the collapse in the world market for coffee and cocoa and a drive to increase yields by producer countries has led to huge swathes of shade-grown coffee and cocoa being cleared to make way for a highly intensive, monoculture pattern of production known as 'full sun'. But this system not only reduces the diversity of flora and fauna, it also requires huge amounts of pesticides and fertilisers. In Côte d'Ivoire, which produces more than half the world's cocoa, more than a third of the crop is now grown in full-sun conditions.

The loggers have been busy in the Americas too, where nearly 70% of all Colombian coffee is now produced using full-sun production. One study carried out in Colombia and Mexico found that, compared with shade coffee, full-sun plantations have 95% fewer species of birds.

In El Salvador, Alex Munro says shade-coffee farms have a cultural as well as ecological significance and people are not happy to see them go. But the financial pressures are great, and few of these coffee farms make much money. 'One farm we studied, a cooperative of 100 families, made just $10,000 a year – $100 per family – and that's not taking labour costs into account.'

The loss of shade-coffee forests has so alarmed a number of North American wildlife organisations that they're now harnessing consumer power to help save these threatened habitats. They are promoting a 'certification' system that can indicate to consumers that the beans have been grown on shade plantations. Bird-friendly coffee, for instance, is marketed by the Smithsonian Migratory Bird Center. The idea is that the small extra cost is passed directly on to the coffee farmers as a financial incentive to maintain their shade-coffee farms.

Not all conservationists agree with such measures, however. Some say certification could be leading to the loss – not preservation – of natural forests. John Rappole of the Smithsonian Conservation and Research Center, for example, argues that shade-grown marketing provides 'an incentive to convert existing areas of primary forest that are too remote or steep to be converted profitably to other forms of cultivation into shade-coffee plantations'.

Other conservationists, such as Stacey Philpott and colleagues, argue the case for shade coffee. But there are different types of shade growing. Those used by subsistence farmers are virtually identical to natural forest (and have a corresponding diversity), while systems that use coffee plants as the understorey and cacao or citrus trees as the overstorey may be no more diverse than full-sun farms. Certification procedures need to distinguish between the two, and Ms Philpott argues that as long as the process is rigorous and offers financial gains to the producers, shade growing does benefit the environment.

Questions 15–19

Do the following statements agree with the information given in Reading Passage 2?

In boxes 15–19 on your answer sheet write

TRUE   *if the statement agrees with the information*
FALSE   *if the statement contradicts the information*
NOT GIVEN   *if there is no information on this*

15 More species survive on the farms studied by the researchers than in the natural El Salvador forests.

16 Nearly three-quarters of the Earth's wildlife species can be found in shade-coffee plantations.

17 Farmers in El Salvador who have tried both methods prefer shade-grown plantations.

18 Shade plantations are important for migrating birds in both Africa and the Americas.

19 Full-sun cultivation can increase the costs of farming.

Tip Strip

- Some people may be mentioned in more than one part of the reading passage. Skim through the passage and highlight all examples of the names.

Questions 20–23

*Look at the following opinions (**Questions 20–23**) and the list of people below.*

Match each opinion to the person credited with it.

*Write the correct letter **A–E** in boxes 20–23 on your answer sheet.*

NB *You can write any letter more than once.*

20 Encouraging shade growing may lead to farmers using the natural forest for their plantations.

21 If shade-coffee farms match the right criteria, they can be good for wildlife.

22 There may be as many species of bird found on shade farms in a particular area, as in natural habitats there.

23 Currently, many shade-coffee farmers earn very little.

A Alex Munroe
B Paul Donald
C Robert Rice
D John Rappole
E Stacey Philpott

Task: Classification

In this type of task you have to match numbered features to a set of general categories. The information in the numbered items will be in a different order from the information in the text and you may have to use information from different sections to answer one question.

1 Scan the text and underline or highlight references to shade-grown methods and full-sun methods. Which paragraph first mentions:
   a) shade-grown methods?
   b) full-sun methods?
2 What are the key words in Question 24? Use these to help you to locate the information you need. Remember to check the sections of the text referring to both methods.

Questions 24–27

Classify the features described below as applying to

A the shade-grown method
B the full-sun method
C both shade-grown and full-sun methods

*Write the correct letter **A–C** in boxes 24–27 on your answer sheet.*

24 can be used on either coffee or cocoa plantations

25 is expected to produce bigger crops

26 documentation may be used to encourage sales

27 can reduce wildlife diversity

You should spend about 20 minutes on **Questions 28–40**, which are based on Reading Passage 3 on page 103.

Questions 28–33

Reading Passage 3 has nine paragraphs **A–I**.

Choose the most suitable heading for paragraphs **A–F** from the list of headings below.

Write the correct number (**i–viii**) in boxes 28–33 on your answer sheet.

Tip Strip
* When matching
  paragraph headings
  you have to choose the
  heading which best
  summarises the main
  idea of the paragraph.
* Each heading will only
  match *one* paragraph.

List of headings	
i	Amazing results from a project
ii	New religious ceremonies
iii	Community art centres
iv	Early painting techniques and marketing systems
v	Mythology and history combined
vi	The increasing acclaim for Aboriginal art
vii	Belief in continuity
viii	Oppression of a minority people

28 Paragraph **A**

29 Paragraph **B**

30 Paragraph **C**

31 Paragraph **D**

32 Paragraph **E**

33 Paragraph **F**

Painters of time

'The world's fascination with the mystique of Australian Aboriginal art.'

Emmanuel de Roux

A   The works of Aboriginal artists are now much in demand throughout the world, and not just in Australia, where they are already fully recognised: the National Museum of Australia, which opened in Canberra in 2001, designated 40% of its exhibition space to works by Aborigines. In Europe their art is being exhibited at a museum in Lyon, France, while the future Quai Branly museum in Paris – which will be devoted to arts and civilisations of Africa, Asia, Oceania and the Americas – plans to commission frescoes by artists from Australia.

B   Their artistic movement began about 30 years ago, but its roots go back to time immemorial. All the works refer to the founding myth of the Aboriginal culture, 'the Dreaming'. That internal geography, which is rendered with a brush and colours, is also the expression of the Aborigines' long quest to regain the land which was stolen from them when Europeans arrived in the nineteenth century. 'Painting is nothing without history,' says one such artist, Michael Nelson Tjakamarra.

C   There are now fewer than 400,000 Aborigines living in Australia. They have been swamped by the country's 17.5 million immigrants. These original 'natives' have been living in Australia for 50,000 years, but they were undoubtedly maltreated by the newcomers. Driven back to the most barren lands or crammed into slums on the outskirts of cities, the Aborigines were subjected to a policy of 'assimilation', which involved kidnapping children to make them better 'integrated' into European society, and herding the nomadic Aborigines by force into settled communities.

D   It was in one such community, Papunya, near Alice Springs, in the central desert, that Aboriginal painting first came into its own. In 1971, a white schoolteacher, Geoffrey Bardon, suggested to a group of Aborigines that they should decorate the school walls with ritual motifs, so as to pass on to the younger generation the myths that were starting to fade from their collective memory. He gave them brushes, colours and surfaces to paint on – cardboard and canvases. He was astounded by the result. But their art did not come like a bolt from the blue: for thousands of years Aborigines had been 'painting' on the ground using sands of different colours, and on rock faces. They had also been decorating their bodies for ceremonial purposes. So there existed a formal vocabulary.

E   This had already been noted by Europeans. In the early twentieth century, Aboriginal communities brought together by missionaries in northern Australia had been encouraged to reproduce on tree bark the motifs found on rock faces. Artists turned out a steady stream of works, supported by the churches, which helped to sell them to the public, and between 1950 and 1960 Aboriginal paintings began to reach overseas museums. Painting on bark persisted in the north, whereas the communities in the central desert increasingly used acrylic paint, and elsewhere in Western Australia women explored the possibilities of wax painting and dyeing processes, known as 'batik'.

F   What Aborigines depict are always elements of the Dreaming, the collective history that each community is both part of and guardian of. The Dreaming is the story of their origins, of their 'Great Ancestors', who passed on their knowledge, their art and their skills (hunting, medicine, painting, music and dance) to man. 'The Dreaming is not synonymous with the moment when the world was created,' says Stephane Jacob, one of the organisers of the Lyon exhibition. 'For Aborigines, that moment has never ceased to exist. It is perpetuated by the cycle of the seasons and the religious ceremonies which the Aborigines organise. Indeed the aim of those ceremonies is also to ensure the permanence of that golden age. The central function of Aboriginal painting, even in its contemporary manifestations, is to guarantee the survival of this world. The Dreaming is both past, present and future.'

G   Each work is created individually, with a form peculiar to each artist, but it is created within and on behalf of a community who must approve it. An artist cannot use a 'dream' that does not belong to his or her community, since each community is the owner of its dreams, just as it is anchored to a territory marked out by its ancestors, so each painting can be interpreted as a kind of spiritual road map for that community.

H   Nowadays, each community is organised as a cooperative and draws on the services of an art adviser, a government-employed agent who provides the artists with materials, deals with galleries and museums and redistributes the proceeds from sales among the artists.

Today, Aboriginal painting has become a great success. Some works sell for more than $25,000, and exceptional items may fetch as much as $180,000 in Australia.

I   'By exporting their paintings as though they were surfaces of their territory, by accompanying them to the temples of western art, the Aborigines have redrawn the map of their country, into whose depths they were exiled,' says Yves Le Fur, of the Quai Branly museum. 'Masterpieces have been created. Their undeniable power prompts a dialogue that has proved all too rare in the history of contacts between the two cultures'.

Questions 34–37

Tip Strip
• Remember that information is given in chronological order in the flow chart, although it may be in a different order in the text.

Complete the flow chart below.

Choose NO MORE THAN THREE WORDS from the passage for each answer.

Write your answers in boxes 34–37 on your answer sheet.

For **34** .... , Aborigines produced ground and rock paintings.

Early twentieth century: churches first promoted the use of **35** .... for paintings.

Mid-twentieth century: Aboriginal paintings were seen in **36** ....

Early 1970s: Aborigines painted traditional patterns on **37** .... in one community.

Questions 38–40

Tip Strip
• Skimming a text quickly before you begin the tasks will help you to locate information later on.

Choose the correct answer, A, B, C or D.

Write your answers in boxes 38–40 on your answer sheet.

38 In Paragraph G, the writer suggests that an important feature of Aboriginal art is

    A its historical context.

    B its significance to the group.

    C its religious content.

    D its message about the environment.

39 In Aboriginal beliefs, there is a significant relationship between

    A communities and lifestyles.

    B images and techniques.

    C culture and form.

    D ancestors and territory.

40 In Paragraph I, the writer suggests that Aboriginal art invites Westerners to engage with

    A the Australian land.

    B their own art.

    C Aboriginal culture.

    D their own history.

Writing module (1 hour)

Strategy

This task consists of plans showing changes to a place over time. Look at both plans carefully and note the changes to the original place and any data that is given. Do NOT describe each diagram individually. Focus on the changes. Remember that you still need to write a summarising statement.

Tip Strip

- Look at the dates. These will indicate the best tense for your answer.
- For help with the vocabulary look at the Language of Change on page 159.

WRITING TASK 1

You should spend about 20 minutes on this task.

The diagrams below show the development of a small fishing village and its surrounding area into a large European tourist resort.

Summarise the information by selecting and reporting the main features, and make comparisons where relevant.

Write at least 150 words.

between 1974 and 2004 the size of

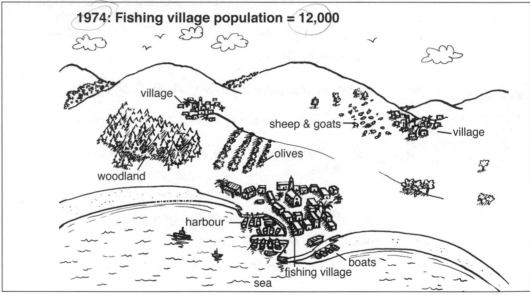

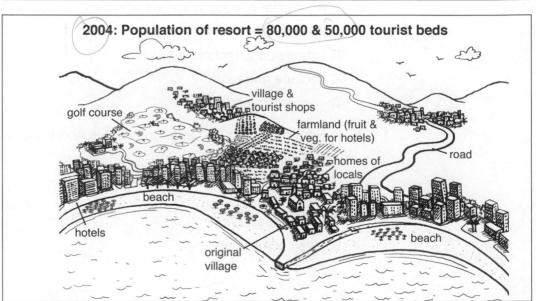

WRITING TASK 2

You should spend about 40 minutes on this task.

Write about the following topic.

Music is played in every society and culture in the world today.

Some people think that music brings only benefits to individuals and societies. Others, however, think that music can have a negative influence on both.

Discuss both these views and give your own opinion.

Give reasons for your answer and include any relevant examples from your own knowledge or experience.

Write at least 250 words.

Speaking module (11–14 minutes)

PART 1

Answer the following examiner questions.

Can you tell me your full name?
What shall I call you?
Which country do you come from?
Whereabouts is your home town?
Tell me about the countryside outside your town.

Now let's talk about your family.

How big is your family?
How often do you spend time together?
What do you enjoy doing as a family?
How do you keep in touch with members of your family?

PART 2

You have one minute to make notes on the following topic. Then talk about it for two minutes.

Tip Strip

- Remember to establish the tense of the prompt.
- If you can't think of something that really took place, don't be afraid to make it up. What is important is to produce a relevant, organised talk.

> Describe something you bought that you were not happy with.
>
> You should say:
>> what you bought
>> why you were not happy with it
>> what you did with it
>
> Explain how you felt about the situation.

Would you buy other things from the same shop / place?
Do you usually enjoy shopping?

PART 3

Think about the issues and answer the questions.

Tip Strip

- The examiner will tell you what topic he / she will ask you about. Listen carefully for these signals, as they may help you to understand the questions.

Let's consider the kinds of products people buy in your country.

Are there more goods available in shops now than in the past? Why / Why not?
Do people generally prefer to buy products from their own or from other countries?
What kinds of products are most affected by fashions from other countries?
Will overseas trends and fashions have more or less impact on what people buy in the future?

Now let's think about protecting consumers.

What kind of techniques do advertisers use to persuade people to buy more?
Who should be responsible for the quality of products: producers, shops or customers?
How could governments protect the rights of consumers?

TEST 5

Listening module (approx 30 minutes + transfer time)

Questions 1–10

Questions 1–7

Choose the correct letter, **A**, **B** *or* **C**.

> *Example*
>
> The woman says she is interested in
>
> **A** part-time employment.
>
> **B** a permanent job.
>
> **C** unpaid work.

1 The librarian says that training always includes

  A computer skills.

  B basic medical skills.

  C interpersonal skills.

2 All library service volunteers have to

  A record their arrival and departure.

  B stay within 'staff only' sections.

  C wear a uniform.

3 The woman would be entitled to a contribution towards the cost of

  A transport by minibus.

  B parking at the library.

  C public transport.

4 One recent library project involved

  A labelling historical objects.

  B protecting historical photographs.

  C cataloguing historical documents.

5 At present, the library is looking for people to

  A record books onto CD.

  B tell stories to children.

  C read books to the blind.

6 The woman says she is interested in a project involving

    A taking library books to people in hospital.

    B delivering library books to people at home.

    C driving the disabled to the library.

7 The woman agrees to work for

    A two hours per week.

    B four hours per week.

    C six hours per week.

Questions 8–10

*Choose **THREE** letters **A–G**.*

Which **THREE** of the following must be provided by all volunteers?

    A civil conviction check

    B signed copy of commitment

    C certificates to indicate qualifications

    D emergency contact information

    E date of birth

    F signature of parent or guardian

    G referees

Tip Strip
• Make sure your completed sentences are grammatically correct.

Questions 11–14

Complete the sentences below.

Write **NO MORE THAN TWO WORDS AND/OR A NUMBER** *for each answer.*

11 'Canadian Clean Air Day' will be held on ....

12 Air pollution may be responsible for .... deaths every year in Canada.

13 The sector most responsible for smog-producing pollutants is ....

14 Scientists now know that even .... of pollutants can be harmful.

Questions 15–20

Complete the notes below.

Write **NO MORE THAN TWO WORDS AND/OR A NUMBER** *for each answer.*

Reducing Air Pollution

Individual action

• respond to the **15** '................. Challenge'

• walk, cycle or car-pool to work

• use public transit

• **16** ....

• **17** .... your domestic equipment

Government action

• emission reduction in the **18** .... region of US and Canada

• move towards **19** .... (e.g. less sulphur in gasoline & diesel)

• reduction of pollutants from **20** .... and power plants.

Questions 21–30

Questions 21–30

Complete the notes below.

Write NO MORE THAN THREE WORDS for each answer.

Field Trip to Kenya

Area of country: the **21** .... of Kenya

Accommodation: Marich Pass Field Studies Centre

- in traditional 'bandas' (bring mosquito **22** ....)

- study areas: **23** .... , lecture room, outdoor areas

Type of environment: both **24** .... and semi-arid plains

Activities:
- interviews (with interpreters)

- **25** .... (environment and culture)

- morphological mapping

- projects (all connected with **26** .... issues)

Jack's group did project on: **27** .... supply and quality issues

Expeditions:
- to Sigor (a **28** ....) to study distribution

- to the Wei Wei valley to study agricultural production

- to a **29** ....

Evaluation:
- logistics – well run

- gave insight into lives of others

- provided input for his **30** ....

Questions 31–40

Strategy

Task: Flow chart completion
As in Reading, flow charts may be used in the Listening module to summarise a process. In Listening, the information will always be given in chronological order.
1 Look at the gapped flow chart below. What is the general topic?
2 What is the topic of the research: a) an Internet company b) a supermarket?

Tip Strip
• Always check the number of words you are allowed to write. If you go over the limit, your answer will be marked wrong.

Questions 31–34

Complete the flow chart below.

*Write **ONE WORD** for each answer.*

Research methodology

STAGE 1

Discussion with supermarket department manager to decide on the store's **31** .... for the website

↓

Decision to investigate website use as a **32** .... way for customers to communicate problems

↓

STAGE 2

Design of questionnaire to identify customers' experiences and **33** .... to problems

↓

Data collected from **34** .... with customers in four branches of the supermarket

↓

Analysis of responses

*Choose the correct letter, **A, B** or **C**.*

35 Which pie chart shows the percentage of respondents who experienced a problem in the supermarket?

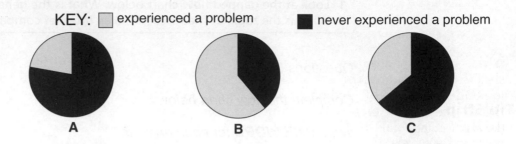

36 Which pie chart shows the reasons why customers failed to report the problem directly to supermarket staff?

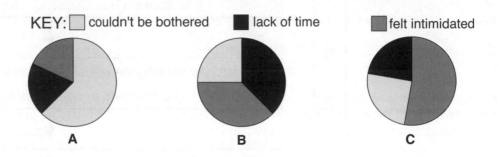

37 How might the student's website help the supermarket, according to the manager?

    A It would support the expansion of the company.

    B It would allow the identification of problem areas.

    C It would make the company appear more professional.

38 The student says one problem is that some customers

    A do not have computer skills.

    B do not have their own computer.

    C do not have access to a computer.

39 Further observation of website use is necessary because of

    A the small size of the sample.

    B the need to evaluate the objectives.

    C the unrepresentative nature of the respondents.

40 One positive result of the website for the supermarket staff could be

    A greater support from management.

    B less chance of unfair complaints.

    C greater cooperation between staff.

READING PASSAGE 1

You should spend about 20 minutes on **Questions 1–13**, which are based on Reading Passage 1 below.

Sustainable architecture – lessons from the ant

Termite mounds were the inspiration for an innovative design in sustainable living

Africa owes its termite mounds a lot. Trees and shrubs take root in them. Prospectors mine them, looking for specks of gold carried up by termites from hundreds of metres below. And of course, they are a special treat to aardvarks and other insectivores.

Now, Africa is paying an offbeat tribute to these towers of mud. The extraordinary Eastgate Building in Harare, Zimbabwe's capital city, is said to be the only one in the world to use the same cooling and heating principles as the termite mound.

Termites in Zimbabwe build gigantic mounds inside which they farm a fungus that is their primary food source. This must be kept at exactly 30.5°C, while the temperatures on the African veld outside can range from 1.5°C at night – only just above freezing – to a baking hot 40°C during the day. The termites achieve this remarkable feat by building a system of vents in the mound. Those at the base lead down into chambers cooled by wet mud carried up from water tables far below, and others lead up through a flue to the peak of the mound. By constantly opening and closing these heating and cooling vents over the course of the day the termites succeed in keeping the temperature constant in spite of the wide fluctuations outside.

Architect Mick Pearce used precisely the same strategy when designing the Eastgate Building, which has no air conditioning and virtually no heating. The building – the country's largest commercial and shopping complex – uses less than 10% of the energy of a conventional building its size. These efficiencies translated directly to the bottom line: the Eastgate's owners saved $3.5 million on a $36 million building because an air-conditioning plant didn't have to be imported. These savings were also passed on to tenants: rents are 20% lower than in a new building next door.

The complex is actually two buildings linked by bridges across a shady, glass-roofed atrium open to the breezes. Fans suck fresh air in from the atrium, blow it upstairs through hollow spaces under the floors and from there into each office through baseboard vents. As it rises and warms, it is drawn out via ceiling vents and finally exits through forty-eight brick chimneys.

To keep the harsh, high veld sun from heating the interior, no more than 25% of the outside is glass, and all the windows are screened by cement arches that jut out more than a metre.

During summer's cool nights, big fans flush air through the building seven times an hour to chill the hollow floors. By day, smaller fans blow two changes of air an hour through the building, to circulate the air which has been in contact with the cool floors. For winter days, there are small heaters in the vents.

This is all possible only because Harare is 1600 feet above sea level, has cloudless skies, little humidity and rapid temperature swings – days as warm as 31°C commonly drop to 14°C at night. 'You couldn't do this in New York, with its fantastically hot summers and fantastically cold winters,' Pearce said. But then his eyes lit up at the challenge. 'Perhaps you could store the summer's heat in water somehow … .'

The engineering firm of Ove Arup & Partners, which worked with him on the design, monitors daily temperatures outside, under the floors and at knee, desk and ceiling level. Ove Arup's graphs show that the temperature of the building has generally stayed between 23°C and 25°C, with the exception of the annual hot spell just before the summer rains in October, and three days in November, when a janitor accidentally switched off the fans at night. The atrium, which funnels the winds through, can be much cooler. And the air is fresh – far more so than in air-conditioned buildings, where up to 30% of the air is recycled.

Pearce, disdaining smooth glass skins as 'igloos in the Sahara', calls his building, with its exposed girders and pipes, 'spiky'. The design of the entrances is based on the porcupine-quill headdresses of the local Shona tribe. Elevators are designed to look like the mineshaft cages used in

Zimbabwe's diamond mines. The shape of the fan covers, and the stone used in their construction, are echoes of Great Zimbabwe, the ruins that give the country its name.

Standing on a roof catwalk, peering down inside at people as small as termites below, Pearce said he hoped plants would grow wild in the atrium and pigeons and bats would move into it, like that termite fungus, further extending the whole 'organic machine' metaphor. The architecture, he says, is a regionalised style that responds to the biosphere, to the ancient traditional stone architecture of Zimbabwe's past, and to local human resources.

Questions 1–5

*Choose the correct answer, **A**, **B**, **C** or **D**.*

Write your answers in boxes 1–5 on your answer sheet.

1 Why do termite mounds have a system of vents?

   A to allow the termites to escape from predators

   B to enable the termites to produce food

   C to allow the termites to work efficiently

   D to enable the termites to survive at night

2 Why was Eastgate cheaper to build than a conventional building?

   A Very few materials were imported.

   B Its energy consumption was so low.

   C Its tenants contributed to the costs.

   D No air conditioners were needed.

3 Why would a building like Eastgate not work efficiently in New York?

   A Temperature change occurs seasonally rather than daily.

   B Pollution affects the storage of heat in the atmosphere.

   C Summer and winter temperatures are too extreme.

   D Levels of humidity affect cloud coverage.

4 What does Ove Arup's data suggest about Eastgate's temperature control system?

   A It allows a relatively wide range of temperatures.

   B The only problems are due to human error.

   C It functions well for most of the year.

   D The temperature in the atrium may fall too low.

5 Pearce believes that his building would be improved by

   A becoming more of a habitat for wildlife.

   B even closer links with the history of Zimbabwe.

   C giving people more space to interact with nature.

   D better protection from harmful organisms.

Tip Strip
• Be careful with Question 3. You need to think about the meaning of the whole paragraph, not just the sentence about New York.

Questions 6–10

Complete the sentences below with words taken from Reading Passage 1.

*Use **NO MORE THAN THREE WORDS** for each answer.*

Write your answers in boxes 6–10 on your answer sheet.

6 Warm air leaves the offices through ……………… .

7 The warm air leaves the building through ……………… .

8 Heat from the sun is prevented from reaching the windows by ……………… .

9 When the outside temperature drops, ……………… bring air in from outside.

10 On cold days, ……………… raise the temperature in the offices.

Questions 11–13

*Answer the question below, using **NO MORE THAN THREE WORDS** from the passage for each answer.*

Write your answers in boxes 11–13 on your answer sheet.

Which three parts of the Eastgate Building reflect important features of Zimbabwe's history and culture?

11 ………………

12 ………………

13 ………………

You should spend about 20 minutes on **Questions 14–26**, which are based on Reading Passage 2 on page 119.

Questions 14–19

Reading Passage 2 has ten paragraphs **A–J**.

Choose the correct heading for Paragraphs **B–G** from the list of headings below.

Write the correct number (**i–x**) in boxes 14–19 on your answer sheet.

List of headings

i A description of the procedure

ii An international research project

iii An experiment to investigate consumer responses

iv Marketing an alternative name

v A misleading name?

vi A potentially profitable line of research

vii Medical dangers of the technique

viii Drawbacks to marketing tools

ix Broadening applications

x What is neuromarketing?

Example:

Paragraph **A**   x

14 Paragraph **B**

15 Paragraph **C**

16 Paragraph **D**

17 Paragraph **E**

18 Paragraph **F**

19 Paragraph **G**

Inside the mind of the consumer

Could brain-scanning technology provide an accurate way to assess the appeal of new products and the effectiveness of advertising?

A

MARKETING people are no longer prepared to take your word for it that you favour one product over another. They want to scan your brain to see which one you really prefer. Using the tools of neuroscientists, such as electroencephalogram (EEG) mapping and functional magnetic-resonance imaging (fMRI), they are trying to learn more about the mental processes behind purchasing decisions. The resulting fusion of neuroscience and marketing is, inevitably, being called 'neuromarketing'.

B

The first person to apply brain-imaging technology in this way was Gerry Zaltman of Harvard University, in the late 1990s. The idea remained in obscurity until 2001, when BrightHouse, a marketing consultancy based in Atlanta, Georgia, set up a dedicated neuromarketing arm, BrightHouse Neurostrategies Group. (BrightHouse lists Coca-Cola, Delta Airlines and Home Depot among its clients.) But the company's name may itself simply be an example of clever marketing. BrightHouse does not scan people while showing them specific products or campaign ideas, but bases its work on the results of more general fMRI-based research into consumer preferences and decision-making carried out at Emory University in Atlanta.

C

Can brain scanning really be applied to marketing? The basic principle is not that different from focus groups and other traditional forms of market research. A volunteer lies in an fMRI machine and is shown images or video clips. In place of an interview or questionnaire, the subject's response is evaluated by monitoring brain activity. fMRI provides real-time images of brain activity, in which different areas 'light up' depending on the level of blood flow. This provides clues to the subject's subconscious thought patterns. Neuroscientists know, for example, that the sense of self is associated with an area of the brain known as the medial prefrontal cortex. A flow of blood to that area while the subject is looking at a particular logo suggests that he or she identifies with that brand.

D

At first, it seemed that only companies in Europe were prepared to admit that they used neuromarketing.

Two carmakers, DaimlerChrysler in Germany and Ford's European arm, ran pilot studies in 2003. But more recently, American companies have become more open about their use of neuromarketing. Lieberman Research Worldwide, a marketing firm based in Los Angeles, is collaborating with the California Institute of Technology (Caltech) to enable movie studios to market-test film trailers. More controversially, the New York Times recently reported that a political consultancy, FKF Research, has been studying the effectiveness of campaign commercials using neuromarketing techniques.

E

Whether all this is any more than a modern-day version of phrenology, the Victorian obsession with linking lumps and bumps in the skull to personality traits, is unclear. There have been no large-scale studies, so scans of a handful of subjects may not be a reliable guide to consumer behaviour in general. Of course, focus groups and surveys are flawed too: strong personalities can steer the outcomes of focus groups, and some people may be untruthful in their responses to opinion pollsters. And even honest people cannot always explain their preferences.

F

That is perhaps where neuromarketing has the most potential. When asked about cola drinks, most people claim to have a favourite brand, but cannot say why they prefer that brand's taste. An unpublished study of attitudes towards two well-known cola drinks, Brand A and Brand B, carried out last year in a college of medicine in the US found that most subjects preferred Brand B in a blind tasting – fMRI scanning showed that drinking Brand B lit up a region called the ventral putamen, which is one of the brain's 'reward centres', far more brightly than Brand A. But when told which drink was which, most subjects said they preferred Brand A, which suggests that its stronger brand outweighs the more pleasant taste of the other drink.

G

'People form many unconscious attitudes that are obviously beyond traditional methods that utilise introspection,' says Steven Quartz, a neuroscientist at Caltech who is collaborating with Lieberman Research. With over $100 billion spent each year on marketing in America alone, any firm that can more accurately analyse how customers respond to brands could make a fortune.

H

Consumer advocates are wary. Gary Ruskin of Commercial Alert, a lobby group, thinks existing marketing techniques are powerful enough. 'Already, marketing is deeply implicated in many serious pathologies,' he says. 'That is especially true of children, who are suffering from an epidemic of marketing-related diseases, including obesity and type-2 diabetes. Neuromarketing is a tool to amplify these trends.'

I

Dr Quartz counters that neuromarketing techniques could equally be used for benign purposes. 'There are ways to utilise these technologies to create more responsible advertising,' he says. Brain-scanning could, for example, be used to determine when people are capable of making free choices, to ensure that advertising falls within those bounds.

J

Another worry is that brain-scanning is an invasion of privacy and that information on the preferences of specific individuals will be misused. But neuromarketing studies rely on small numbers of volunteer subjects, so that seems implausible. Critics also object to the use of medical equipment for frivolous rather than medical purposes. But as Tim Ambler, a neuromarketing researcher at the London Business School, says: 'A tool is a tool, and if the owner of the tool gets a decent rent for hiring it out, then that subsidises the cost of the equipment, and everybody wins.' Perhaps more brain-scanning will some day explain why some people like the idea of neuromarketing, but others do not.

Tip Strip

- Information relating to the same person may be found in different places in the text.
- People may be referred to in different ways within the text – e.g. whole name, or surname only.

Look at the following people (Questions 20–22) and the list of opinions below.

Match each person with the opinion credited to him.

Write the correct letter **A–F** in boxes 20–22 on your answer sheet.

20 Steven Quartz

21 Gary Ruskin

22 Tim Ambler

List of opinions

A Neuromarketing could be used to contribute towards the cost of medical technology.

B Neuromarketing could use introspection as a tool in marketing research.

C Neuromarketing could be a means of treating medical problems.

D Neuromarketing could make an existing problem worse.

E Neuromarketing could lead to the misuse of medical equipment.

F Neuromarketing could be used to prevent the exploitation of consumers.

Tip Strip

- This summary focuses on the main ideas of the passage rather than examples of specific experiments.

Questions 23–26

Complete the summary below using words from the passage.

Choose **ONE WORD ONLY** from the passage for each answer.

Write your answers in boxes 23–26 on your answer sheet.

Neuromarketing can provide valuable information on attitudes to particular **23** .... It may be more reliable than surveys, where people can be **24** .... , or focus groups, where they may be influenced by others. It also allows researchers to identify the subject's **25** .... thought patterns. However, some people are concerned that it could lead to problems such as an increase in disease among **26** ....

The accidental rainforest

According to ecological theory, rainforests are supposed to develop slowly over millions of years. But now ecologists are being forced to reconsider their ideas

When Peter Osbeck, a Swedish priest, stopped off at the mid-Atlantic island of Ascension in 1752 on his way home from China, he wrote of 'a heap of ruinous rocks' with a bare, white mountain in the middle. All it boasted was a couple of dozen species of plant, most of them ferns and some of them unique to the island.

And so it might have remained. But in 1843 British plant collector Joseph Hooker made a brief call on his return from Antarctica. Surveying the bare earth, he concluded that the island had suffered some natural calamity that had denuded it of vegetation and triggered a decline in rainfall that was turning the place into a desert. The British Navy, which by then maintained a garrison on the island, was keen to improve the place and asked Hooker's advice. He suggested an ambitious scheme for planting trees and shrubs that would revive rainfall and stimulate a wider ecological recovery. And, perhaps lacking anything else to do, the sailors set to with a will.

In 1845, a naval transport ship from Argentina delivered a batch of seedlings. In the following years, more than 200 species of plant arrived from South Africa. From England came 700 packets of seeds, including those of two species that especially liked the place: bamboo and prickly pear. With sailors planting several thousand trees a year, the bare white mountain was soon cloaked in green and renamed Green Mountain, and by the early twentieth century the mountain's slopes were covered with a variety of trees and shrubs from all over the world.

Modern ecologists throw up their hands in horror at what they see as Hooker's environmental anarchy. The exotic species wrecked the indigenous ecosystem, squeezing out the island's endemic plants. In fact, Hooker knew well enough what might happen. However, he saw greater benefit in improving rainfall and encouraging more prolific vegetation on the island.

But there is a much deeper issue here than the relative benefits of sparse endemic species versus luxuriant imported ones. And as botanist David Wilkinson of Liverpool John Moores University in the UK pointed out after a recent visit to the island, it goes to the heart of some of the most dearly held tenets of ecology. Conservationists' understandable concern for the fate of Ascension's handful of unique species has, he says, blinded them to something quite astonishing – the fact that the introduced species have been a roaring success.

Today's Green Mountain, says Wilkinson, is 'a fully functioning man-made tropical cloud forest' that has grown from scratch from a ragbag of species collected more or less at random from all over the planet. But how could it have happened? Conventional ecological theory says that complex ecosystems such as cloud forests can emerge only through evolutionary processes in which each organism develops in concert with others to fill particular niches. Plants co-evolve with their pollinators and seed dispersers, while microbes in the soil evolve to deal with the leaf litter.

But that's not what happened on Green Mountain. And the experience suggests that perhaps natural rainforests are constructed far more by chance than by evolution. Species, say some ecologists, don't so much evolve to create ecosystems as make the best of what they have. 'The Green Mountain system is a man-made system that has produced a tropical rainforest without any co-evolution between its constituent species,' says Wilkinson.

Not everyone agrees. Alan Gray, an ecologist at the University of Edinburgh in the UK, argues that the surviving endemic species on Green Mountain, though small in number, may still form the framework of the new ecosystem. The new arrivals may just be an adornment, with little structural importance for the ecosystem.

But to Wilkinson this sounds like clutching at straws. And the idea of the instant formation of rainforests sounds increasingly plausible as research reveals that supposedly pristine tropical rainforests from the Amazon to south-east Asia may in places be little more than the overgrown gardens of past rainforest civilisations.

The most surprising thing of all is that no ecologists have thought to conduct proper research into this human-made rainforest ecosystem. A survey of the island's flora conducted six years ago by the University of Edinburgh was concerned only with endemic species. They characterised everything else as a threat. And the Ascension authorities are currently turning Green Mountain into a national park where introduced species, at least the invasive ones, are earmarked for culling rather than conservation.

Conservationists have understandable concerns, Wilkinson says. At least four endemic species have gone extinct on Ascension since the exotics started arriving. But in their urgency to protect endemics, ecologists are missing out on the study of a great enigma.

'As you walk through the forest, you see lots of leaves that have had chunks taken out of them by various insects. There are caterpillars and beetles around,' says Wilkinson. 'But where did they come from? Are they endemic or alien? If alien, did they come with the plant on which they feed or discover it on arrival?' Such questions go to the heart of how rainforests happen.

The Green Mountain forest holds many secrets. And the irony is that the most artificial rainforest in the world could tell us more about rainforest ecology than any number of natural forests.

Questions 27–32

Do the following statements agree with the information given in Reading Passage 3?

In boxes 27–32 on your answer sheet write

TRUE   if the statement agrees with the information
FALSE   if the statement contradicts the information
NOT GIVEN if there is no information on this

27 When Peter Osbeck visited Ascension, he found no inhabitants on the island.

28 The natural vegetation on the island contained some species which were found nowhere else.

29 Joseph Hooker assumed that human activity had caused the decline in the island's plant life.

30 British sailors on the island took part in a major tree planting project.

31 Hooker sent details of his planting scheme to a number of different countries.

32 The bamboo and prickly pear seeds sent from England were unsuitable for Ascension.

Questions 33–37

*Complete each sentence with the correct ending **A–G** from the box below.*

*Write the correct letter **A–G** in boxes 33–37 on your answer sheet.*

33 The reason for modern conservationists' concern over Hooker's tree planting programme is that

34 David Wilkinson says the creation of the rainforest in Ascension is important because it shows that

35 Wilkinson says the existence of Ascension's rainforest challenges the theory that

36 Alan Gray questions Wilkinson's theory, claiming that

37 Additional support for Wilkinson's theory comes from findings that

---

A other rainforests may have originally been planted by man.

B many of the island's original species were threatened with destruction.

C the species in the original rainforest were more successful than the newer arrivals.

D rainforests can only develop through a process of slow and complex evolution.

E steps should be taken to prevent the destruction of the original ecosystem.

F randomly introduced species can coexist together.

G the introduced species may have less ecological significance than the original ones.

Questions 38–40

*Choose the correct letter, **A**, **B**, **C** or **D**.*

Write your answers in boxes 38–40 on your answer sheet.

38 Wilkinson suggests that conservationists' concern about the island is misguided because

   A it is based on economic rather than environmental principles.

   B it is not focusing on the most important question.

   C it is encouraging the destruction of endemic species.

   D it is not supported by the local authorities.

39 According to Wilkinson, studies of insects on the island could demonstrate

   A the possibility of new ecological relationships.

   B a future threat to the ecosystem of the island.

   C the existence of previously unknown species.

   D a chance for the survival of rainforest ecology.

40 Overall, what feature of the Ascension rainforest does the writer stress?

   A the conflict of natural and artificial systems

   B the unusual nature of its ecological structure

   C the harm done by interfering with nature

   D the speed and success of its development

Writing module (1 hour)

Strategy

Some Task 1 diagrams show what a device consists of and how it works. If there are several diagrams they may show how the device has developed. In this case, describe the first device briefly and then describe how it was changed or improved in the later stages. Try to link the information across the diagrams and remember to give a summarising statement.

WRITING TASK 1

Tip Strip
- Read the task prompt carefully as this will give you help in how to approach the task. In this case 'stages in the development' suggests how you can structure your answer.
- For help with vocabulary look at the Language of Technology on page 163.

You should spend about 20 minutes on this task.

The diagrams below show stages in the development of simple cooking equipment.

Summarise the information by selecting and reporting the main features, and make comparisons where relevant.

Write at least 150 words.

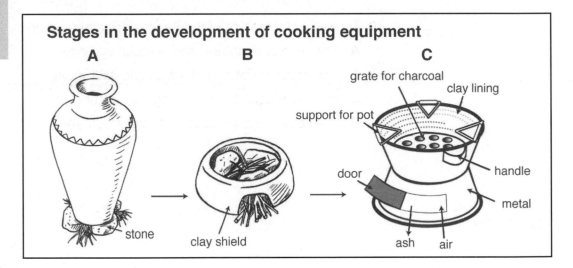

Stages in the development of cooking equipment

A   B   C

grate for charcoal
clay lining
support for pot
handle
metal
door
ash air
stone
clay shield

WRITING TASK 2

Tip Strip
- When making suggestions for solving problems, use tentative language, such as *perhaps*, *possibly*, and modal verbs, e.g. *might*, *could*, etc.
- For help with vocabulary look at the Language of Cause and Effect on page 160, and the Language of the Urban Environment on page 165.

You should spend about 40 minutes on this task.

Write about the following topic:

In recent years some countries have experienced very rapid economic development. This has resulted in much higher standards of living in urban areas but not in the countryside.

This situation may bring some problems for the country as a whole.

What are these problems?

How might they be reduced?

Give reasons for your answer and include any relevant examples from your own knowledge or experience.

Write at least 250 words.

Speaking module (11–14 minutes)

PART 1

Answer the following examiner questions.

Are you a student or do you have a job?
What qualifications do you hope to get from your studies?
OR:
What qualifications did you have to have for your job?
Do you meet many people in your job / studies? Why / Why not?

Now let's talk about clothes.

What kind of clothes do you wear for work / college?
Do you prefer wearing formal or casual clothes? Why?
Do you like to get clothes as gifts from friends or family? Why / Why not?

PART 2

You have one minute to make notes on the following. Then talk about it for two minutes.

Tip Strip
• Think about the tense you need to use for this task.

> Describe a family event you are looking forward to.
>
> You should say:
> > what the event is
> > where it will be held
> > what you will do at this event
>
> Explain why you are looking forward to this family event.

Did you help to plan this event?
Does your family often have special events?

PART 3

Think about the issues and answer the questions.

Tip Strip
• You are not expected to know about these topics, but you should be able to think about them in relation to your own context. Try to explore the topic and ask the examiner for clarification or examples if you're not sure what he or she means.

Let's talk about family celebrations.

What type of special occasions are generally celebrated in your country?
How important is it for families to celebrate occasions together? Why?
Are family occasions as important today as they were for former generations?

Let's think about any recent social changes in your country.

How has the role of elderly people in the family changed in recent times?
Who has more power and influence in the family today, young people or grandparents?
In the future what kind of units or groups will people live in, do you think?
What impact have modern lifestyles had on neighbourhood communities? Why?

Listening module (approx 30 minutes + transfer time)

Questions 1–10

Questions 1–10

Complete the form below.

Write **NO MORE THAN THREE WORDS AND/OR A NUMBER** *for each answer.*

Tip Strip

- **Question 3:** You will hear the information about the main road and its number before the information you need to answer Question 3. Notice that the preposition *in* is written before the gap.
- **Question 10:** The woman introduces this topic, but you need to listen to the man's reply for the exact word you need.

Report on abandoned vehicle	
Example	*Answer*
Name of caller	<u>Mrs Shefford</u>
Address	41, **1** ....
	Barrowdale
	WH4 5JP
Telephone	**2** ....
Vehicle location	in **3** .... near main road (A69)
Type of vehicle	**4** ....
Make	Catala
Model	**5** ....
Present colour of vehicle	**6** ....
Vehicle number	S 322 GEC
General condition	poor – one **7** .... , cracked windscreen
Length of time at site	**8** ....
Land belongs to	**9** ....
Last owner	no information available
Other notes	vehicle does not belong to a **10** .... resident

Questions 11–20

Questions 11–17

Complete the sentences below.

*Write **NO MORE THAN TWO WORDS AND/OR A NUMBER** for each answer.*

The story of John Manjiro

11 Manjiro started work as a .... when he was still a young boy.

12 He spent .... on a deserted island before he was rescued.

13 He became friends with William Whitfield, who was a ship's
    ....

14 The cost of Manjiro's .... in America was covered by the
    Whitfield family.

15 Manjiro eventually returned to Japan, where he carried out important
    work as a teacher and ....

16 Fairhaven and Tosashimizu are now officially ....

17 Every two years, the John Manjiro .... is held in Fairhaven.

Questions 18–20

Label the map below.

*Write the correct letter **A–I** next to
Questions 18–20.*

Tip Strip
• **Questions 18–20:**
Notice the direction of
the arrows on the roads
– this will help you
follow the directions
given.

18 Whitfield family house   ....

19 Old Oxford School   ....

20 School of Navigation   ....

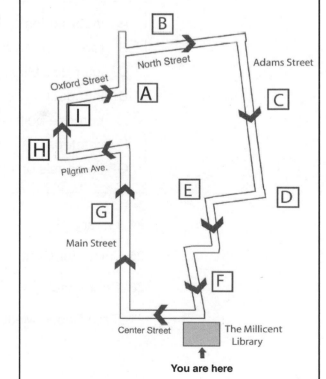

Questions 21–30

Questions 21–23

Tip Strip

• **Question 21:** Notice that you are listening for the <u>main thing</u> Julia feels she has gained.

*Choose the best answer, **A**, **B** or **C**.*

21 What is the main thing Julia feels she has gained from her experience in retail?

    A better understanding of customer attitudes

    B improved ability to predict fashion trends

    C more skill in setting priorities in her work

22 Why is Julia interested in doing the postgraduate course?

    A It will enable her to develop new types of technology.

    B It will allow her to specialise in a design area of her choice.

    C It will provide managerial training focusing on her needs.

23 What would Julia like to do after she has completed the postgraduate course?

    A work overseas

    B start her own business

    C stay in an academic environment

Questions 24–27

What does each university facility have?

*Choose your answers from the box and write the correct letter **A–G** next to Questions 24–27.*

    A laboratories

    B rooms for individual study

    C inter-disciplinary focus

    D introductory course

    E purpose-built premises

    F cafeteria

    G emphasis on creative use

---

24 Library   ………

25 Computer Centre   ………

26 Photomedia   ………

27 Time Based Media   ………

Tip Strip

- A change of activity type often goes with a new topic in the recording. Listen for 'signposting language' to indicate when the topic is changing.

- Remember that in sentence and summary completion tasks, the words you write must be grammatically correct.

SECTION 4

Tip Strip

- **Questions 31–40:** Here you are listening for the main ideas – in the text, these may be preceded or followed by discussion of specific examples.

- **Question 40:** Your answer must include an adjective to reflect the speaker's main point here.

Tip Strip

When you are transferring answers to the answer sheet:

- NEVER copy anything that is already written on the question paper, either before or after your answer, e.g. for Question 39 you should NOT copy the article *the*.

- Check that you have not written words in your answer that are already written on the question paper (e.g. just before or just after the gap).

- Check that you are writing next to the correct number.

- Check that your spelling is correct and your handwriting is clear.

Questions 28–30

Complete the summary below.

Write **NO MORE THAN TWO WORDS** *for each answer.*

MA in Fashion Design: Assessment

Assessment includes three **28** .... which take place at the end of the stages of the degree. Final assessment is based on a project, and includes the student's **29** .... , in the form of a written report, and the **30** .... , to which representatives of fashion companies are invited.

Questions 31–40

Questions 31–40

Complete the notes below.

Write **NO MORE THAN THREE WORDS** *for each answer.*

Laughter

The nature of laughter

- laughter is a **31** .... process – involves movement and sound

- it is controlled by our **32** ....

Reasons for laughter

- only 10% of laughter is caused by jokes / funny stories

- may have begun as sign of **33** .... after a dangerous situation

- nowadays, may help to develop **34** .... within a group

- connected to **35** .... (e.g. use of humour by politicians or bosses)

- may be related to male / female differences (e.g. women laugh more at male speakers)

- may be used in a **36** .... way to keep someone out of a group

Benefits of laughter

- safe method for the **37** .... of emotions such as anger and sadness

- provides good aerobic exercise

- leads to drop in levels of stress-related **38** ....

- improves the **39** ....

- can stop **40** .... and improve sleep

Reading module (1 hour)

Astronaut ice cream, anyone?

Freeze-drying is a technique that can help to provide food for astronauts. But it also has other applications nearer home.

Freeze-drying is like suspended animation for food; you can store a freeze-dried meal for years, and then, when you're finally ready to eat it, you can completely revitalisc it with a little hot water. Even after several years, the original foodstuff will be virtually unchanged.

The technique basically involves completely removing the water from some material, such as food, while leaving the rest of the material virtually intact. The main reason for doing this is either to preserve the food or to reduce its weight. Removing the water from food keeps it from spoiling, because the microorganisms such as bacteria that cause spoiling cannot survive without it. Similarly, the enzymes which occur naturally in food cannot cause ripening without water, so removing water from food will also stop the ripening process.

Freeze-drying significantly reduces the total weight of the food because most food is largely made up of water; for example, many fruits are more than 80–90% water. Removing this makes the food much lighter and therefore makes transportation less difficult. The military and camping-supply companies freeze-dry foods to make them easier for an individual to carry and NASA has also freeze-dried foods for the cramped quarters on board spacecraft.

The process is also used to preserve other sorts of material, such as pharmaceuticals. Chemists can greatly extend pharmaceutical shelf life by freeze-drying the material and storing it in a container free of oxygen and water. Similarly, research scientists may use freeze-drying to preserve biological samples for long periods of time. Even valuable manuscripts that had been water damaged have been saved by using this process.

Freeze-drying is different from simple drying because it is able to remove almost all the water from materials, whereas simple drying techniques can only remove 90–95%. This means that the damage caused by bacteria and enzymes can virtually be stopped, rather than just slowed down. In addition, the composition and structure of the material is not significantly changed, so materials can be revitalised without compromising the quality of the original.

This is possible because in freeze-drying, solid water – ice – is converted directly into water vapour, missing out the liquid phase entirely. This is called 'sublimation', the shift from a solid directly into a gas. Just like evaporation, sublimation occurs when a molecule gains enough energy to break free from the molecules around it. Water will sublime from a solid (ice) to a gas (vapour) when the molecules have enough energy to break free but the conditions aren't right for a liquid to form. These conditions are determined by heat and atmospheric pressure. When the temperature is above freezing point, so that ice can thaw, but the atmospheric pressure is too low for a liquid to form (below 0.06 atmospheres (ATM)) then it becomes a gas.

This is the principle on which a freeze-drying machine is based. The material to be preserved is placed in a freeze-drying chamber which is connected to a freezing coil and refrigerator compressor. When the chamber is sealed the compressor lowers the temperature inside it. The material is frozen solid, which separates the water from everything around it on a molecular level, even though the water is still present. Next, a vacuum pump forces air out of the chamber, lowering the atmospheric pressure below to 0.06 ATM. The heating units apply a small amount of heat to the shelves in the chamber, causing the ice to change phase. Since the pressure in the chamber is so low, the ice turns directly into water vapour, which leaves the freeze-drying chamber, and flows past the freezing coil. The water vapour condenses onto the freezing coil in the form of solid ice, in the same way that water condenses as frost on a cold day.

The process continues for many hours (even days) while the material gradually dries out. This time is necessary to avoid overheating, which might affect the structure of the material. Once it has dried sufficiently, it is sealed in a moisture-free package. As long as the package is secure, the material can sit on a shelf for years and years without degrading, until it is restored to its original form with a little hot water. If everything works correctly, the material will go through the entire process almost completely unscathed.

In fact, freeze-drying, as a general concept, is not new but has been around for centuries. The ancient Incas of Peru used mountain peaks along the Andes as natural food preservers. The extremely cold temperatures and low pressure at those high altitudes prevented food from spoiling in the same basic way as a modern freeze-drying machine and a freezer.

Questions 1–5

Complete the notes below.

Choose **NO MORE THAN THREE WORDS** from the passage for each answer.

Write your answers in boxes 1–5 on your answer sheet.

Tip Strip
• Take care with spelling when copying words from the passage.

Uses of freeze-drying:

• food preservation

• easy **1** .... of food items

• long-term storage of **2** .... and biological samples

• preservation of precious **3** ....

Freeze-drying

• is based on process of **4** ....

• is more efficient than **5** ....

Questions 6–9

Label the diagram below.

Choose **NO MORE THAN TWO WORDS** from the passage for each answer.

Write your answers in boxes 6–9 on your answer sheet.

A simplified freeze-drying machine

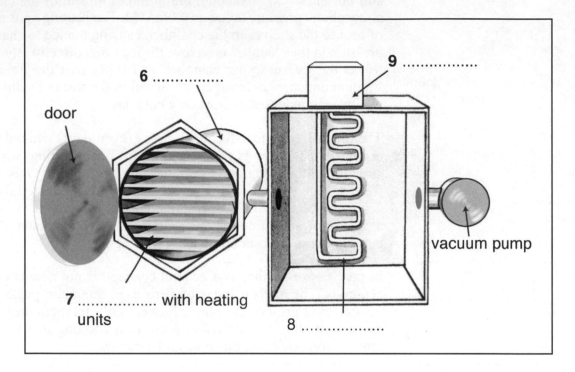

6 ....

door

9 ....

vacuum pump

7 .... with heating units

8 ....

Questions 10–13

Complete the summary below.

Choose **NO MORE THAN THREE WORDS AND/OR A NUMBER** from the passage for each answer.

Write your answers in boxes 10–13 on your answer sheet.

Freeze-drying prevents food from going bad by stopping the activity of microorganisms or **10** .... Its advantages are that the food tastes and feels the same as the original because both the **11** .... and .... are preserved. The process is carried out slowly in order to ensure that **12** .... does not take place. The people of one ancient mountain civilisation were able to use this method of food preservation because the conditions needed were present at **13** ....

Tip Strip
• **Question 13:** Check your answer goes with the preposition *at*.

THE WILD SIDE OF TOWN

The countryside is no longer the place to see wildlife, according to Chris Barnes. These days you are more likely to find impressive numbers of skylarks, dragonflies and toads in your own back garden.

The past half century has seen an interesting reversal in the fortunes of much of Britain's wildlife. Whilst the rural countryside has become poorer and poorer, wildlife habitat in towns has burgeoned. Now, if you want to hear a deafening dawn chorus of birds or familiarise yourself with foxes, you can head for the urban forest.

Whilst species that depend on wide open spaces such as the hare, the eagle and the red deer may still be restricted to remote rural landscapes, many of our wild plants and animals find the urban ecosystem ideal. This really should be no surprise, since it is the fragmentation and agrochemical pollution in the farming lowlands that has led to the catastrophic decline of so many species.

By contrast, most urban open spaces have escaped the worst of the pesticide revolution, and they are an intimate mosaic of interconnected habitats. Over the years, the cutting down of hedgerows on farmland has contributed to habitat isolation and species loss. In towns, the tangle of canals, railway embankments, road verges and boundary hedges lace the landscape together, providing first-class ecological corridors for species such as hedgehogs, kingfishers and dragonflies.

Urban parks and formal recreation grounds are valuable for some species, and many of them are increasingly managed with wildlife in mind. But in many places their significance is eclipsed by the huge legacy of post-industrial land – demolished factories, waste tips, quarries, redundant railway yards and other so-called 'brownfield' sites. In Merseyside, South Yorkshire and the West Midlands, much of this has been spectacularly colonised with birch and willow woodland, herb-rich grassland and shallow wetlands. As a consequence, there are song birds and predators in abundance over these once-industrial landscapes.

There are fifteen million domestic gardens in the UK, and whilst some are still managed as lifeless chemical war zones, most benefit the local wildlife, either through benign neglect or positive encouragement. Those that do best tend to be woodland species, and the garden lawns and flower borders, climber-covered fences, shrubberies and fruit trees are a plausible alternative. Indeed, in some respects gardens are rather better than the real thing, especially with exotic flowers extending the nectar season. Birdfeeders can also supplement the natural seed supply, and only the millions of domestic cats may spoil the scene.

As Britain's gardeners have embraced the idea of 'gardening with nature', wildlife's response has been spectacular. Between 1990 and the year 2000, the number of different bird species seen at artificial feeders in gardens increased from 17 to an amazing 81. The BUGS project (Biodiversity in Urban Gardens in Sheffield) calculates that there are 25,000 garden ponds and 100,000 nest boxes in that one city alone.

We are at last acknowledging that the wildlife habitat in towns provides a valuable life support system. The canopy of the urban forest is filtering air pollution, and intercepting rainstorms, allowing the water to drip more gradually to the ground. Sustainable urban drainage relies on ponds and wetlands to contain storm water runoff, thus reducing the risk of flooding, whilst reed beds and other wetland wildlife communities also help to clean up the water. We now have scientific proof that contact with wildlife close to home can help to reduce stress and anger. Hospital patients with a view of natural green space make a more rapid recovery and suffer less pain.

Traditionally, nature conservation in the UK has been seen as marginal and largely rural. Now we are beginning to place it at the heart of urban environmental and economic policy. There are now dozens of schemes to create new habitats and restore old ones in and around our big cities. Biodiversity is big in parts of London, thanks to schemes such as the London Wetland Centre in the south west of the city.

This is a unique scheme masterminded by the Wildfowl and Wetlands Trust to create a wildlife reserve out of a redundant Victorian reservoir. Within five years of its creation the Centre has been hailed as one of the top sites for nature in England and made a Site of Special Scientific Interest. It consists of a 105-acre wetland site, which is made up of different wetland habitats of shallow, open water and grazing marsh. The site attracts more than 104 species of bird, including nationally important rarities like the bittern.

We need to remember that if we work with wildlife, then wildlife will work for us – and this is the very essence of sustainable development.

Tip Strip
- The subheading contains some words that may be unfamiliar to you. However, you can work out that these words refer to types of wildlife. You do not need to know exactly what they are in order to follow the writer's argument.
- **Question 14:** Use the context of the whole sentence to deduce the meaning of *burgeoned* in Paragraph 1. Does this paragraph give information about the <u>proportions</u> of wildlife presently living in rural and urban areas?

Do the following statements agree with the information given in Reading Passage 2?

In boxes 14–19 on your answer sheet write

TRUE   *if the statement agrees with the information*
FALSE   *if the statement contradicts the information*
NOT GIVEN *if there is no information on this*

14 There is now more wildlife in UK cities than in the countryside.

15 Rural wildlife has been reduced by the use of pesticides on farms.

16 In the past, hedges on farms used to link up different habitats.

17 New urban environments are planned to provide ecological corridors for wildlife.

18 Public parks and gardens are being expanded to encourage wildlife.

19 Old industrial wastelands have damaged wildlife habitats in urban areas.

Questions 20–23

Answer the questions below, using **NO MORE THAN THREE WORDS AND/OR A NUMBER** from the passage for each answer.

Write your answers in boxes 20–23 on your answer sheet.

Tip Strip
- **Question 20:** Look for information about gardens in urban areas. You need to identify a type of wildlife, not a particular plant or animal.
- **Questions 20–23:** Remember that correct answers may be below the maximum number of words allowed. Only include the words essential for the meaning.

20 Which type of wildlife benefits most from urban gardens?

21 What type of garden plants can benefit birds and insects?

22 What represents a threat to wildlife in urban gardens?

23 At the last count, how many species of bird were spotted in urban gardens?

Questions 24–26

*Choose **THREE** letters **A–G**.*

Write your answers in boxes 24–26 on your answer sheet.

In which **THREE** ways can wildlife habitats benefit people living in urban areas?

    A They can make the cities greener.

    B They can improve the climate.

    C They can promote human well-being.

    D They can extend the flowering season.

    E They can absorb excess water.

    F They can attract wildlife.

    G They can help clean the urban atmosphere.

Question 27

Tip Strip

• Question 27 tests global understanding. Start by looking at the last paragraph, but think about the meaning of the whole text, using the title and subtitle to help you.

*Choose the correct answer, **A**, **B**, **C** or **D**.*

Write your answer in box 27 on your answer sheet.

27 The writer believes that sustainable development is dependent on

    A urban economic policy.

    B large restoration schemes.

    C active nature conservation.

    D government projects.

You should spend about 20 minutes on **Questions 28–40**, which are based on Reading Passage 3 below.

Questions 28–33

Reading Passage 3 has eleven paragraphs **A–K**.

Choose the correct heading for Paragraphs **A–F** from the list of headings below.

Write the correct number (**i–viii**) in boxes 28–33 on your answer sheet.

Tip Strip

- When you have done Questions 28–30, look briefly through Paragraphs G–K in the text to get a general idea of the content. This will help you to locate the answers to the remaining questions.

List of headings

i	Avoiding tiredness in athletes
ii	Puzzling evidence raises a question
iii	Traditional explanations
iv	Interpreting the findings
v	Developing muscle fibres
vi	A new hypothesis
vii	Description of a new test
viii	Surprising results in an endurance test

---

28 Paragraph **A**

29 Paragraph **B**

30 Paragraph **C**

31 Paragraph **D**

32 Paragraph **E**

33 Paragraph **F**

Running on empty

A revolutionary new theory in sports physiology.

A For almost a century, scientists have presumed, not unreasonably, that fatigue – or exhaustion – in athletes originates in the muscles. Precise explanations have varied, but all have been based on the 'limitations theory'. In other words, muscles tire because they hit a physical limit: they either run out of fuel or oxygen or they drown in toxic by-products.

B In the past few years, however, Timothy Noakes and Alan St Clair Gibson from the University of Cape Town, South Africa, have examined this standard theory. The deeper they dig, the more convinced they have become that physical fatigue simply isn't the same as a car running out of petrol. Fatigue, they argue, is caused not by distress signals springing from overtaxed muscles, but is an emotional response which begins in the brain. The essence of their new theory is that the brain, using a mix of physiological, subconscious and conscious cues, paces the muscles to keep them well back from the brink of exhaustion. When the brain decides it's time to quit, it creates the distressing sensations we interpret as unbearable muscle fatigue. This 'central governor' theory remains controversial, but it does explain many puzzling aspects of athletic performance.

C   A recent discovery that Noakes calls the 'lactic acid paradox' made him start researching this area seriously. Lactic acid is a by-product of exercise, and its accumulation is often cited as a cause of fatigue. But when research subjects exercise in conditions simulating high altitude, they become fatigued even though lactic acid levels remain low. Nor has the oxygen content of their blood fallen too low for them to keep going. Obviously, Noakes deduced, something else was making them tire before they hit either of these physiological limits.

D   Probing further, Noakes conducted an experiment with seven cyclists who had sensors taped to their legs to measure the nerve impulses travelling through their muscles. It has long been known that during exercise, the body never uses 100% of the available muscle fibres in a single contraction. The amount used varies, but in endurance tasks such as this cycling test the body calls on about 30%.

E   Noakes reasoned that if the limitations theory was correct and fatigue was due to muscle fibres hitting some limit, the number of fibres used for each pedal stroke should increase as the fibres tired and the cyclist's body attempted to compensate by recruiting an ever-larger proportion of the total. But his team found exactly the opposite. As fatigue set in, the electrical activity in the cyclists' legs declined – even during sprinting, when they were striving to cycle as fast as they could.

F   To Noakes, this was strong evidence that the old theory was wrong. 'The cyclists may have felt completely exhausted,' he says, 'but their bodies actually had considerable reserves that they could theoretically tap by using a greater proportion of the resting fibres.' This, he believes, is proof that the brain is regulating the pace of the workout to hold the cyclists well back from the point of catastrophic exhaustion.

G   More evidence comes from the fact that fatigued muscles don't actually run out of anything critical. Levels of glycogen, which is the muscles' primary fuel, and ATP, the chemical they use for temporary energy storage, decline with exercise but never bottom out. Even at the end of a marathon, ATP levels are 80–90% of the resting norm, and glycogen levels never get to zero.

H   Further support for the central regulator comes from the fact that top athletes usually manage to go their fastest at the end of a race, even though, theoretically, that's when their muscles should be closest to exhaustion. But Noakes believes the end spurt makes no sense if fatigue is caused by muscles poisoning themselves with lactic acid, as this would cause racers to slow down rather than enable them to sprint for the finish line. In the new theory, the explanation is obvious. Knowing the end is near, the brain slightly relaxes its vigil, allowing the athlete to tap some of the body's carefully hoarded reserves.

I But the central governor theory does not mean that what's happening in the muscles is irrelevant. The governor constantly monitors physiological signals from the muscles, along with other information, to set the level of fatigue. A large number of signals are probably involved, but, unlike the limitations theory, the central governor theory suggests that these physiological factors are not the direct determinants of fatigue, but simply information to take into account.

J Conscious factors can also intervene. Noakes believes that the central regulator evaluates the planned workout, and sets a pacing strategy accordingly. Experienced runners know that if they set out on a 10-kilometre run, the first kilometre feels easier than the first kilometre of a 5-kilometre run, even though there should be no difference. That, Noakes says, is because the central governor knows you have farther to go in the longer run and has programmed itself to dole out fatigue symptoms accordingly.

K St Clair Gibson believes there is a good reason why our bodies are designed to keep something back. That way, there's always something left in the tank for an emergency. In ancient times, and still today, life would be too dangerous if our bodies allowed us to become so tired that we couldn't move quickly when faced with an unexpected need.

Questions 34–40

Classify the following ideas as relating to

A *the Limitations Theory*
B *the Central Governor Theory*
C *both the Limitations Theory and the Central Governor Theory*

*Write the correct letter, **A**, **B** or **C**, in boxes 34–40 on your answer sheet.*

NB *You may use any letter more than once.*

34 Lactic acid is produced in muscles during exercise.

35 Athletes can keep going until they use up all their available resources.

36 Mental processes control the symptoms of tiredness.

37 The physiological signals from an athlete's muscles are linked to fatigue.

38 The brain plans and regulates muscle performance in advance of a run.

39 Athletes' performance during a race may be affected by lactic acid build-up.

40 Humans are genetically programmed to keep some energy reserves.

Tip Strip
• **Question 34:** Is this something that is claimed by Noakes, or that is given as an accepted idea?
• **Question 35:** Look at the example of the car in Paragraph B. Is this repeating the same idea as Paragraph A, or the opposite idea?

Writing module (1 hour)

WRITING TASK 1

You should spend about 20 minutes on this task.

The tables below give information about the world population and distribution in 1950 and 2000, with an estimate of the situation in 2050.

Tip Strip
- Try to group the information according to trends. Do not simply write a list of figures for different areas.

Summarise the information by selecting and reporting the main features, and make comparisons where relevant.

Write at least 150 words.

World Population 1950–2050			
World Population	**1950**	**2000**	**2050**
(billions)	2.5	6.0	9.0 (estimate)

Distribution of World Population by Region			
Africa	9%	13%	20%
Asia	56%	60%	59%
Europe	22%	12%	7%
Latin America	6%	9%	9%
North America	7%	5%	4%
Oceania	<1%	1%	1%

WRITING TASK 2

Tip Strip
- Skim the strategy for this type of Task 2 in Test 1 on page 34.

You should spend about 40 minutes on this task.

Write about the following topic:

The exploration and development of safe alternatives to fossil fuels should be the most important global priority today.

To what extent do you agree or disagree?

Give reasons for your answer and include any relevant examples from your own knowledge or experience.

Write at least 250 words.

Speaking module (11–14 minutes)

PART 1

Answer the following examiner questions.

Tip Strip
- Pay attention to the time markers and tense of this topic.

Tell me about the town or city you live in now.

How long have you lived in this city?
Do tourists visit your city? Why / Why not?
What places do you think tourists should see in your city?
What is the best way for tourists to travel around your city? Why?

Now tell me about the kind of music you listen to.

What kind of music do you prefer? Why?
Have you ever been to a music concert? Why / Why not?
Why do you think music is important to people?

PART 2

You have one minute to make notes on the following topic. Then talk about it for two minutes.

> Describe a TV or radio programme you enjoyed when you were a child.
>
> You should say:
> > what the programme was about
> > when it was on
> > where you watched or listened to it
>
> Explain why you enjoyed this programme when you were a child.

Would you still like this programme today?
Did your friends enjoy this programme too?

PART 3

Think about the issues and answer the questions.

Let's talk about TV and radio in your country.

In your country, which do people prefer: watching TV or listening to radio? Why?
What kind of programmes are most popular?
Do men and women tend to like the same kind of programmes? Why / Why not?

Now let's think about the effects of TV.

Some people think that watching TV can be a negative influence. Would you agree?
What benefits can TV bring people?
What priorities do you think TV stations should have?

What about developments in programming?

What kind of 'interactive' programmes are there in your country?
Are these a good or a bad development? Why?
What kind of programmes will there be in the future, do you think?

Reading module (1 hour)

About the General Training Reading module
The General Training Reading module has three sections.
Section 1 is related to everyday situations and may have several short informational texts.
Section 2 contains one or more short texts on practical topics related to education and training.
Section 3 has one longer text on a topic of general interest.

There are forty questions, and a variety of task types similar to those in the Academic Reading module. You should aim to spend about the same amount of time on each section.

SECTION 1   *You should spend about 20 minutes on* **Questions 1–13**.

Clear Lighting

Use energy more efficiently and help save the planet by switching to low-energy light bulbs.

Many of us still use traditional bulbs around the house. But simply replacing one traditional 100-watt bulb in your home with a low-energy equivalent will save you the amount of electricity required to make 1,200 cups of tea. It will also reduce your annual electricity bill, so as well as using less energy, you'll be paying less money. This is because traditional bulbs only use 10% of the electrical energy to produce light, while the remaining 90% is wasted as heat. Low-energy bulbs, which are also known as compact fluorescent lamps, or CFLs, are more efficient because most of the electrical energy is used to generate actual light instead.

CFLs are more expensive to buy, costing an average of £6 each compared to 40p for a traditional equivalent, but they work out cheaper in the long run because they use less electricity and are much more durable, lasting at least six times longer.

However, they do have some drawbacks. For example, they can have a slow start-up, taking some time to reach their full brightness, so you are recommended to use them where they will be left on for longer periods, such as your living room or hallway. This also avoids frequent switching on and off, which may also shorten the life of the bulb.

CFLs are also noticeably dimmer when used in cold conditions, such as in a garage or outside, as this can reduce the bulb's efficiency, so this is not recommended. Finally, CFLs are also likely to be up to three times heavier than traditional bulbs, which may make them unsuitable for some light fittings, so you should always check these before changing your bulbs.

Questions 1–7

Look at the information about lighting on page 143.

Complete the sentences below with words taken from the passage.

*Write **NO MORE THAN THREE WORDS** for each answer.*

Write your answers in boxes 1–7 on your answer sheet.

1   If you change your type of light bulb you could save both energy and
    ....

2   Conventional bulbs convert most of the energy they use into ....

3   You do not need to replace CFLs very often because they are very
    ....

4   When they are first switched on, CFLs may have a ....

5   Constantly using the light switch may .... of a CFL.

6   Low temperatures may reduce the .... of CFLs.

7   CFLs may weigh more than other bulbs, so you must only use them with
    appropriate ....

Rights in the workplace

This leaflet explains your legal rights when you are at work, including what your employer must (and must not) do for you.

Do I need a contract?

A written contract of employment is useful to have because it sets out what you can expect from your job and from your employer. There are laws to protect workers, whether or not they have a written contract.

Every worker has the right to be paid and to enjoy a reasonably safe place of work. You also have certain legal rights, such as the right not to be discriminated against at work because of your sex, race or disability.

What can I do if I don't have a written contract?

Every employee has a legal right to receive a written statement which sets out your terms of employment. You should get this within eight weeks of starting your job. The terms include basic things like the name of your employer and where you will be working, the date you started work, how much you will earn and when you will be paid. It will also include terms about your hours of work, your holiday entitlement and any benefits, such as holiday and sickness pay and pensions. It should also state the length of notice you both have to give, as well as any disciplinary rules.

In many cases, employers don't do all of this. They either give employees a short offer letter or nothing at all. This is partly because an employer can't be fined for not giving you a proper contract.

If you want a contract, but your employer won't give you one, all you can do is apply to an employment tribunal for a list of what should be included in your written statement.

Questions 8–13

Do the following statements agree with the information given in the extract above?

In boxes 8–13 on your answer sheet write

TRUE   *if the statement agrees with the information*
FALSE   *if the statement contradicts the information*
NOT GIVEN   *if there is no information on this*

8   Employers have to provide written contracts for their employees.

9   There are laws to ensure that people are treated equally at work.

10 A written statement has the same value as a contract.

11 Employers should give written terms of employment to employees in the first two months of the job.

12 Employers must contribute towards their employees' pensions.

13 An employment tribunal can force employers to issue contracts.

Adult Education Courses: Computing skills for all levels

A   Introduction to Computing
This 10-week course is for those with only a little experience but no confidence in your computing skills. It aims to help you to get to know your way around the computer, to understand the jargon and to use the basic applications of word processing, database and spreadsheets. Fees: £25 payable at start of course.

B   Computer Literacy and Information Technology
A certificated course offering three or more modules chosen from, e.g. word processing, database, spreadsheets, spreadsheet graphic data and computer art. This course is suitable for those with a basic understanding of computers. Fees: £10 per module, payable at start of course.

C   Integrated Business Technology 1
This 30-week programme consists of five set modules that must be successfully completed in order to gain the intermediate level Certificate in IBT. Word processing, database, spreadsheets, spreadsheet graphic data and integrated documents are all covered. This is a challenging course leading to a good level of accuracy, presentation, business understanding and skill. Entry qualification – Certificate in Computer Literacy and IT. Fees: £75 payable at start of programme, or £25 payable at the start of each 10-week session.

D   Text / Word Processing Levels 1, 2 and 3
Students wishing to apply will be assessed and entered for the appropriate exam course. All abilities are catered for, including absolute beginners with no previous keyboard experience [Level 1 group]. Fees: £20, £25 or £30 according to level. Additional examination fee of £10 – both payable in advance of course to reserve a place.

E   Integrated Business Technology 2
Six set modules must be successfully completed in order to gain the certificate for this 60-week course. The modules will include Electronic Communication, File Management, Source Data Processing, Automated Presentation Production and Publication Production. This is a high-level course aimed at further developing business understanding, presentation and effective computing skills. Applicants must have the IBT intermediate level certificate and an intermediate level qualification in Desk Top Publishing, as well as experience of using email. Fees: £125 payable at start of course only. Booking essential for course places.

Questions 14–20

Look at the information on five computer courses on the page opposite.

For which course are the following statements true?

Write the correct letter **A–E** in boxes 14–20 on your answer sheet.

NB *You may use any letter more than once.*

14 People who know nothing about computers can join this course.

15 This course does not lead to any formal qualification.

16 Students can pay for parts of this course at different times.

17 This is an advanced-level course.

18 Those applying for this course only need one relevant qualification.

19 Students on this course can choose the number of components they want to do.

20 Students have to pay extra money to take the final test on this course.

ENROL NOW AT YOUR CENTRE

Welcome to our new Adult Community Education brochure.
You will find a wide range of learning opportunities which reflect the County Council's commitment to community-based adult learning.

How to join a course
Our courses are very popular so we advise you to enrol early to avoid disappointment.
- By post: complete the booking form and return it together with your cheque to the main centre organising your course.
- In person: at one of our main centres. Details of opening times can be found under the information for each centre.
- At an information week: this is held at our main centres prior to the beginning of term. You can meet your tutor to make sure you have chosen the right course before you enrol.
- At the first session: only if there are places available, so please telephone the centre beforehand.

Further information
- You can telephone your main centre for the latest information on the availability of courses.
- Ask for a course description sheet, which will give you more details on the suitability of each course.
- Come to a main centre at the beginning of term where you can talk to members of staff.
- Visit our website at www.midland.edu.uk/adult

Lifelong learning for all – additional needs
We aim to accommodate students with disabilities into our provision wherever possible. Your main centre can give you information on special equipment and/or individual learner support which may be available to enable you to join our course. Disabled access does vary from centre to centre, however, so please check with your centre before enrolling.

Child care
Many of our centres offer crèche facilities, which are staffed by experienced and qualified workers. Please book early, as places are limited.

How much do courses cost?
The prices are displayed in three bands and are inclusive of tuition and registration fees. However, there may be additional costs such as examination fees, materials and books. You can find out about these at the main centre.
Band A: Full fee.
Band B: Fee payable by people over the age of 60.
Band C: Fee payable by low-income groups on recognised benefits.
NB If you are claiming a reduction in fees you will be required to bring evidence of your entitlement when you enrol, and at the start of each term.

Questions 21–27

Look at the information opposite about enrolling for adult courses.

Complete the sentences below with words taken from the passage.

*Write **NO MORE THAN THREE WORDS** for each answer.*

Write your answers in boxes 21–27 on your answer sheet.

21 People who mail their applications have to send a .... together with payment.

22 Before all the courses start, the main centres hold ....

23 It is not always possible to enrol at .... of popular courses.

24 For more information about course content, students can talk to tutors, check the website or request a ....

25 Many centres have special facilities and services for students with physical problems, but not all centres have ....

26 Course fees only cover the cost of ....

27 People such as senior citizens and those with little money can get a ....

*You should spend about 20 minutes on **Questions 28–40**, which are based on Reading Passage 3 below.*

Battle of the Bag

The world has declared war on the plastic bag. What did this harmless item do to attract such a negative reaction? Caroline Williams explains.

For a growing number of environmentalists, the humble plastic bag has become public enemy number one – an unnecessary evil that must be stopped. The only people who have a good word to say about plastic bags are the plastic-bag industry, unsurprisingly. They claim that plastic bags are nowhere near the world's worst environmental problem and say the reason they are under attack is because they are an easy and emotive target that reflects individuals' guilt about general environmental responsibility. So who is right?

Since it was introduced in the 1970s, the plastic bag – made from high-density polyethylene – has become part of our lives, and today most people around the world don't use anything else to carry their shopping. Estimates differ, but it is thought that the UK gets through at least 9 billion plastic bags a year. Globally, we carry home between 500 billion and a trillion every year. That is 150 bags a year for every person on Earth, or, to put it another way, a million a minute and rising. In the UK, even though up to 7 billion plastic bags may be reused, they still end up in rubbish bins, while a few become street litter. But ultimately the vast majority end up in landfill sites as waste. Only a fraction are incinerated for energy production and an even smaller number are recycled into heavy-duty plastic.

Startling as these statistics may be, they do not explain why plastic bags have become so hated, as they still constitute only 1% of UK litter. Claire Wilton of the environmental group Friends of the Earth claims that plastic bags are 'a waste of resources in that we use them once and throw them away'. But there are bigger and better examples of fossil fuel waste, so the issue is also about visible pollution.

Samantha Fanshawe of the UK Marine Conservation Society points out that, 'Plastic bags exceed what you would anticipate to be their pollution impact because they are so much more mobile than other types of litter.' Once the wind reaches them, they become a highly visible problem, blowing around streets and getting caught in the branches of trees.

But plastic bags can also have a devastating effect on wildlife, and the problem is increasing. One victim was a Minke whale washed up in northern France in 2002, with 800 kilograms of plastic bags and other packaging blocking its stomach. The Planet Ark Environmental Foundation in Australia estimates that tens of thousands of marine animals and birds are killed every year, and since most marine animals die far out at sea, the real death toll may be much higher.

Denmark was among the first to try reducing these problems in 1994 when they introduced a tax on packaging, including carrier bags. This led to a 66% drop in take-up at the checkout, despite the fact that it was the retailers and not their customers who had to pay up. Taiwan followed in 2001, charging consumers about two pence for a plastic bag. The tax was criticised by industry and the public as being confusing and unfair but still managed to slash plastic bag usage by 69%.

In 2002, Bangladesh took a more drastic approach, bringing in a total ban on the production and sale of polyethylene and introducing a £5 on-the-spot fine for using a plastic bag. If a blanket ban seems a little extreme, it was prompted by more than just green thinking. In a country with limited waste disposal and virtually no bins, most of the 10 million or so plastic bags used every day were dropped in the street, then washed into rivers and sewers where they choked the country's drainage system. Blocked drains are widely held responsible for the devastating monsoon floods of 1988 and 1989. In the two years since the ban, the once floundering jute-bag industry has been resurrected and street children are reportedly doing a roaring trade in handmade paper bags. A resurgence of rebel plastic-bag manufacturers this year has prompted a government crackdown, with manufacturers facing up to ten years in jail and a fine of £9000.

Elsewhere, governments rich and poor are making attempts to bin the bag. The government of the north Indian state of Himachal Pradesh is also taking a hard line. There, being caught in possession of a polyethylene bag could get you seven years behind bars and a £1000 fine. In 2002, Ireland introduced a tax of 15 cents on plastic carriers, payable by the consumer. Within months the number of bags taken from shops fell by 90%, and in the two years since then, the 'PlasTax' has raised €23 million for waste management initiatives.

According to Wilton, 'Plastic bags are symbolic of a society in which we use things without thinking and then throw them away. Governments have realised that, by focusing on something so symbolic, they can get messages across to people about their behaviour and how it affects the environment.'

The plastic bag industry, unsurprisingly, takes issue with being blamed for general environmental irresponsibility. But even with the facts on their side, manufacturers seem resigned. 'Green marketing wins out every time,' says spokesman Peter Woodall.

Questions 28–31

Label the diagram below.

Choose **ONE WORD OR A NUMBER** from the passage for each answer.

Write your answers in boxes 28–31 on your answer sheet.

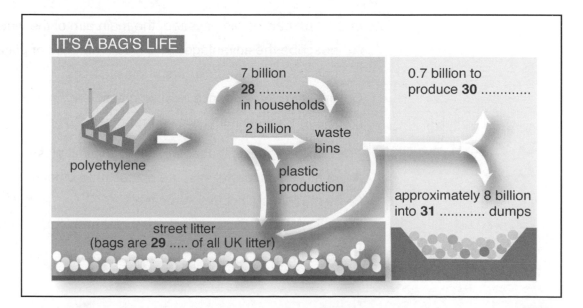

Questions 32–38

Look at the following situations and the list of places (A–E) below.

Match each situation with the place it relates to.

Write the correct letter A–E in boxes 32–38 on your answer sheet.

You may use any letter more than once.

32 The use of plastic bags fell by approximately two-thirds.

33 An unsuccessful local product became popular again.

34 Action against plastic bags was unpopular, but successful.

35 Money from plastic bag taxation is available for environmental projects.

36 Discarded bags may have caused national disasters.

37 Shops had to pay a tax on plastic bags.

38 People can be sent to prison for using plastic bags.

A Denmark

B Taiwan

C Bangladesh

D Himachal Pradesh (India)

E Ireland

Questions 39–40

Choose the correct letter, A, B, C or D.

Write your answers in boxes 39 and 40 on your answer sheet.

39 In the first part of this passage, the main aim of the writer is to

    A describe the advantages and disadvantages of plastic bags.

    B criticise the manufacturers of plastic bags.

    C evaluate the evidence against plastic bags.

    D present relevant statistics about plastic bags.

40 The writer suggests that action taken against plastic bags

    A is more successful in some places than others.

    B is much too strict in some cases.

    C will solve our biggest environmental problem.

    D will put manufacturers out of business.

Writing module (1 hour)

Strategy

Here are some points to remember:

1 For General Training Task 1 you always need to write a letter, so your answer must look like a letter on the page.
2 The prompt describes a situation. This will give you information about who you should write to, so you will know whether the letter should be formal or informal. This is important for the language you use and the opening and closing of the letter.
3 The situation also gives you the reason for writing the letter. Make this very clear in your answer.
4 The three bullet points tell you what information to include. Expand the bullets with your own ideas.
5 The bullet points also help you to organise your letter. Use clear links between the sections.

WRITING TASK 1

Tip Strip

- Remember to fill in a name if your letter is to someone you know. If the letter is formal, semi-formal or informal make sure your ending is appropriate, e.g. *Yours sincerely, Kind regards, With love,*

You should spend about 20 minutes on this task.

A Canadian friend recently sent you a present by post. You want to thank him/her.

Write a letter to your friend. In your letter

- **say how you felt when you received the present**

- **describe what you like about it**

- **explain how you will use the present**

Write at least 150 words.

You do NOT need to write your own address.

Begin your letter as follows:

   Dear .... ,

Strategy

General Training Task 2 is very similar to Academic Writing Task 2, except that the topics may be more personal. All the Task 2 Writing modules are useful preparation for General Training Task 2 writing. Look at the Strategy sections for the Writing module in Test 2 for a step-by-step approach to this specific task type.

WRITING TASK 2

Tip Strip

• Read the prompt carefully to see how many questions you need to answer before you make your plan.

• For help with vocabulary look at the Language of Cause and Effect on page 160.

You should spend about 40 minutes on this task.

You have been asked to write about the following topic.

People who travel to another country to live, work or study for a period of time often suffer badly from homesickness.

Why is this?

What are the best ways to reduce this problem?

Give reasons for your answer and include any relevant examples from your experience.

Write at least 250 words.

ASSESSING YOUR WRITING

ACADEMIC WRITING TASK 1

Read the task carefully and compare the two sample answers below and on page 156.

You should spend about 20 minutes on this task.

The chart below gives information about the percentage of the adult population who were overweight in four different countries in 1980, 1990 and 2000. (Figures are given for the year, or the nearest year available.)

Summarise the information by selecting and reporting the main features, and make comparisons where relevant.

Write at least 150 words.

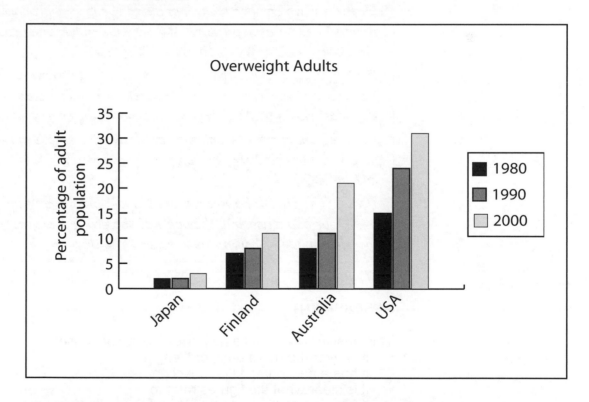

SAMPLE ANSWER A

The chart gives information about the percentage of the adult population who were overweight in Japan, Finland, Australia and the US in 1980, 1990 and 2000.

In 1980 Japan had 2% overweight, Finland had 7%, Australia about 8% and the US 15%. In 1990 Japan was still 2%, Finland 8%, Australia had about 11% and the USA 24%. In 2000 maybe all the countries had more fast food because Japan was 3%, Finland 11%, Australia 21% and USA 31%.

(79 words)

ASSESSMENT

Although this answer has no grammar or vocabulary mistakes it would get a low IELTS band because:
- it is significantly underlength (It would lose a lot of marks for this)
- the introduction is copied from the rubric with only slight changes
- it is not clear what the figures relate to
- there is no focus on trends, the figures are just listed
- there is no comparison between the figures
- there is little organisation: no paragraphs, no signals, no linking
- the candidate tries to explain the information in the last sentence
- there is no summarising statement
- the range of grammar and vocabulary is extremely limited
- there is a lot of repetition

SAMPLE ANSWER B

This chart shows changes in the proportion of overweight people in the adult population of countries in four different regions in 1980, 1990 and 2000.

First of all we can see that Japan had the lowest proportion of overweight adults in all three given years. It also showed the smallest change across the period, rising only 1% to reach 3% by 2000.

Both Finland and Australia had over 5% of adults overweight in 1980, but the increase in figures for Australia was much greater in the following decades, rising to 11% in 1990 and almost doubling Finland at 21% in 2000.

However, the highest proportion of overweight adults in each of the given years was in the USA. The percentage rose from 15% in 1980 to a dramatic 31% in 2000.

Overall, the chart shows that the proportion of overweight adults is rising in all four countries, but the scale of the problem is greater and the rate of increase much higher in Australia and the US.

(167 words)

ASSESSMENT

This answer would get a high IELTS band because:
- it is over the minimum word length
- it has a paraphrased introduction
- it is clear what the figures refer to
- it focuses on the main trends and supports these with figures
- it groups and compares the main sets of data
- the answer is clearly organised using paragraphs, signals, linkers
- there is a clear summarising statement
- the answer describes the information rather than trying to explain it
- a good range of vocabulary and grammar is used
- there is no repetition

ACADEMIC WRITING TASK 2

Read the task carefully and compare the two sample answers below and on page 158.

You should spend about 40 minutes on this task.

Write about the following topic.

Some people think men and women have different natural abilities that make them suitable for different types of work. Others, however, believe that both men and women can be equally suited to do any type of work.

Discuss both these views and give your own opinion.

Give reasons for your answer and include any relevant examples from your own knowledge and experience.

Write at least 250 words.

SAMPLE ANSWER C

I agree that men and women have different natural abilities. This makes them suitable for different types of work. Women are good at looking after children and men are good at earning money for the family. Women are more suited to jobs where they look after people and men are more suited to jobs where they make decisions. Women are emotional and men are strong and can fight. Women are kinder than men. Men are good at being the boss. This is what happens in most countries and this proves that men and women have different natural abilities that make them suitable for different types of work.

(107 words)

ASSESSMENT

Even though there are no grammar or vocabulary errors in this answer it would get a low IELTS band because:
- it is significantly underlength (It would lose a lot of marks for this)
- the introduction is copied from the rubric with only slight changes
- the conclusion is also copied from the rubric
- the response does not discuss both points of view
- it is difficult to identify what the main ideas are
- the ideas are not developed or supported
- ideas are simply listed rather than being organised into an argument
- the response is not organised into paragraphs so it is hard to follow
- there are very few links between sentences
- the writing is repetitive

SAMPLE ANSWER D

It is understandable that some people believe that the physical and genetic differences between men and women equip them for different activities and skills. Because women have babies, they have traditionally worked in the home in most cultures. In addition, employed women have tended to dominate the so-called 'caring professions' such as teaching, nursing or social work, and this has reinforced the idea that women are particularly suited to such jobs.

However, it is very difficult to separate this notion from our cultural traditions and to arrive at any clear idea of what natural abilities belong to one or the other gender. As more and more women in different countries get jobs outside the home, it is clear that they are able to perform jobs that were traditionally only held by men. With high levels of education, even the highest positions in science, politics or law, for example, can be held successfully by women. Therefore, those who claim that the sexes can do the same jobs equally seem to have a good point, especially in terms of intellectual work.

There is also increasing scientific evidence that individual differences between people may be more important than gender differences. In other words, some women may be physically stronger than some men, while some male individuals may be more sensitive, or more caring than some women.

In my opinion, only science will be able to identify what is 'natural' to each gender. But in the meantime, I think that in the modern world individual men and women can be trained to develop similar abilities. Differences in aptitude and talents are greater at the individual level than at the gender level.

(277 words)

ASSESSMENT

This answer would get a high IELTS band because:

- it is over the minimum word length
- it discusses both points of view
- it clearly states the writer's opinion and conclusion
- it has a paraphrased introduction
- there is a clear structure to the argument
- good paragraphing makes it easy to follow
- ideas are supported and developed
- there are clear links between sentences and paragraphs
- a good range of language is used with no repetition

Now check your own written answers using the same criteria for assessment.

VOCABULARY PAGES

1 The Language of Change

X **increased / rose / grew** from … to …
Y **decreased / fell / dropped / declined** from … to …

There was a / an **increase / rise / growth** in X
There was a **decrease / fall / drop / decline** in Y

X **peaked** at / **reached a peak** of …
Y **levelled off** at …
Z **fluctuated** between …

X **remained constant** at …

X rose **gradually** to reach … in 2005
     steadily
     sharply
     dramatically

There was a **gradual** fall to … in 2005
     steady
     sharp
     dramatic

rising / soaring / falling / plummeting prices …

X had **doubled / halved** by 2005

this **trend continued / was reversed** in …

1 Complete the text using expressions from the box below. Use each word or phrase only once.

> steady increase   declined   peaked
>
> growth   dropped dramatically   fall
>
> soaring   fluctuate

Changes in Urban Crime Rate

A few years ago people living in urban areas were very anxious about the **1** ………… crime rates. These **2** ………… four years ago and the government then responded by recruiting more police officers. Subsequently, the **3** ………… in the number of officers on the streets has definitely helped to reverse the trend. Overall crime rates have steadily **4** ………… over the past three years and the number of young offenders, in particular, has **5** ………… from 17% of all city crime to only 7%. We all hope that this trend will continue and the rate will continue to **6** ………… over the next year or two. But even if the figures **7** ………… rather than stabilising, the huge **8** ………… of confidence in the police is likely to continue as a positive force in the community.

2 Underline the language of change in each of the sentences below. Then decide if sentences a) and b) have parallel meanings, or different meanings.

1. a) Pesticide pollution has led to a gradual decline in the number of bird species.
   b) The number of bird species has plummeted because of pesticide pollution.

2. a) With rising personal incomes come rising expectations.
   b) People's expectations grow as their incomes increase.

3. a) The rural population has halved in the last twenty years.
   b) The number of people living in the countryside has soared in recent decades.

4. a) Unemployment peaked in 1983.
   b) In 1983 the unemployment rate was at its highest, but then started to decrease.

5. a) The level of sales tends to fluctuate on a seasonal basis.
   b) No matter what the season, sales figures usually remain quite constant.

3 Complete the text below using the correct forms of the words in brackets.

The need for hi-tech medical equipment

The market needs more hi-tech companies that can develop surface engineering to meet the new and **1** ………… (grow) need for advanced surfaces for laboratory items such as glass slides. This technology is needed because of the **2** ………… (increase) high requirements of diagnostic testing in the fields of medicine and life sciences. The sensitivity of tests can be more than **3** ………… (double) by treating the surface of a slide with new chemical coatings. Yet the **4** ………… (grow) and development of this specialised industry has been slow. This gap in the market, however, could encourage greater research links between businesses and universities which **5** ………… (decline) in this field in recent years. By **6** ………… (increase) this kind of technical cooperation, medical diagnosis could be greatly improved.

2 The Language of Cause and Effect

X **causes** Y / Y **is caused by** X
X is **a (common) cause of** Y
X **results in** Y / Y **results from** X
X **leads to** Y
X **makes** Y do something
X **contributes to** Y
X is **so … that** it can … Y
X, and **so** Y
X, **therefore** Y
Thanks to X, Y
the effects of X are Y
X **is explained by** Y
X **is a source of** Y
since X, Y
Y is **(largely) due to** X
Y **(is) (partly) because (of)** X
If X, **(then)** Y
the more / less the X, **the more / less the** Y

1 Complete the text using expressions from the box below. Use each word or phrase only once.

> *so much*   *largely because*
>
> *the causes of*   *since*   *due to*
>
> *contributed further to*

Malaria in England

Malaria was already common in fifteenth-century England and the growth in international trade in the sixteenth century **1** ………… the spread of this disease.

For many years it was thought that it was **2** ………… 'bad air'. However, by the late 1800s **3** ………… malaria were becoming clearer, with the discovery of malaria parasites, and new methods of treatment were developed.

The number of imported cases of the disease has recently risen sharply, **4** ………… of the growth of global travel. However, an epidemic of malaria is unlikely to occur in the UK today, **5** ………… housing and public health conditions have improved **6** ………… that the disease could swiftly be brought under control, say specialists.

2 Complete the text below using the correct forms of the words in brackets.

The effects of tourism

The explosion in the tourist industry can **1** ………… (*explain*) by more affordable transport and greater wealth among some of the world's population. It is true that tourism sometimes **2** ………… (*result*) in an improvement in the standard of living of local people, as well as **3** ………… (*contribute*) to increased understanding of other cultures. However, many of the **4** ………… (*effect*) of tourism are negative. Atmospheric pollution **5** ………… (*cause*) by air travel, while the building of hotels **6** ………… (*lead*) to shortage of resources such as water. So tourism sometimes **7** ………… (*cause*) the destruction of the very places that people want to visit.

3 Underline the language of cause and effect in each of the sentences below. Then decide if sentences a) and b) have parallel meanings, or different meanings.

1 a) Sufficiently low temperatures will make the water droplets freeze.
   b) If the temperature is sufficiently low, the water droplets will freeze.

2 a) Cultural differences may be a source of misunderstandings.
   b) Misunderstandings may lead to cultural differences.

3 a) The rougher the surface of the road, the noisier the traffic will be.
   b) Traffic noise results from rough road surfaces.

4 a) This habitat supports many rare species, and so it must be preserved.
   b) A large number of rare species live in this habitat and its preservation is therefore necessary.

5 a) Thanks to the discovery of new applications for aspirin, it is still manufactured today.
   b) The reason why aspirin is still manufactured today is that new applications have been discovered.

3 The Language of Comparison and Contrast

A is (almost / exactly) **the same as** B
C is (a little / completely) **different from** A
D is **as** likely to succeed **as** E

Comparative and superlative forms
Short adjectives
X is (slightly / much) cheap**er than** Y / **than** it was before
Z is (by far) **the** cheap**est** of them all / that it has ever been
Longer adjectives
X is (slightly / considerably / far) **more** expensive **than** Z / **than** (we'd) expected
Y is (by far) **the most** expensive of all / that I have seen
X is (considerably / much) **less** expensive **than** Y / **than** they had expected
Z is (by far) **the least** expensive in the group / that we have found

Markers
In / By contrast / On the other hand / however / while / whereas / although
Compared to / with
Similarly / Both … and … / Like …

---

1 Complete the text using expressions from the box below. Use each word or phrase only once.

difference	as many as	the same
higher	a lot more frequent	high as
most	far fewer	differently
much more		

Sea change

Sea levels are **1** .... now than they have been for the last 100 years, though this change has affected regions **2** .... because the Earth's crust is not uniformly **3** ....
The oceans cover 70% of the planet, so any perceptible **4** .... in their depth or temperature is a dangerous development. Of course, sea levels have been as **5** .... this before, but then human civilisation was not a factor. Now our planet is **6** .... densely populated and **7** .... 39% of the world's people live in coastal regions. The people who are the **8** .... at risk are those living in developing countries, where floods and natural disasters seem to have become **9** .... but where there are **10** .... resources for dealing with them.

---

2 Choose the correct markers to complete the passage below.

Energy sources

The vast majority of the energy used in northern Europe today still comes from fossil fuels, **1** *on the other hand / although* the push for newer, less-polluting sources has begun. **2** *Similarly / Both* wind and solar power have been at the forefront of the research, but the problem of reliability has not really been overcome in the northern regions because of climatic considerations. **3** *Compared to / In contrast*, hotter countries have benefited from solar technology for decades now, **4** *while / however* the colder north has had little success. **5** *On the other hand / While* wave power has proved to be more consistent in terms of producing a steady energy supply. The output to date, **6** *whereas / however*, has been small.

---

3 In academic texts, contrasts are often made by using two words or phrases with opposite meanings. Complete the sentences using expressions from the box below.

several kilos	simple	in the past
differently	more common	today
exactly the same	few	complex
a few grams		

1 The device works .... from natural systems, but the result is ....
2 The mechanism seems rather .... but it works on clear, ... principles.
3 There used to be very .... of these machines available, but they are .... now.
4 One machine weighs .... but the core mechanism weighs only ....
5 The world population was much smaller .... but .... we have an overcrowded planet.

4 The Language of Education and Research

Academic courses
assessment, course, examination, module, practice, project, report, semester, topic

Research
Nouns: aim, article, category, class, closed question, (anecdotal) evidence, experiment, evaluation, hypothesis, interview, literature search, pilot project, questionnaire, respondent, sample, survey, theory, volunteer

Adjectives: random, systematic

Verbs: carry out, evaluate, investigate, prove, select, suggest

1 Complete the text using expressions from the box below. Use each word or phrase only once.

interviews	investigate	sample
questionnaire	aim	respondents
articles	carried out	suggest
closed questions		

Research project on organic food

We did a research project on attitudes towards organic food. Our **1** .... was to **2** .... whether some age groups were more likely to buy organic food than others.

We **3** .... a literature survey and found several relevant books and **4** .... We decided to use face-to-face **5** .... as the basis for our research and we prepared a **6** .... with a combination of **7** .... (with yes/no answers) and open questions.

We interviewed a random **8** .... of people whom we stopped in the street, and had a total of 37 **9** ....

Our results **10** .... that women of 25–40 years old are the most likely to buy organic food.

2 Complete the text using words from the box below. You may need to change the form of the word.

research	examine	semester	project
theory	topic	report	assess (x 2)

Postgraduate course in Sustainable Development

The postgraduate course in Sustainable Development involves the study of various **1** .... of development together with practical applications. The course has two stages, a taught course stage which takes up most of the first two **2** .... , and the **3** .... stage, which involves extended **4** .... on a **5** .... agreed with the department. The course is modular, and each module is **6** .... at the end of the semester in which it is taught. An MSc degree is awarded on the basis of the five module **7** .... , the project **8** .... , which must be between 10,000 and 15,000 words, and the final **9** .... , which takes place at the end of the course.

3 Underline the language of education and research in each of the sentences below. Then decide if sentences a) and b) have parallel meanings, or different meanings.

1. a) Our survey provides evidence that attitudes towards global warming are changing.
   b) Our survey proves that attitudes towards global warming are changing.

2. a) The researchers selected a random sample of volunteers for the experiment.
   b) Volunteers for the experiment were selected in a systematic way by the researchers.

3. a) The group will carry out evaluation of the pilot project before beginning the main study.
   b) The pilot project will be evaluated by the group before they begin the main study.

4. a) We found plenty of anecdotal evidence for the effect of weather on people's moods.
   b) We found a large amount of data on the effect of weather on people's moods.

5. a) The components can be assigned to three distinct classes.
   b) Three distinct categories can be identified among the components.

5 The Language of Technology

General words
device, machine, structure, system, process

Parts of structures
base, foundation, layer, surface

Parts of machines
fan, filter, pump, motor, engine

Mechanical processes (verbs)
bend, collect, combine, connect, extract, force, leave, located, manufacture, pass through, remain, utilise

Things involved in technology
energy, materials, resources, skills

1   Complete the text using words from the box below. Use each word only once.

energy	bending	machinery	utilise
extract	manufacture	skill	resources

Technology in use

In the past it was thought that only man could make and **1** ………… tools, but now it is known that some animals have this **2** ………… too. Chimpanzees use pieces of wood to **3** ………… ants from ant-hills, while captive birds have been observed **4** ………… a piece of wire and using it to get food out of a tube. However, only man is able to make use of natural **5** ………… such as metals, and sources of **6** ………… such as heat and electricity, in order to **7** ………… sophisticated **8** ………… .

2   Look at this diagram of a vacuum cleaner, then complete the text using words from the box below. Use each word once only. You may need to change the form of the word.

remain	base	connect	fan	collect
leave	force	pass	filter	locate

The vacuum cleaner

A conventional vacuum cleaner has a **1** ………… which rests on the ground, **2** ………… to a vertical section with a handle. Dust is **3** ………… by a rotating brush in the base. An electric motor activates a **4** ………… , which **5** ………… dust and air into the dust bag **6** ………… in the vertical section of the vacuum cleaner. The air **7** ………… through a **8** ………… and **9** ………… the vacuum

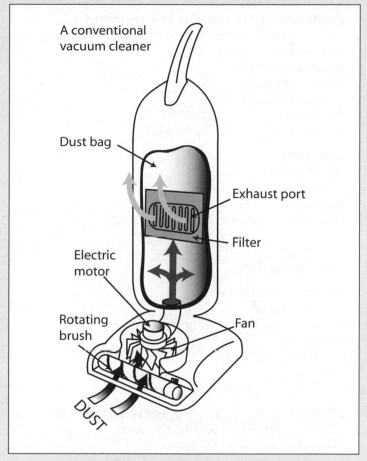
A conventional vacuum cleaner

Dust bag
Exhaust port
Filter
Electric motor
Rotating brush
Fan
DUST

cleaner through the exhaust port, while the dust **10** ………… in the dust bag.

3   Underline the language of technology in each of the sentences below. Then decide if sentences a) and b) have parallel meanings, or different meanings.

1   a) Hydrogen and oxygen combine to form water.
    b) Water is formed from the combination of oxygen and hydrogen.

2   a) The experiment uses a process by which water is supercooled.
    b) The experiment uses a device which supercools water.

3   a) Roman roads had a foundation layer of stone, with a middle layer of softer material, and a layer of flat stones on top.
    b) Roman roads had a surface of flat stones under which were two layers, an upper one of softer material and a lower one of stone.

4   a) Pumps were used to bring the water up from under the ground.
    b) Water was pumped up to the surface of the ground.

6 The Language of Man and the Natural World

Features of the natural environment
unspoilt wilderness / landscapes
indigenous wildlife
species diversity
flora and fauna
unique habitats
nutrients
to survive / support / sustain …

Dangers
monoculture
industrial development
toxins / poisons
introduced species / invasive species
to pose a threat (to)
to pollute
to contaminate

Human solutions
conservation
protected zones / national parks
sustainable agriculture
farming techniques
land recovery

1   Complete the text using words from the box below. Use each word only once.

conservation   unique   protected
industrial   survival   unspoilt   flora
species   threat   wildlife

The dangers of development

In today's world there is a constant battle between 1 …………… development and countryside 2 …………… . In many places where areas of 3 …………… wilderness have been designated as 4 …………… zones, governments suddenly announce plans that allow the developers to move in. The subsequent impact of such projects is usually devastating for indigenous types of 5 …………… such as flowers and insects and many 6 …………… habitats are permanently destroyed. While the need for jobs and homes for increasing populations has to be accepted, the developers need to understand the 7 …………… their activities pose to the 8 …………… of many 9 …………… of fauna and 10 …………… .

2   Complete the text below using the correct form of the words in brackets.

Growing for gold and for a clean land

A New Zealand geologist has developed a way of using biotechnology to help the 1 …………… (environment) recovery of 2 …………… (pollute) areas by harvesting gold from plants. He claims this process can be used to extract gold, mercury and other minerals from 3 …………… (contaminate) gold mines. He has conducted successful field trials in the Amazon, where local miners use 4 …………… (toxin) mercury to extract gold and then simply leave the sites and move on. The process uses chemicals to break down gold to a water-soluble form. Once the metals are mixed with water, crop plants such as corn and canola can absorb them along with other 5 …………… (nutrient) they need for growth. It is estimated that one kilogram of gold can 6 …………… (recover) per hectare in this way. The New Zealand team also trained locals in farming 7 …………… (technique), so once the land is clean, these people can reclaim it for 8 …………… (sustain) agriculture.

3   Underline the topic related language in each of the sentences below. Then decide if sentences a) and b) have parallel meanings, or different meanings.

1 a) Large areas of rainforest have been lost to agriculture.
  b) Cultivation of the land has helped to regenerate the natural rainforest.

2 a) Indigenous plants are not threatened by non-native species in national parks.
  b) Introduced species are often invasive in national parks.

3 a) It has been discovered that some organisms are able to survive in extremely harsh conditions.
  b) We now know that even the most extreme habitats can sustain some life forms.

4 a) Monoculture is a threat to species diversity.
  b) Fewer species can survive in areas where a single crop is grown intensively.

5 a) Some species of insects and birds are dependent on the vegetation found only in tropical rainforests.
  b) Some plants that are unique to tropical rainforests support specific species of insects and birds.

7 The Language of the Urban Environment

Features of the city
residential areas, neighbourhoods, local community
residents, neighbours
housing, houses, house design
architecture
infrastructure
education, health, leisure, public transport, shopping facilities
employment opportunities
(higher) standard of living
city centre, inner-city areas, city limits, city outskirts
suburbs

Problems of the city
urbanisation
overcrowding, densely-populated areas
air pollution, litter, waste disposal
traffic (jams, congestion, queues, noise, fumes)
(lack of) space, planning
commuters

1 Complete the text using expressions from the box below. Use each word or phrase only once.

infrastructure	public transport	
standard of living	urban	overcrowding
urbanisation	facilities	traffic

Moving to the city

It is expected that within a couple of decades, 75% of the world population will be living in **1** .... areas. What attracts people to the cities are the access to educational and medical **2** .... and the greater employment opportunities. These contribute to a higher **3** .... than many people could find in a rural environment. However, this process of **4** .... puts a huge strain on a city's systems. The packed buses and long queues at bus stops are an early indicator of how **5** .... is affecting **6** .... , while the congestion levels and noise of **7** .... in the streets can highlight the problems of an undeveloped or poorly-maintained **8** ....

2 Complete the text below using the correct form of the words in brackets.

Moving outside the city

In many capital cities today people are moving out of the old city centres and becoming **1** .... (*reside*) in newly-developed **2** .... (*suburbs*) areas. Here people can afford **3** .... (*house*) that is more **4** .... (*space*) than the high-rise apartment block of the centre, and the **5** .... (*architecture*) designs are often more convenient for modern lifestyles. But what is often hard to find in these new **6** .... (*neighbour*) is any real sense of local community. Because many people continue to work in the city, they often end up spending more time **7** .... (*commute*) than they spend at home. And often such environments lack any large **8** .... (*community*) centre where people can have the opportunity to meet and mingle with neighbours.

3 Underline the language linked to the topic of the urban environment in each of the sentences below. Then decide if each pair of sentences have parallel meanings, or different meanings.

1 a) The inner-city areas usually have lots of rubbish lying around.
   b) Street litter is a feature of the inner-city areas.

2 a) Apartments that are near the main urban highways need to have specialised windows that reduce noise levels.
   b) Flats built next to main urban highways need double glazing to protect them from traffic noise.

3 a) Housing is less expensive in under-populated areas.
   b) In densely-populated areas, housing costs more.

4 a) The cities are encroaching on rural areas because of urban sprawl.
   b) Migration to the cities is depopulating rural areas.

5 a) Cities grow quickly when there is lots of building and development.
   b) Rapid urban expansion is a sympton of increased urbanisation.

8 General Academic Language

General nouns
action, activity, application, area, aspect, factor, field, invention, phenomenon, production, role, service, site, work

Feelings and ideas
attitude, belief, principle, relationship, significance

Social features
society, organisation, trade, commerce

Key verbs
consume, develop, invent, locate, originate, produce, transform

Adjectives
diverse, varied

Useful phrases
an impact on, a threat to, has its roots in, demands made on, taken into account

1 Complete the text below using the words in brackets in the correct forms.

What is culture?

The word 'culture' is used in several different ways. It may refer to **1** ………… (*active*) such as art, music, literature and so on, and to all the **2** ………… (*work*) of art produced by people working in these **3** ………… (*field*). However, it may also have a broader **4** ………… (*signify*), and refer to the ideas, **5** ………… (*believe*) and customs that are shared and accepted by people in a society. The special ceremonies that mark births, marriages and deaths and the **6** ………… (*principle*) which guide people's behaviour and **7** ………… (*relationship*) are all **8** ………… (*aspect*) of this type of culture. In addition, 'culture' may also refer to similar **9** ………… (*phenomenon*) taking place in **10** ………… (*organisation*) such as large companies, where particular **11** ………… (*attitude*) or types of behaviour are accepted and others are regarded as unacceptable.

2 Underline the general academic words in each of the sentences below. Then decide if sentences a) and b) have parallel meanings, or different meanings.

1. a) Nanotechnology has applications in fields as varied as medicine, electronics and computer science.
   b) Nanotechnology can be used in areas as diverse as medicine, electronics and computer science.

2. a) Some historians claim that civilisation has its roots in trade and commerce.
   b) Civilisation originated in trade and commerce, claim some historians.

3. a) Noise and pollution are two factors which must be taken into account when choosing a site for a new airport.
   b) Those choosing where to locate a new airport must try to avoid the effects of noise and pollution.

4. a) The role of the doctor has changed considerably in recent years.
   b) There have been significant increases in the demands made on doctors in recent years.

3 Complete the text using words from the box below. You may need to change the form of the word.

produce	consume	threaten	
develop	impact	service	invent
transform	society	act	

The industrial revolution

The term 'industrial revolution' originally referred to the **1** ………… that took place in Great Britain during the eighteenth and nineteenth centuries, **2** ………… it from an agricultural to a manufacturing society. The **3** ………… of the steam engine and of machines for spinning and weaving cloth meant that the **4** ………… of textiles and other **5** ………… goods, which had previously taken place in people's homes could now be carried out on a large scale in factories. This led to huge **6** ………… , economic and technological changes.

But the **7** ………… of these changes was not all positive. The **8** ………… of disease from a rapidly increasing urban population meant that government **9** ………… was urgently needed to provide the growing population with housing, **10** ………… such as water and waste disposal, and transportation.

ANSWER KEY

TEST 1

Test 1 LISTENING

Section 1
Strategy

1 An enquiry about bookcases. The title is written above the notes on the question paper.
2 The general topics that will be discussed – they therefore give an overview of the structure of the talk.
3 **a)** Details of seller **b)** Both bookcases **c)** Second bookcase **d)** First bookcase
4 **a)** 1, 3, 8 **b)** 2 **c)** 9
   All the maps have a roundabout with four roads leading off, the university and a side road. However, the order of these three things is different, and the side road is sometimes on the left and sometimes on the right. Key language will relate to the features of the map – *road*, *roundabout*, *university* – and the differences between the diagrams – *on the left / right*, *before / after the roundabout / university*.

Exam task
1 75 cm(s)/centimetres   2 wood
3 £15.00■£15■fifteen pounds   4 cream
5 adjustable   6 cupboard
7 doors   8 £95.00■£95■ninety-five pounds
9 Blake   10 B

Section 2
Strategy

1 The topic is a charity art sale. There are two task types (summary completion and table completion).
2 The information is given in complete sentences. Question 13 needs an adjective, 12 a number (a time) and 11 a place.
3 At the end of the first task.
4 The artists, personal information about them, and the type of painting they do. This information is given in the headings of the table.
5 Personal information – b, c, e. Type of painting – a, d.
6 Across the rows
7 Six questions (14, 15, 17, 18, 19, 20). Question 15 must be plural ('a number of'), 14, 18, 19 and 20 could also be plural.

Exam task
11 café   12 7.30 (p.m.)■seven thirty■half past seven
13 (the) disabled   14 birds
15 (art) exhibitions   16 abstract
17 designer   18 portraits
19 two/2 years/yrs   20 photographs/photos

Section 3
Strategy

1 A project. This is in the question.
2 Obligation/Choice.
3 **a)** – C **b)** – A (notice that you need to listen for a statement and a reply here) **c)** – B
4 Basically the same topic – the project – although the notes also include information about assessment. This information comes from the heading(s).

Exam task
21 A   22 C   23 B   24 C   25 B
26 interests (and) style■style (and) interests   27 visuals
28 range   29 source(s)   30 content

Section 4
Strategy

1 b
2 31: extremophiles/live in
   32: organisms/Antarctica
   33: life forms
3 **a)** isolated areas **b)** hostile conditions
4 b)
5 (suggested answers)
   34 sun's heat/create
   35: deeper/soil/salt
   36: salt/protect/low temperatures
   37 living things/water
   38 salt/process/freezing
   39 environment/similar/Antarctica
   40 extraterrestrial life/planets
6 **a)** 38 **b)** 39 **c)** 37

Exam task
31 B   32 B   33 A   34 microclimate
35 concentration   36 frost   37 liquid
38 supercooling   39 Mars   40 locations

Test 1 READING

Reading Passage 1
Strategy: Finding out what the text is about

1 snow gun – to create snow on ski slopes when there is insufficient natural snow.

Strategy: Matching paragraph headings

1 **a)** the problem – *But ski resort owners … close everything down.* **b)** the solution – *Fortunately, a device called … needed.*
2 It is tempting because it mentions the need for snow, but there is nothing in Paragraph A about *different varieties* of snow.
3 Heading ix is tempting because it mentions a process, but Paragraph B is all about a *natural* process, not an artificial one.

Exam task

1	ix	The snow gun works very differently from a natural weather system, but it accomplishes exactly the same thing.
2	iii	resort owners also use denser, wet snow … then regularly coat the trails with a layer of dry snow
3	viii	Many ski slopes now do this with a central computer system
4	i	man-made snow makes heavy demands on the environment.
5	vi	man-made snow has a number of other uses as well.

Strategy: Diagram labelling
1 The snow gun – the diagram has a title.
2 Paragraph C
3 The right
4 No more than two

Exam task

6	compressed	and the other leading from an air compressor. When the compressed air passes …
7	(tiny) droplets	the water splits up into tiny droplets.
8	ice crystals	blown out of the gun … ice crystals will form,

Strategy: Sentence completion
1 dry snow/slopes/wet snow (Paragraph D)
2 *slopes which receive heavy use/build up*

Exam task

9	depth	Many resorts build up the snow depth this way
10	temperature humidity	The wetness of snow is dependent on the temperature and humidity outside,
11	energy	considerable amounts of energy are needed to run the large air-compressing pumps,
12	insulation	farmers often use man-made snow to provide insulation for winter crops.
13	aircraft	the tests that aircraft must undergo

Reading Passage 2
Strategy: Finding out what the text is about
1 a) the last b) the first
2 a) (other animals are mentioned briefly, but the word *tigers* occurs throughout the text)

Strategy: Locating information in paragraphs
1 *Surely, then, it is a little strange that attacks on humans are not more frequent.*

2 Yes – that tigers attack most living creatures including large, fierce ones.

Exam task

14	C	But I think the explanation may be more simple
15	A	Tigers can and do kill almost anything they meet in the jungle
16	F	Many incidents of attacks on people involve villagers squatting or bending over
17	B	Some people might argue that these attacks were in fact common in the past.
18	E	Section beginning: If you try to think like a tiger, …

Strategy: True/False/Not Given
1 Tigers/Bandhavgarh National Park
2 This is Not Given – there is no information about tigers being – or not being – a protected species.

Exam task

19	NG	Paragraph A mentions tigers in the Bandhavgarh National Park, but there is no information about their status as a protected species.
20	T	Paragraph B: British writers … gave the impression that village life … involved a state of constant siege by man-eating tigers.
21	T	Paragraph C: Has the species programmed the experiences … into its genes to be inherited as instinct? Perhaps.
22	NG	Paragraph D mentioned the views of naturalists before Lorenz, but there is no information about Lorenz's claims.
23	F	Paragraph D: Since the growth of ethology in the 1950s, we have tried to understand animal behaviour from the animal's point of view.

Strategy: Multiple-choice questions
1 people in cars
2 A is contradicted (*unless the car is menacing the tiger or its cubs, in which case …*). D is not stated, although the cubs are mentioned.

Exam task

24	C	Paragraph E: If you try to think like a tiger, a human in a car might appear just to be part of the car,
25	B	Paragraph E: From the front the man is huge, but looked at from the side he all but disappears. This must be very disconcerting.

26	D	Paragraph F: A squatting human is half the size and presents twice the spread of back,

Reading Passage 3
Strategy: Finding out what the text is about
1 the history of aspirin
2 b) a chronological account. The paragraph openings support this as many give dates or time references.

Strategy: Sentence completion using words from a box
1 Egyptian and Greek doctors – the second paragraph
2 G is tempting as it refers to the willow tree. However, the Egyptian and Greek doctors were not aware of the actual chemical involved – only of the fact that parts of the tree had beneficial effects.

Exam task

27	E	Paragraph 2: Ancient Egyptian physicians used extracts from the willow tree … the Greek physician Hippocrates recommended the bark of the willow tree
28	G	Paragraph 2: The race was on to identify the active ingredient and to replicate it synthetically. … Friedrich Bayer & Co, succeeded
29	D	Paragraph 4: scientific advance was closely linked to the industrial revolution. … In the case of aspirin that happened piecemeal … fertilised by the century's broader economic, medical and scientific developments
30	H	Paragraph 5: huge amounts of money were put into promoting it as an ordinary everyday analgesic.
31	A	Paragraph 5: discoveries were made regarding the beneficial role of aspirin in preventing heart attacks, strokes and other afflictions.
32	C	Paragraph 6: aspirin … was around for over 70 years without anybody investigating the way in which it achieved its effects, because they were making more than enough money out of it as it was.

Strategy: Yes/No/Not Given
1 The second, third and fourth paragraphs
2 One scientist in a laboratory with some chemicals and a test tube/significant breakthroughs
3 Yes
Exam task

33	Y	Paragraph 3: One scientist in a laboratory with some chemicals and a test tube could make significant breakthroughs
34	NG	Paragraph 4 mentions the industrial revolution and scientific research but there is no information about a change in focus
35	N	Paragraph 4: In the case of aspirin that happened piecemeal – a series of minor, often unrelated advances,
36	NG	Paragraph 5 refers to the entry of new analgesic drugs into the market, but there is no information about relative sales.
37	Y	Section of Paragraph 6 beginning: So the relationship between big money and drugs is an odd one.

Strategy: Summary completion using words from a box
1 Part of the text. The title indicates this.
2 a) the first sentence b) the second sentence
3 scientists working in the public sector/big pharmaceutical companies/major drug companies
Exam task

38	E major drug companies	Paragraph 5: and the pharmaceutical companies then focused on publicising these new drugs.
39	F profitable	Paragraph 7: There's no profit in aspirin any more.
40	C state	Paragraph 8: More public money going into clinical trials, says Jeffreys.

Test 1 WRITING

Writing Task 1
Exercise 1
1 the United States
2 From 1950 to present; present to 2025
3 US energy consumption & US energy production
4 Energy units
5 the amount of energy imported to bridge the gap
Exercise 2
3 changes in the gap between energy production and consumption
Exercise 3
1 The graph shows changes in
2 the gap between US energy consumption and production
3 since 1950.
4 It also estimates trends
5 up to 2025.
Exercise 4
a 1, 2, 5
Exercise 5
a 3, 1, 4, 5, 2

b Para 1: 3
Para 2: 1, 4 & 5
Para 3: 2

Exercise 6

a 3

b *In conclusion, the graph suggests that*
To sum up, we can see that
In general, the graph indicates that

Band 9 Sample Answer

NB: There is no single correct answer to the writing task.
This is one example of a Band 9 response.

TASK 1

The graph shows changes in the gap between US energy
consumption and production since 1950. It also estimates
trends up to 2025.

Between 1950 and 1970 both production and
consumption increased from just over 30 units to about
65, and although consumption was consistently higher, the
difference was marginal during this period.

However, production grew only gradually over the next
30 years to reach 70 units in 2000. In contrast, growth in
consumption was steeper and more fluctuating, reaching
95 units by 2000. Energy imports needed to bridge this
gap therefore increased from very little in 1970 to a
substantial 25 units in 2000.

Projections up to 2025 indicate that this trend is likely
to continue, with the gap between production and
consumption widening. By 2025 it is expected that
consumption will reach 140 units, while production will
reach only 90, so more than 30% of energy consumed [50
units] will have to be imported.

Overall, the graph indicates that energy production in the
US is not keeping up with consumption, so imports will
continue to increase.
(177 words)

Writing Task 2

1 1, 4, 6

2 **b** All three structures are interchangeable in these
sentences.
1 **Even though** *people can work from home,*
***nevertheless** it is unrealistic to think they would all
want to.*
***It is certainly true that** people can work from
home.* **However***, it is unrealistic to think they would
all want to.*
***It may be the case that** people can work from
home,* **but** *it is unrealistic to think they would all
want to.*
2 ***It is certainly true that** distance learning is very
efficient.* **However***, there would be a lack of social
contact for students.*
3 ***It may be the case that** this presents a possible
solution,* **but** *it would be a very unpopular one.*

3 2, 4, 3, 1

4 **a** f, c, a, e, d, b ■ f, c, a, e, b, d

5 **a** 1b, 4c, 6a

b

1 *Traffic in cities today is a problem.* **This is obvious
from** *the number of vehicles on our roads and the
jams we experience every day.*

2 *Probably these are mainly due to individuals
travelling for work, study or shopping purposes.*
This is evident in *rush hours every morning and
evening.*

3 *Today people can do these things at home.* **We can
see this in** *the options IT gives us today.*

6 *It is evident that*
It is certainly true that
It is the case that
Probably this is mainly due to

7 **Band 9 Sample Answer**

It is certainly true that today traffic in cities throughout the
world has become a major problem. This is obvious from
the number of vehicles on our roads and the amount of
pollution they cause. Probably the traffic problem is due to
individuals travelling for work, study or shopping purposes,
and this is evident in the rush hours we experience every
morning and evening.

It is also true that today such daily commuting is not
always necessary because people can do these things
from home. We can see this in the options Information
Technology gives us today. For instance, on-line work,
distance learning and shopping facilities are all available via
the Internet.

However, even if everyone had access to the technology
and the opportunity to work from home, it is unrealistic
to think that everyone would want to. Even though the
technology for working, studying or shopping on-line
makes this option a possibility, nevertheless it would mean
people had less freedom of choice and less social contact
in their lives. This would have a large impact on society as a
whole.

So, in conclusion, I think that while this practice could
reduce the traffic problems in our cities, it is most unlikely
to be an acceptable solution. In terms of other solutions,
perhaps we need to think more carefully about facilitating
public transport and limiting private cars in our city centres.
The development of public transport that is not road-
based, such as sky trains or subways, would probably be a
more acceptable alternative measure to reduce jams on our
roads.
(260 words)

Test 1 SPEAKING

Part 1

1 3, 4, 6

2a (i) b, (ii) c, (iii) a

Part 2

3 **1** present perfect: how long you've had this routine
2 conditional *would* in explain prompt
3 present tense: what you do, when you do it

4 Make sure notes are in note form and cover the prompts, e.g.:

mornings – class / seminars
evenings – lectures or library
2nd year – but some changes
want more taught classes

5 4, 1, 3, 2
6 1 More or less.
  2 No, I wouldn't go that far.

Part 3
7 1 last one
  2 *How are work or study schedules today different …*
  3 *Do young people and old people have …*
8 2, 3, 5
9 a) 2, 7, 8 b) 4, 5, 6 c) 1, 3

TEST 2

Test 2 LISTENING

Section 1
Strategy
1 The topic is renting a flat. The example suggests this, and the heading of the table shows that this is the topic of the whole listening. (The rubric heard on the recording will also give some information about the topic and context.)
2 Two – multiple choice and table completion.
3 1 – b, 2 – c, 3 – a
4 ✓ refers to each flat's good points, and ✗ refers to the bad points. (This information is given in the heading to column 3.)
5 a) question 5 b) Questions 4, 7 and maybe 9 c) 8 d) 6

Exam task
1 B   **2** A   **3** C   **4** bus station
5 £450   **6** noisy   **7** Hills Avenue
8 dining room   **9** (very) modern   **10** quiet

Section 2
Strategy
1 a
2 b
3 two (lower ground and upper ground). The Piazza.
4 Meeting Point
5 (16) Main Entrance, Piazza, Statue (17) Lower Ground Floor, Cloakroom

Exam task
11 Sundays
12 1998
13 100,000 one/a hundred thousand
14 government
15 research
16 Conference Centre/Center
17 Information Desk
18 bookshop
19 King(')s Library
20 stamp display

Section 3
Strategy
1 A project on work placement – this is given as a title at the beginning of the task.
2 c) a)
3 b) Introduction (1) d) Findings (2) a) Findings (3) c) Findings (4)

Exam task
21 B   **22** C   **23** A   **24** B   **25** A
26 organisation   **27** definition   **28** aims
29 Key Skills   **30** evidence

Section 4
Strategy
1 Bilingualism – This word comes in each sentence 31–35 and also in questions 38–40. (It is also given in the introduction to the task in the recording.)
2 a) the first b) the second c) the first
3 a) can be defined as b) two or more c) caused problems with d) is now rejected e) it did not consider f) It is now thought g) suggests that

Exam task
31 proficiency   **32** learning
33 social (and) economic   **34** positive
35 adults
36 A   **37** A   **38** B   **39** C   **40** A

Test 2 READING

Reading Passage 1
Strategy: Finding out what the text is about
1 risk/s
2 a) describing a problem

Task: Matching paragraph headings
3 (verbs) *underestimating/overestimating*, (adjective) *better*. because people 'make terrible decisions about the future'.
4 He originally studied psychology, but became interested in the science of decision-making. His ideas are generally accepted now (he was awarded the Nobel Prize and is in demand by businesses).

Exam task

1 (B)	vi	When Kahneman and his colleagues first started work, the idea of applying psychological insights to economics and business decisions was seen as rather bizarre. But in the past decade the fields of behavioural finance and behavioural economics have blossomed, and in 2002 Kahneman shared a Nobel Prize in economics for his work.
2 (D)	ix	Once a figure has been mentioned, it takes a strange hold over the human mind.

3 (E)	iii	No one likes to abandon a cherished belief, and the earlier a decision has been taken, the harder it is to abandon it.
4 (F)	viii	People also tend to put a lot of emphasis on things they have seen and experienced themselves, which may not be the best guide to decision-making.
5 (G)	i	people spend proportionally too much time on small decisions and not enough on big ones.
6 (H)	iv	crying over spilled milk is not just a waste of time; it also often colours people's perceptions of the future.

Strategy
Task: Multiple choice
1 The key words are *initially / Kahneman / work / unusual*
2 Paragraph B – refers to Kahneman starting work, to his career, and to him receiving the Nobel Prize for his work.
3 *bizarre*
4 *first started work* reflects the idea of *initially*.

Exam task

7	D	Paragraph B: When Kahneman and his colleagues first started work, the idea of applying psychological insights to economics and business decisions was seen as rather bizarre.
8	B	Paragraph C: most people … see too much blue sky ahead, even if past experience suggests otherwise. … people's forecasts of future stock market movements are … optimistic … The same goes for their hopes of ever-rising prices for their homes
9	D	In Paragraph E, drug companies and analysts are given as examples of people who may be unwilling to give up one course of action.
10	A	Paragraph F: In finance, too much emphasis on information close at hand helps to explain the tendency by most investors to invest only within the country they live in.

Strategy: Short answer questions
1 The relevant paragraph is C.
2 The two occupations are managers and sportsmen.

Exam task

11	managers (and/or) sportsmen	Paragraph C: Such optimism can be useful for managers or sportsmen, and sometimes turns into a self-fulfilling prophecy.
12	driving	Paragraph C: far fewer than half the respondents admit to having below average skills in, say, driving.
13	Pharmaceutical (companies)	Paragraph I: Pharmaceutical companies, which are accustomed to many failures and a few big successes in their drug-discovery programmes, are fairly rational about their risk-taking.

Reading Passage 2
Strategy: Finding out what the text is about
1 film
2 a) the past
3 It is international in focus
4 Because this question is testing the main idea of the passage

Strategy: True/False/Not Given
1 They relate to one part of the reading passage – the first two paragraphs – which are mainly about the early history of film in Europe and America.
2 Paragraph 1 discusses the invention of cinema.
3 The phrase is *a sideshow at a funfair*.
4 Yes. In the same sentence, *they saw* has parallel meaning to *the inventors of cinema regarded …* . (*they* refers back to *they invented it*.)

Exam task

14	T	Paragraph 1: At first, they saw their clumsy new camera-projectors merely as … mechanical curiosities which might have a use as a sideshow at a funfair.
15	F	Paragraph 1: Then the best of the pioneers looked beyond the fairground properties of their invention. A few directors … saw that the flickering new medium was more than just a diversion.
16	NG	Paragraph 1 mentions *mechanical curiosities* but there is no information about the relationship between art and technology.
17	T	The last part of Paragraph 1 describes the different approaches to cinema in California, Germany, the Soviet Union and Italy.

18	F	Paragraph 2: America and Europe can be forgiven for assuming that they were the only game in town … It never occurred to its financial backers that another continent might borrow their magic box

Strategy: Note completion

1 The relevant section is Paragraph 3. This is the only paragraph which has China as its main topic.
2 a) 20 b) 19
3 The possible phrases are: (19) *without soundtracks*/*elements of realism* (20) *among the best ever made*

Exam task

19	D silent	Paragraph 3: China produced more than 500 films, mostly conventionally made in studios in Shanghai, without soundtracks.
20	F outstanding	Paragraph 3: are regularly voted among the best ever made in the country.
21	B negative	Paragraph 4: they addressed social and peasant themes in an optimistic and romantic way
22	H powerful	Paragraph 5: in Tokyo the director chose the stories and hired the producer and actors.
23	E social	Paragraph 6: Mizoguchi's films … analysed the way in which the lives of the female characters … were constrained by the society of the time.
24	A emotional	Paragraph 6: he evolved a sinuous way of moving his camera in and around a scene, … often retreating at moments of confrontation or strong feeling.
25	G little	Paragraph 7: His camera seldom moved.

Strategy: Multiple choice – main idea of passage

1 The first and the last. The last paragraph is usually most important as it often includes the writer's conclusion.
2 b) Asian cinema
3 b) the special qualities of Asian cinema

Exam task

26	B	Paragraph 8: it is the beliefs which underlie cultures such as those of China and Japan that explain the distinctiveness of Asian cinema at its best. … it is their different sense of what a person is, and what space and action are, which makes them new to western eyes.

Reading Passage 3
Strategy: Finding out what the text is about

1 b) transport (Roads and vehicles are referred to in the title and subtitle) and d) technology (the subtitle refers to noise and the future)
2 The paragraph openings refer to roads, road surfaces, research and manufacturing.
3 b) a problem and one solution (Kuijpers' solution – the paragraphs refer to *his* road surface (E), *the* stones/*the* two layers (F), *the* … manufacturing process (G), *The* foundation (H), *his* resonators (I))

Strategy: Locating information in paragraphs

1 Topic sentence: *The noise produced by busy roads is a growing problem.* Question 30 is related to the topic of road noise and its problems, but Paragraph A does not mention economic reasons for reducing road noise.
2 Paragraph B is also about road noise and mentions three economic reasons for reducing it – building expenses, house sales and productivity.

Exam task

27	G	It emerges from the factory rolled, like a carpet, onto a drum 1.5 metres in diameter. On site, it is unrolled …
28	D	Kuijpers has developed a method of road building that he thinks can create the ultimate quiet road. His secret is … (the description of the formation of the road surface then follows)
29	J	The success of Kuijpers' design will depend on how much it eventually costs.
30	B	road builders have to spend money erecting sound barriers … Houses become harder to sell … and people are not as efficient or productive at work.
31	I	On large highways, trucks tend to use the inside lane
32	C	the three most important factors: surface texture, hardness and ability to absorb sound.

Strategy: Diagram labelling

1 *Cross section* means that we imagine the road has been cut in half so we can see the inside. The top part is the 'upper layer' and the lowest part is the 'foundation'.

2 Paragraph C introduces Kuijpers, but the road structure is not described until Paragraph D (the upper layer). Paragraph E describes the lower layer. Paragraph F gives more information about both layers, and Paragraph H describes the foundation.

33	asphalt	Paragraph D: Hot asphalt, mixed with small stones, is spread into the mould
34	9/nine	Paragraph F: the ones below are approximately twice that size – about 9 millimetres.
35	concrete	Paragraph H: It consists of a sound-absorbing concrete base

Strategy: Table completion
1 function (of components of the different parts of the road)
2 structure
3 Paragraph H (Again, information on structure is given first.)

Exam task

36	E air flow	Paragraph F: the surface can absorb any air that is passing through a tyre's tread, damping oscillations
37	J drainage	Paragraph F: they make it easier for the water to drain away
38	G sound energy	Paragraph H: the energy of the sound dissipates into the concrete as heat.
39	C rubbish	Paragraph H: This flow will help flush out waste material
40	A frequencies	Paragraph I: Kuijpers can even control the sounds that his resonators absorb, … This could prove especially useful since different vehicles produce noise at different frequencies.

Test 2 WRITING

Writing Task 1
1 Understanding the information
  1.1 b
  1.2 range of activities, club facilities and opening hours
  1.3 the percentage of male and female members who expressed opinions in the survey
2 Differences and similarities between male and female members' opinions – contrasting information.
3 The most thorough paraphrase is:
  (1) This table (2) compares (3) the opinions of male and female club members about (4) the services in a (5) particular sports club.
4 1 very satisfied & satisfied because they are both positive
  2 Male members (95% feel happy about this)

3 Fewer women think the range is satisfactory (70%)
4 Club facilities
5 Opening hours (97% are very happy or satisfied)
6 Fewer men are happy with opening hours (63%) and over a third are not satisfied (37%)
7 However, In contrast, while … , whereas … , On the other hand.
5 1 comparisons, contrast markers, superlatives
  2 happier; most in agreement; most happy; compare with
  3 a the men and the women; women and their counterparts; males and females, both genders
    b happy with, content with, feel positive about;
    c dissatisfied with; unhappy about; less/least satisfied with
6 1 In conclusion; Overall; To sum up;
  2 What the members are least happy about – so they can make changes.
  3 Overall, the men are least happy with the opening hours, while the women seem to be least satisfied with the range of club activities.

8 Task 1 Band 9 Sample Answer
The table compares the opinions of male and female club members about the services provided by a city sports club.

  We can see from the responses that the male members are generally happy or satisfied with the range of activities at the club, with only 5% dissatisfied. In contrast, however, only about two-thirds of female members were positive about the activity range and almost a third were dissatisfied.

  The genders were more in agreement about the club facilities. Only 14% of women and 10% of men were unhappy with these, and the majority (64 and 63% respectively) were very positive.

  Finally, the female respondents were much happier with the club opening hours than their male counterparts. Almost three-quarters of them were very satisfied with these and only 3% were unhappy, whereas nearly 40% of the men expressed their dissatisfaction.

  Overall, the table indicates that female members are most unhappy with the range of activities, while male members feel that opening hours are the least satisfactory aspect of the club.
(171 words)

Writing Task 2
1 1 Not enough students study subjects that are useful for society.
  2 That governments can encourage students to study useful subjects by funding these but not others.
  3 For example:
    Increase enrolment in relevant subjects;
    produce more graduates who can fill employment gaps;
    reduce graduate unemployment in less needed fields.

4 For example:
Loss of individual choice;
Unfair – discriminates against other subjects and against poorer students;
May lead to waste as people without interest or talent for that field may drop out.

2 1 Argue that there are more advantages or more disadvantages and why.
2 No – you may argue that there are more advantages *or* more disadvantages according to your opinions.

4 a 6, 2, 7, 8, 1, 4, 3, 5
b a 4, b 6, c 8, d1, e 2, f 7, g 5, h 3

5 Possible answers:
1 This kind of policy would be unfair *because it would discriminate between different subjects and would give poorer students less choice than richer ones.*
2 It could attract people who are unsuited to that particular field *by offering financial incentives, rather than academic interests.*
3 Students may drop out more often or choose not to get jobs in the target subjects, *which means the government spending could be wasted or used inefficiently.*

6 1 *would be unfair* 2 *It could attract* 3 *Students may drop out*

8 2 1 Have I identified and addressed the **issues**?
2 Have I directly answered the **question**, or directly followed the **instructions**?
3 Have I **supported** my ideas?
4 Have I used clear **signals** to organise my argument?
5 Have I used features of academic writing appropriate for this question, such as **hypothetical** or tentative language?
6 Have I written at least **250** words?

Task 2 Band 9 Sample Answer
In every country there are fashions among students about which subjects are the best to study at university. Sometimes the popularity of a subject is determined by how much money a graduate could subsequently earn in that field. Or subjects that are perceived as relatively 'easy' may also become popular, in spite of later difficulties of finding appropriate employment. It is up to governments to give incentives to students to choose subjects that match the needs of their society.

Obviously one way to do this would be for the government to pay the fees of those choosing such subjects. The advantage would certainly be that higher numbers of students would enrol and would later fill the employment gaps.

However, the disadvantages of such a policy would be considerable. For example, the students attracted by the funding may not have any real interest in or aptitude for that subject. Such students may drop out before graduation or after working only a short time in a related job. Furthermore, funding one group of students but not others would penalise those with a genuine interest and ability for another field. Such discrimination would certainly affect the whole of higher education of the country and students would develop very negative attitudes towards going to university altogether. This would be very counter-productive for any country.

In conclusion I think that there are many other incentives for students that could be considered, such as making courses more interesting to take, or the job rewards greater after graduation. The educational policy proposed above, however, would certainly have more long-term disadvantages than benefits for society.
(267 words)

Test 2 SPEAKING

1 a Why did you choose this job/subject?
b What skills do you need for that job?
c What job would you like to do in the future? Why?

2 1 Do you think you get enough free time?
2 What do you enjoy doing in your free time?
3 How important is it to use your free time usefully?

3 1 a part of the world you would like to visit/what you would like to do there/explain why you would like to visit
2 how you know about it
3 You are expected to talk about somewhere you have never been, but would like to visit. However, if you find it difficult to choose a part of the world, then you can talk about somewhere you know and pretend that you haven't been there.

5 3, 2, 1, 4, 6, 5

6 a What makes some places very attractive to tourists?
b Will international tourism increase or decrease in the future? Why?
c Do people travel abroad more or less than they did in the past? Why/Why not?
d Are there any drawbacks of tourism?

7 1, 3, 4 are all appropriately general.

8 1 b, 2 a, 3 b, 4 c

TEST 3

Test 3 LISTENING

Section 1
Strategy
1 To apply for money from the council for a project
2 Four
3 Ralph Pearson – it is connected with a theatre group (performing a play for children)

Exam task
1 230 South Road   **2** 18
3 activities (and/&) workshops   **4** £250
5 interactive   **6** material(s)
7 insurance   **8** publicity
9 programme   **10** not available/unavailable

Section 2
Strategy
1 The order of the numbered items (as in all IELTS Listening Tasks).

2 No, there are some extra ones.
3 letters
Exam task
11 A   **12** C   **13** B   **14** A   **15** C
16 B   **17** E   **18** G   **19** H   **20** C

Section 3
Strategy
1 Three answers
2 Things which haven't been decided yet.
3 b, d, f
Exam task
21 investigate   **22** sunny (and) warm   **23** change
24 F   **25** D   **26** C   **27** B
28–30 B, F, H (in any order)

Section 4
31–32 A, D (in either order)   **33–34** B, E
35 12,000   **36** minority   **37** all
38 teachers   **39** (the) evaluation   **40** poor

Test 3 READING

Reading Passage 1

1	B	Paragraph B: it's probably because the brain is better at holding onto information than it is at knowing what information is important.
2	A	Paragraph C: Unfortunately, superficial, repetitive pop tunes are, by their very nature, more likely to stick than something more inventive.
3	D	Paragraph D: he asked volunteers to replay the theme from the TV show *Dallas* in their heads.

Strategy
Matching
1 The names are listed in the order in which they appear in the passage.
2 Theories. This information is given in the rubric.
3 Chaffin's theory is that 'song-in-head syndrome' is an example of a feature of memory that is generally useful, but not useful in this case. There is no matching sentence for this theory in Questions 4–7.

4	E	Paragraph H: in one experiment students who heard a history text set as the lyrics to a catchy song remembered the words better than those who simply read them, says Sandra Calvert
5	D	Paragraph G: a phenomenon called 'chunking', in which people remember musical phrases as a single unit of memory, says Caroline Palmer
6	F	Paragraph I: Before the written word could be used to record history, people memorised it in songs, says Leon James
7	B	Paragraph E: But it can become fatigued or depressed, which is when people most commonly suffer from song-in-head syndrome and other intrusive thoughts, says Susan Ball
8	I	'This message functions to unite society …
9	G	Particular chunks may be especially 'sticky' if you hear them often or if they follow certain predictable patterns
10	E	And once the unwanted song surfaces, it's hard to stuff it back down into the subconscious. 'The more you try to suppress a thought, the more you get it,' says Ball.
11	D	The annoying playback probably originates in the auditory cortex. Located at the front of the brain
12	A	You hear a pop song on the radio – or even just read the song's title
13	F	so I will not play them in the early morning

Reading Passage 2

14	NG	Paragraph 1 mentions wealth and poverty but there is no information about the attitudes of wealthy people.
15	Y	Paragraph 2: there may be political or social barriers to achieving a rich world
16	N	Paragraph 2: In thinking about the future of civilization, we ought to start by asking what people want.
17	Y	Paragraph 3: Increasing productivity that results in decreasing costs for such goods has been responsible for the greatest gains in the standard of living, and there is every reason to believe that this will continue.
18	NG	Paragraph 4 mentions that raw materials can be recycled, but there is no information about new types of raw materials.
19	Y	Paragraph 4: And long before all fossil fuels are exhausted, their rising prices may compel industrial society not only to become more energy efficient but also to find alternative energy sources

Strategy

1 one word only

2 space, population. This topic is dealt with in the middle of the text.

20	agriculture / farms / farmland	Paragraph 5: However, in fact the increasing amount of land consumed by <u>agriculture</u> is a far greater danger than urban sprawl. Stopping the growth of farms is the best way to preserve many of the world's remaining wild areas. But is a dramatic downsizing of farmland possible?
21	parks	Paragraph 5: Since 1950 more land in the US has been set aside in <u>parks</u> than has been occupied by urban and suburban growth.
22	productivity	Paragraph 5: Taking the best Iowa maize growers as the norm for world food productivity, it has been calculated that less than a tenth of present cropland could support a population of 10 billion.
23	protein	Paragraph 6: Nigel Calder suggested that 'nourishing but unpalatable primary food produced by industrial techniques – like yeast from petroleum – may be fed to animals … so that people in underdeveloped countries can have adequate supplies of <u>animal protein</u> … '
24	DNA	Paragraph 7: Once their <u>DNA</u> has been extracted … domesticated species of livestock … should be allowed to become extinct
25	game	Paragraph 7: However, <u>game</u> such as wild deer, rabbits and wild ducks will be ever more abundant

26	A	Paragraph 8: rising expectations of mobility … could become a necessity of tomorrow's global population – particularly if its members choose to live widely dispersed in a post-agrarian wilderness.
27	D	Paragraph 9: But before long our aircraft and cars will be piloted by computers which are never tired or stressed.

Reading Passage 3

28	E	Paragraph 1: the technology once used by Polynesians to colonize islands in the Pacific
29	B	Paragraph 1: Finney pointed out that … archaeologists will someday study off-Earth sites to trace the development of humans in space. He realized that it was unlikely … in the near future, but he was convinced that one day such work would be done.
30	H	Paragraph 2: There is a growing awareness, however, that it won't be long before both corporate adventurers and space tourists reach the Moon and Mars. … measures need to be taken to protect these sites.
31	A	Paragraph 2: scholars cite other potentially destructive forces such as souvenir hunting and unmonitored scientific sampling, as has already occurred in explorations of remote polar regions.
32	F	Paragraph 3: equating the remains of human exploration of the heavens with 'space junk' leaves them vulnerable to scavengers.
33	D	Paragraph 3: This presents some interesting dilemmas … Does the US own Neil Armstrong's famous first footprints on the Moon but not the lunar dust in which they were recorded?

Task: Flow chart completion

1 It is a proper name, so the exact words will be given in the text.

2 When *Surveyor 3* is mentioned in Paragraphs 5 and 6, the past perfect tense is used, because the writer is describing events that happened before the *Apollo 12* landing.

34	sneezed	Paragraph 8: While the camera was being installed in the probe prior to the launch, someone <u>sneezed</u> on it.
35	two/2	Paragraphs 7 and 8: these aerospace artefacts … for more than <u>two</u> years.
36	removed	Paragraph 7: The astronaut-archaeologists carefully <u>removed</u> the probe's television camera
37	analysis	Paragraph 8: One result of the <u>analysis</u> astonished them.

38	life	Paragraph 8: For a moment it was thought Conrad and Bean had discovered evidence for <u>life</u> on the Moon
39, 40	C, D (in either order)	C – mainly Paragraphs 2 and 3; D – throughout text especially Paragraph 9

Test 3 WRITING

Academic writing Task 1
Band 9 Sample Answer

The two diagrams give figures for water use in different parts of the world in 2000. The first indicates that almost three-quarters of world consumption (70%) was for agriculture, while 22% was used for industry and a mere 8% for domestic purposes.

This pattern is almost identical to that for China in 2000, whereas India used even more water (92%) for agriculture and only 8% for industrial and domestic sectors. In contrast, New Zealand used almost equal proportions for agriculture and household use, 44% and 46% respectively, and a slightly higher 10% was consumed by industry.

The pattern in Canada is almost the reverse of the world average, with a mere 8% of water consumed by agriculture and a massive 80% by industry. Only 12% was used by the domestic sector, which was almost a quarter of the NZ industrial consumption.

Overall, the data show that water use in the two developing countries is closer to the world patterns of consumption.
(161 words)

Academic writing Task 2
Band 9 Sample Answer

I would agree that young people today play a bigger role in society than their parents' or grandparents' generation did. This is mainly due to the large social and technological changes that have increased the experience gap between the generations. For instance, young people today are generally better educated, and because they have been trained from a young age to use computer technology, they have Internet access to information in a way that was unimaginable for earlier generations.

This means that they are probably better informed than their parents or grandparents were at their age, and their hi-tech skills give them confidence in dealing with the very rapid changes in technology that are so uncomfortable for older people.

In addition, younger people are often the most affected by globalisation. They follow fashions in clothes, music and social habits that are common among young people throughout the world. So they have become powerful consumers who influence big global markets today.

As a result of all these developments, relationships with older people are often difficult. Teachers and parents are no longer treated with respect, and experience is undervalued

because young people think they know everything, or at least can learn about everything from the Internet. In many cultures this has led to a lack of discipline in schools, family breakdowns and even serious social problems.

However, the current generation gap is the responsibility of both younger and older generations. Both have to make efforts to understand each other and a good starting point would be for families to spend more time together than they normally do today.
(264 words)

TEST 4

Test 4 LISTENING

Section 1
Exam task
1 19.75 **2** theme **3** quiet
4 children **5** breakfast (is) **6** (free) sky(-)dive
7 A **8** C **9** B **10** C

Section 2
Strategy
1 the names of organisations **2** b) d) f)
Exam task
11 B **12** A **13** C **14** C
15–17 [in any order] schools, local councils, companies
18 020 7562 4028 **19** £27.50 **20** 3 hours/hrs

Section 3
Strategy
1 (21) strongest aspect (22) least happy (23) in more depth
2 a noun
Exam task
21 (the/their) technique
22 (answering) (the/students') questions
23 (the/their) solutions
24 A **25** B **26** B **27** C
28 end(ing)
29 limitations
30 literature

Section 4
Exam task
31 clean (and) safe■safe (and) clean **32** basic needs
33 local government **34** residents
35 economic **36** secondary school
37 films **38** Women's Centre
39 skills **40** status

Test 4 READING

Reading Passage 1

1	D	So he intends to build five or six factories in cities where there are large quantities of bottles

2	E	The only problem that they could foresee was possible contamination if some glass came from sources other than beverage bottles.
3	G	It is already in use in central America to filter water on banana plantations
4	B	green glass is worth only $25 a tonne. Clear glass … is worth double that amount.
5	D	Current estimates of the UK market for this glass for filtering drinking water, sewage, industrial water, swimming pools and fish farming
6	F	'We have looked at a number of batches and it appears to do the job'
7	A	Backed by $1.6m from the European Union and the Department for Environment, Food and Rural Affairs
8	C	He concedes that he has given what is basically recycled glass a 'fancy name' to remove the stigma of what most people would regard as an inferior product.
9	G	Mr Dryden has set up a network of agents round the world to sell AFM.
10	E	the government's drinking water inspectorate will be asked to perform tests and approve it for widespread use by water companies.

11	natural resource	Paragraph B: The idea is not only to avoid using up an increasingly scarce natural resource, sand
12	recycling industry	Paragraph B: but also to solve a crisis in the recycling industry.
13	drinkable liquids/ beverages	Paragraph C: he needs bottles that have already contained drinkable liquids
14	(real) sand	Paragraph C: tests show that AFM does the job better than sand

Reading Passage 2

15	NG	Paragraph 1 mentions the number of insect and tree species found on the farms studied, but there is no information about the number of species in the forests of El Salvador.
16	F	Paragraph 3: In addition, coffee (and chocolate) is usually grown in tropical rain forest regions that are biodiversity hotspots. 'These habitats support up to 70% of the planet's plant and animal species
17	NG	Paragraph 4 mentions farmers and shade plantations, but there is no reference to farmers trying both.
18	T	Paragraph 5: In Ghana, West Africa … 90% of the cocoa is grown under shade, and these forest plantations are a vital habitat for wintering European migrant birds. In the same way, the coffee forests of Central and South America are a refuge for wintering North American migrants.
19	T	Paragraph 6: 'full sun'. But this system … requires huge amounts of pesticides and fertilisers.

20	D	Paragraph 9: John Rappole … argues that shade-grown marketing provides 'an incentive to convert existing areas of primary forest … into shade-coffee plantations'.
21	E	Paragraph 10: Ms Philpott argues that as long as the process is rigorous and offers financial gains to the producers, shade growing does benefit the environment.
22	C	Paragraph 5: Bird diversity in shade-grown coffee plantations rivals that found in natural forests in the same region, says Robert Rice
23	A	Paragraph 8: Alex Munro says shade-coffee farms have a cultural as well as ecological significance and people are not happy to see them go. But the financial pressures are great, and few of these coffee farms make much money.

Strategy: Classification
1 a) Paragraph 2 b) Paragraph 6
2 coffee, cocoa

24	C	Paragraph 4 describes shade-grown farming of coffee and cocoa Paragraph 6 describes full-sun farming of these two crops
25	B	Paragraph 6: a drive to increase yields by producer countries has led to … shade-grown coffee and cocoa being cleared to make way for a … pattern of production known as 'full sun'.
26	A	Paragraph 9: They are promoting a 'certification' system that can indicate to consumers that the beans have been grown on shade plantations.
27	B	Paragraph 3: Species diversity is much higher where coffee is grown in shade conditions. Paragraph 6: 'full sun'. But this system not only reduces the diversity of flora and fauna

Reading Passage 3

28	(A) vi	in Australia … they are already fully recognised … In Europe their art is being exhibited … while the future Quai Branly museum … plans to commission frescoes by artists from Australia.
29	(B) v	the founding myth of the Aboriginal culture … the land which was stolen from them … in the nineteenth century.
30	(C) viii	they were undoubtedly maltreated by the newcomers.
31	(D) i	He was astounded by the result.
32	(E) iv	Aboriginal … had been encouraged to reproduce on tree bark the motifs found on rock faces. … the churches … helped to sell them to the public
33	(F) vii	'For Aborigines, that moment has never ceased to exist.

34	thousands of years	Paragraph D: for thousands of years Aborigines had been 'painting' on the ground using sands of different colours, and on rock faces.
35	(tree) bark	Paragraph E: In the early twentieth century, Aboriginal communities … had been encouraged to reproduce on tree bark the motifs found on rock faces.

36	overseas museums	Paragraph E: between 1950 and 1960 Aboriginal paintings began to reach overseas museums.
37	school walls	Paragraph D: In 1971 … Geoffrey Bardon, suggested to a group of Aborigines that they should decorate the school walls with ritual motifs

38	B	Paragraph G: An artist cannot use a 'dream' that does not belong to his or her community, since each community is the owner of its dreams
39	D	Paragraph G: just as it is anchored to a territory marked out by its ancestors
40	C	Paragraph I: Their undeniable power prompts a dialogue that has proved all too rare in the history of contacts between the two cultures.

Test 4 WRITING

Writing Task 1
Band 9 Sample Answer
The two plans illustrate how a small coastal village in Europe grew into a large tourist centre between 1974 and 2004.

The figures show that over these thirty years, the local population increased dramatically from only 12,000 to 80,000, swelling to a possible 130,000 during the tourist season.

During this period large numbers of high-rise hotels were built along the coastline on both sides of the original village. The harbour and coastal woodlands were replaced by a sandy beach and a golf course for the tourists. Similarly, the olive groves inland were replaced with fruit and vegetable farms for the tourist market.

The original village and those further inland on the hillsides were developed with more homes for locals and more shops for the tourist trade. A main road leading from the hills to the coast was built to cope with the increased traffic to the village.

In conclusion, not only the original village, but also the whole surrounding area had been transformed into a well-populated tourist resort by 2004.
(170 words)

Writing Task 2
Band 9 Sample Answer
Generally, music is considered to be one of the most popular and ancient modes of human expression. It features largely in all histories and all cultures and indeed has been one of the main ways of passing on cultural traditions to new generations. Because of this, many people view music as a positive influence for societies. They also believe that the influence on individuals is wholly

beneficial as it is a long-established way of communicating and helping us to understand the whole range of human emotion and experience in a more spiritual language than words can represent.

However, there are different kinds of music and the qualities of classical music traditions are not necessarily part of the music many people experience today. In the modern world there is a huge music industry that sells piped music to supermarkets and advertisers. We are also constantly exposed to loud, modern music from people's CD players, iPods or car radios. So the view of music today as a kind of noise pollution produced by selfish people, is also a common and negative one.

But it is difficult to think of a world without music. Certainly there is bad music that may have negative influences, particularly on the young. But people's taste in music tends to change as they get older, and it would be difficult to find someone who had no positive musical associations at all.

In conclusion, I think that music can have both positive and negative influences on people and society, but it is an integral part of human expression that we cannot really separate from our lives.

(267 words)

TEST 5

Test 5 LISTENING

Section 1
Exam task
1 B   2 A   3 C   4 B   5 A   6 A   7 B
8–10 B, D, G [in any order]

Section 2
Exam task
11 June 6th   12 5,000   13 transportation
14 low levels   15 Commuter   16 plant trees
17 upgrade   18 border   19 clean(er) fuels   20 factories

Section 3
Exam task
21 north(-)west   22 spray
23 (a) (small) library   24 mountains
25 field observation   26 development
27 water   28 market town
29 national park   30 dissertation

Section 4
Strategy
1 Research methodology
2 b)
Exam task
31 requirements   32 private
33 attitudes   34 interviews
35 B   36 C   37 B   38 B   39 A   40 C

Test 5 READING

Reading Passage 1

1	B	Paragraph 3: they farm a fungus that is their primary food source. This must be kept at exactly 30.5°C … The termites achieve this remarkable feat by building a system of vents …
2	D	Paragraph 4: Eastgate's owners saved $3.5 million … because an air-conditioning plant didn't have to be imported.
3	A	Paragraph 8: This is all possible only because Harare … has … <u>rapid</u> temperature swings – <u>days</u> as warm as 31°C commonly drop to 14°C at <u>night</u>. 'You couldn't do this in New York, with its fantastically hot summers and fantastically cold winters,'
4	C	Paragraph 9: the temperature of the building has generally stayed between 23°C and 25°C, with the exception of the annual hot spell … in October
5	A	Paragraph 11: Pearce said he hoped plants would grow wild in the atrium and pigeons and bats would move into it

Strategy: Sentence completion
1 b)
2 Key words are *warm air*/*offices*

6	ceiling vents	Paragraph 5: As it rises and warms, it is drawn out via <u>ceiling vents</u>
7	(the) (brick) chimneys	Paragraph 5: and finally exits through forty-eight brick <u>chimneys</u>
8	cement arches	Paragraph 6: To keep the harsh, high veld sun from heating the interior, … all the windows are screened by <u>cement arches</u> that jut out more than a metre.
9	(the) big fans	Paragraph 7: During summer's cool nights, <u>big fans</u> flush air through the building seven times an hour to chill the hollow floors.
10	(the) (small) heaters	Paragraph 7: For winter days, there are small <u>heaters</u> in the vents.

Strategy: Short answer questions involving a list

1 parts of a building
2 features of Zimbabwe's history and culture – these do not have to be written down

11–13	(the) entrances (the) elevators (the) fan covers (IN ANY ORDER)	Paragraph 10: The design of the <u>entrances</u> is based on the porcupine-quill headdresses of the local Shona tribe. <u>Elevators</u> are designed to look like the mineshaft cages used in Zimbabwe's diamond mines. The shape of the <u>fan covers</u>, and the stone used in their construction, are echoes of Great Zimbabwe, the ruins that give the country its name.

Reading Passage 2

14	(B) v	But the company's name may itself simply be an example of clever marketing. BrightHouse does not scan people …
15	(C) i	Paragraph C summarises the steps of the procedure of brain scanning
16	(D) ix	Lieberman Research Worldwide … is collaborating … to enable movie studios to market-test film trailers … FKF Research, has been studying … campaign commercials
17	(E) viii	There have been no large-scale studies
18	(F) iii	An unpublished study carried out last summer … found that most subjects preferred Pepsi
19	(G) vi	any firm that can more accurately analyse how customers respond to brands could make a fortune.

20	F	Paragraph I: Brain-scanning could, for example, be used to determine when people are capable of making free choices, to ensure that advertising falls within those bounds.
21	D	Paragraph H: 'Already, marketing is deeply implicated in many serious pathologies … Neuromarketing is a tool to amplify these trends.'
22	A	Paragraph J: But as Tim Ambler, a neuromarketing researcher … says: '… if the owner of the tool gets a decent rent for hiring it out, then that subsidises the cost of the equipment …'
23	brands	Paragraph G: any firm that can more accurately analyse how customers respond to brands could make a fortune.
24	untruthful	Paragraph E: some people may be untruthful in their responses to opinion pollsters.
25	unconscious	Paragraph G: People form many <u>unconscious</u> attitudes that are obviously beyond traditional methods that utilise introspection
26	children	Paragraph H: 'Already, marketing is deeply implicated in many serious pathologies,' he says. 'That is especially true of children …'

Reading Passage 3

27	NG	Paragraph 1: 'all it boasted was a couple of dozen species of plant
28	T	Paragraph 1: most of them ferns and some of them unique to the island.
29	F	Paragraph 2: he concluded that the island had suffered some natural calamity
30	T	Paragraph 2: He suggested an ambitious scheme for planting trees and … the sailors set to with a will.
31	NG	Paragraph 3 mentioned the arrival of seeds, but there is no information about Hooker sending details of his scheme.
32	F	Paragraph 3: including those of two species that especially liked the place: bamboo and prickly pear.

33	B	Paragraph 4: Modern ecologists throw up their hands in horror at what they see as Hooker's environmental anarchy. The exotic species wrecked the indigenous ecosystem, squeezing out the island's endemic plants.
34	F	Paragraph 5: And as botanist David Wilkinson … pointed out … the introduced species have been a roaring success.
35	D	Paragraph 6: Conventional ecological theory says that complex ecosystems … can emerge only through evolutionary processes in which each organism develops in concert with others
36	G	Paragraph 8: Alan Gray … argues that the surviving endemic species … may still form the framework of the new ecosystem. The new arrivals may just be an adornment
37	A	Paragraph 9: as research reveals that supposedly pristine tropical rainforests from the Amazon to south-east Asia may in places be little more than the overgrown gardens of past rainforest civilisations.

38	B	Paragraph 11: But in their urgency to protect endemics, ecologists are missing out on the study of a great enigma.
39	A	Paragraph 12: '… various insects. There are caterpillars and beetles around,' says Wilkinson. 'But where did they come from?' … Such questions go to the heart of how rainforests happen.
40	D	All topics are mentioned, but D is the main idea.

Test 5 WRITING

Writing Task 1
Band 9 Sample Answer
The three diagrams illustrate how basic cooking devices developed from simple fires to more complex equipment.

The first stage was a simple cooking pot balanced on three stones over a fire of twigs and grass. The second shows how the same equipment was improved by building a shield made of clay around the fire. This was obviously to prevent heat loss and to protect the fire from winds.

The final diagram shows a further stage in which the fire is completely enclosed by a metal base in order to increase the control of the heat and the level of protection. There is a door at the front where air can enter and ashes can be removed. Charcoal is used as the fuel and it is burnt on a grate that sits inside a shield lined with clay. In addition there are metal supports so that a pot can balance on the stove and a handle for easy transportation.

Overall, the features of the stove in diagram C indicate that the efficiency of the cooking equipment was greatly improved.
(178 words)

Writing Task 2
Band 9 Sample Answer
From the evidence of developing countries all over the world it seems inevitable that economic growth is generated in the business and industrial centres of the major cities. As a result, urban citizens have access to jobs and facilities that improve their living standards considerably. However, it is usually the case that these are not equally enjoyed by people in the countryside and this generates several problems for the countries concerned.

First of all, people from the countryside will try to move to the cities to get more employment opportunities and better access to the facilities available there. But this increase in the urban population puts great pressure on housing and services, and leads to the creation of massive slum areas where conditions may be lower than in the rural villages. These are often left under-populated and this can impact on food production and can have severe affects for people in both urban and rural areas.

Finally, as a country's economy develops, there may be an increasing sense of inequality as the towns get richer and the villages get poorer, and this may lead to more crime and even civil unrest.

The key to reducing these problems seems to lie in improving the standards of living and the facilities available in the countryside. Perhaps incentives can be offered to factories and companies to relocate; road and rail networks can be built to make such relocation possible; doctors and teachers could be required to spend part of their professional lives in rural areas, etc.

In conclusion, however, improving rural living standards requires investment and political will that is sometimes not easy to generate.
(272 words)

TEST 6

Test 6 LISTENING

Section 1
1 Lower Green(e) Street/St.   2 01778 552387
3 (a) field   4 (a) van   5 (a) Flyer 2000
6 blue   7 flat tyre/tire   8 8/eight days
9 Hill Farm Estate   10 local

Section 2
11 fisherman   12 six/6 months   13 captain
14 education   15 (an) interpreter   16 sister cities
17 Festival   18 I   19 B   20 E

Section 3

21 A   22 B   23 B   24 D   25 G   26 C
27 E   28 progress reviews   29 (critical) reflection
30 exhibition

Section 4

31 physical   32 instincts   33 relief
34 (social) bonds   35 power   36 negative
37 release   38 hormones   39 immune system
40 bad dreams

Test 6 READING

Reading Passage 1

1	transportation	Paragraph 3: Removing this makes the food much lighter and therefore makes transportation less difficult.
2	pharmaceuticals	Paragraph 4: The process is also used to preserve other sorts of material, such as pharmaceuticals.
3	manuscripts	Paragraph 4: Even valuable manuscripts that had been water damaged have been saved by using this process.
4	sublimation	Paragraph 6: in freeze-drying, solid water – ice – is converted directly into water vapour, missing out the liquid phase entirely. This is called 'sublimation'
5	simple drying (techniques)	Paragraph 5: Freeze-drying is different from simple drying because it is able to remove almost all the water from materials, whereas simple drying techniques can only …
6	(freeze-drying) chamber	Paragraph 7: The material to be preserved is placed in a freeze-drying chamber
7	shelves	Paragraph 7: The heating units apply a small amount of heat to the shelves in the chamber
8	freezing coil	Paragraph 7: water vapour, which leaves the freeze-drying chamber, and flows past the freezing coil.
9	(refrigerator) compressor	Paragraph 7: a freeze-drying chamber which is connected to a freezing coil and refrigerator compressor. When the chamber is sealed the compressor lowers …
10	enzymes	Paragraph 2: Similarly, the enzymes which occur naturally in food cannot cause ripening without water …
11	composition (and/the) structure	Paragraph 5: the composition and structure of the material is not significantly changed
12	overheating	Paragraph 8: This time is necessary to avoid overheating, which might affect the structure of the material.
13	high altitudes	Paragraph 9: The extremely cold temperatures and low pressure at those high altitudes prevented food from spoiling

Reading Passage 2

14	NG	Paragraph 1 describes changes in wildlife in the countryside and towns, and examples of two types of wildlife, but there is no information about general proportions of wildlife.
15	T	Paragraphs 2 and 3: agrochemical pollution in the farming lowlands … has led to the catastrophic decline of so many species. By contrast, most urban open spaces have escaped the worst of the pesticide revolution
16	T	Paragraph 3: Over the years, the cutting down of hedgerows on farmland has contributed to habitat isolation and species loss.
17	NG	Paragraph 3 mentions ecological corridors, but there is no mention of anyone planning them.
18	NG	Paragraph 4 mentions changes in the management of public parks and gardens, but there is no mention of their expansion.
19	F	Paragraph 4: As a consequence, there are song birds and predators in abundance over these once-industrial landscapes.

20	woodland species	Paragraph 5: Those that do best tend to be woodland species
21	exotic flowers	Paragraph 5: Indeed, in some respects gardens are rather better than the real thing, especially with exotic flowers extending the nectar season.
22	(domestic) cats	Paragraph 5: only the millions of domestic cats may spoil the scene.
23	81	Paragraph 6: Between 1990 and the year 2000, the number of different bird species seen … in gardens increased from 17 to an amazing 81.
24–26	C, E, G (IN ANY ORDER)	Paragraph 7: (G) The canopy of the urban forest is filtering air pollution Paragraph 7: (E) Sustainable urban drainage relies on ponds and wetlands to contain storm water runoff, thus reducing the risk of flooding, … Paragraph 7: (C) contact with wildlife … can help to reduce stress and anger. Hospital patients … make a more rapid recovery and suffer less pain.
27	C	See last three paragraphs especially

Reading Passage 3

28	(A) iii	For almost a century, scientists have presumed
29	(B) vi	Noakes and … Gibson … have examined this standard theory. … The essence of their new theory …
30	(C) ii	'Puzzling evidence' is raised by experiments involving exercise at high altitudes. The 'Question' relates to the 'something else' referred to in the last sentence.
31	(D) vii	Probing further, Noakes conducted an experiment … (+ this paragraph explains the basis for its design)
32	(E) viii	But his team found exactly the opposite.
33	(F) iv	he says, '… their bodies actually had considerable reserves … '

34	C	Paragraph C: Lactic acid is a by-product of exercise, and its accumulation is often cited as a cause of fatigue. (This is given as a fact, and it underlies both theories.)
35	A	Paragraph A: In other words, muscles tire because they hit a physical limit: …
36	B	Paragraph F: the brain is regulating the pace of the workout to hold the cyclists well back from the point of catastrophic exhaustion.
37	C	Paragraph E: Noakes reasoned that if the limitations theory was correct and fatigue was due to muscle fibres hitting some limit Paragraph I: The governor constantly monitors physiological signals from the muscles, along with other information, to set the level of fatigue.
38	B	Paragraph J: Noakes believes that the central regulator evaluates the planned workout, and sets a pacing strategy accordingly.
39	A	Paragraph H: … makes no sense if fatigue is caused by muscles poisoning themselves with lactic acid …
40	B	Paragraph K makes this point.

Test 6 WRITING

Writing Task 1
Band 9 Sample Answer

The table shows dramatic increases in the total world population from 2.5 billion in 1950 to 6 billion in 2000, with an expected increase to 9 billion in 2050.

However, this trend is affecting parts of the world differently. Throughout the period Asia is expected to retain the largest share of the world population (56 to 59%) so their population will probably continue to increase in line with world growth. Meanwhile, regions like Africa and Latin America have experienced similar rates of increase in their populations up to 2000 (4% and 3% of the total, respectively), but Africa is expected to grow much faster as it rises to 20% of the total by 2050.

In contrast, more industrialised regions saw a large fall in their proportion of the global population, from almost a quarter in 1950 in Europe to only 12% by 2000 and from 7% to 5% in North America. This decline is expected to continue to a mere 11% of the total in both regions together by 2050.

Overall the figures suggest that population increases will continue in less developed regions, but not in the more industrialised ones.
(190 words)

Writing Task 2
Band 9 Sample Answer

It is true to say that fossil fuels are still our main source of energy today, and as more countries develop their industries and their economies, the scale of their use continues to grow.

However, we are now well aware of the consequences of relying on this energy source for our natural environment. Global warming and the damage to the protective ozone layer are caused by carbon dioxide and other by-products of fossil fuels. So I certainly agree that these problems are global rather than national ones. They threaten our whole planet and no action by a single country could solve them. Furthermore these problems are urgent as nobody knows when our natural world will be so damaged that it will no longer be able to support us.

While some countries already use safer alternative energy sources, such as wind, water or solar power, it seems that there has not been sufficient investment in developing the technology to make such alternatives viable for all. So it should definitely be a global priority to invest in such research and development.

Of course there are other global priorities that we also need to address, such as poverty and disease. But while it may be the case that these problems are just as important as the energy problem, there is a sense that time is ticking away for our planet and any solutions to the energy issue will take some time to achieve.

So in conclusion, I would agree that finding alternatives to fossil fuels is certainly the most pressing global priority, if not the most important one for our world today.
(269 words)

GENERAL TRAINING

READING Section 1

1	money	you'll be paying less <u>money</u>.
2	heat	the remaining 90% is wasted as <u>heat</u>.
3	durable	they … are much more <u>durable</u>, lasting at least six times longer.
4	slow start-up	they can have a <u>slow start-up</u>, taking some time to reach their full brightness,
5	shorten the life	frequent switching on and off … may also shorten the life of the bulb.
6	efficiency	cold conditions … can reduce the bulb's <u>efficiency</u>
7	(light) fittings	heavier than traditional bulbs, which may make them unsuitable for some <u>light fittings</u>,

8	F	There are laws to protect workers, whether or not they have a written contract. (i.e. employers do not *have* to provide contracts)
9	T	legal rights, such as the right not to be discriminated against at work because of your sex, race or disability.
10	NG	The passage mentions both, but there is no information about them having the same value.
11	T	… a written statement which sets out your terms of employment. You should get this within eight weeks of starting your job.
12	NG	The text mentions pensions, but there is no information about employers having to contribute.
13	F	If you want a contract, but your employer won't give you one, all you can do is apply to an employment tribunal for a list of what should be included in your written statement.

Section 2

14	D	including absolute beginners with no previous keyboard experience,
15	A	(No mention of qualifications)
16	C	or £25 payable at the start of each 10-week session.
17	E	This is a high-level course
18	C	Entry qualification – Certificate in Computer Literacy and IT
19	B	offering three or more modules
20	D	Additional examination fee of £10 –
21	booking form	complete the booking form and return it together with your cheque
22	an information week	an information week: this is held at our main centres prior to the beginning of term.
23	the first session	At the first session: only if there are places available,
24	course description sheet	a course description sheet … will give you more details on the suitability of each course.
25	disabled access	Disabled access does vary from centre to centre,

26	tuition and registration	The prices … are inclusive of tuition and registration
27	reduction in fees	If you are claiming a reduction in fees

Section 3

28	reused	up to 7 billion plastic bags may be <u>reused</u>,
29	1%	they still constitute only <u>1%</u> of UK litter.
30	energy	Only a fraction are incinerated for <u>energy</u> production
31	landfill sites	But ultimately the vast majority end up in <u>landfill sites</u> as waste.
32	B	'still managed to slash plastic bag usage by 69%.'
33	C	the once floundering jute-bag industry has been resurrected
34	B	The tax was criticised … but still managed to slash plastic bag usage
35	E	the 'Plas Tax' has raised €23 million for waste management initiatives.
36	C	Blocked drains are widely held responsible for the devastating monsoon floods of 1988 and 1989.
37	A	a tax on packaging, … the retailers … had to pay up.
38	D	being caught in possession of a polyethylene bag could get you seven years behind bars
39	C	(The text gives and evaluates evidence both for and against the danger caused by plastic bags)
40	A	This is an implication question. The writer implies that action taken in Bangladesh is justified, by mentioning the problems it solves, but the comments about Taiwan, for example, are less positive.

GT WRITING Task 1
Band 9 Sample Answer

Dear Chris,

I can't tell you how surprised I was when the package from Canada arrived. The postman brought it last Saturday and I was very excited when I saw that it was from you. Then when I opened it and saw the beautiful silk scarf you've sent me for my birthday I have to say I was truly delighted. Thank you so much!

You remembered my taste in colours very well, so I really love the mix of blues and greys in the design, and the silk feels very soft. I can't thank you enough for the gift. I know that I intend to wear it every weekend when I go out with the family – and we'll have to take some pictures so you can see how good it looks, even if I say so myself.

So thank you once again, Chris. Give my regards to your folks, but lots of love to you and Peter.

I'll write to you soon and send that photo!
Best wishes, Misha
(166 words)

GT WRITING Task 2
Band 9 Sample Answer

I think most people who travel away from home for any length of time will feel homesick at the beginning because missing their own home and country is a natural reaction. However, I think it becomes less of a problem as people adapt to the new environment and start to enjoy new relationships and experiences. Today many young people study abroad and for them it is probably their first time away from family, friends and everything that is familiar. The country they have moved to may have a completely different culture and language, so they need to adjust to this and learn how to communicate in new ways. This can be very tiring, but until they can do so they will feel out of place and unable to form new relationships.

Professionals who have moved abroad for work may have left older parents behind, or even young children. For them, the separation can be worse because they feel so far from the people they feel responsible for.

I personally think that people should try and prepare themselves for study or work abroad. They need to learn the new language, and to try to be as adaptable and independent as they can. At the same time, however, they need to set up ways of communicating quickly and easily with people back home, by using email for instance, so that they know what is happening there and do not need to worry. If people are aware of the problems, they can do a lot to reduce their homesickness and make their stay abroad a positive, exciting experience.
(265 words)

VOCABULARY PAGES

1 The Language of Change   (page 159)

1 1 soaring   2 peaked   3 steady increase
   4 declined   5 dropped dramatically
   6 fall   7 fluctuate   8 growth

2 1 a) Pesticide pollution has led to a gradual <u>decline</u> in the number of bird species.
    b) The number of bird species has <u>plummeted</u> because of pesticide pollution.
   (different meanings)
  2 a) With <u>rising</u> personal incomes come <u>rising</u> expectations.
    b) People's expectations <u>grow</u> as their incomes <u>increase</u>.
   (parallel meanings)

3 a) The rural population has <u>halved</u> in the last twenty years.
  b) The number of people living in the countryside has <u>soared</u> in recent decades.
  (different meanings)
4 a) Unemployment <u>peaked</u> in 1983.
  b) In 1983 the unemployment rate was at its highest, but then started to <u>decrease</u>.
  (parallel meanings)
5 a) The level of sales tends to <u>fluctuate</u> on a seasonal basis.
  b) No matter what the season, sales figures usually <u>remain quite constant</u>.
  (different meanings)
3 1 growing   2 increasingly
  3 doubled   4 growth
  5 have declined/have been declining
  6 increasing

2 The Language of Cause and Effect   (page 160)
1 1 contributed further to   2 due to
  3 the causes of   4 largely because
  5 since   6 so much
2 1 be explained   2 results   3 contributing
  4 effects   5 is caused   6 leads
  7 causes
3 1 a) Sufficiently low temperatures will <u>make</u> the water droplets freeze.
  b) <u>If</u> the temperature is sufficiently low, the water droplets will freeze.
  (parallel meanings)
  2 a) Cultural differences may be <u>a source of</u> misunderstandings.
  b) Misunderstandings may <u>lead to</u> cultural differences.
  (different meanings)
  3 a) <u>The rougher</u> the surface of the road, <u>the noisier</u> the traffic will be.
  b) Traffic noise <u>results from</u> rough road surfaces.
  (parallel meanings)
  4 a) This habitat supports many rare species, <u>and so</u> it must be preserved.
  b) A large number of rare species live in this habitat and its preservation is <u>therefore</u> necessary.
  (parallel meanings)
  5 a) <u>Thanks to</u> the discovery of new applications for aspirin, it is still manufactured today.
  b) <u>The reason why</u> aspirin is still manufactured today is that new applications have been discovered.
  (parallel meanings)

3 The Language of Comparison and Contrast (page 161)
1 1 higher   2 differently   3 the same
  4 difference   5 high as   6 much more
  7 as many as   8 most   9 a lot more frequent
  10 far fewer
2 1 although   2 Both   3 In contrast

4 while   5 On the other hand   6 however
3 1 differently/exactly the same
  2 complex/simple
  3 few/more common
  4 several kilos/a few grams
  5 in the past/today

4 The Language of Education and Research (page 162)
1 1 aim   2 investigate   3 carried out
  4 articles   5 interviews   6 questionnaire
  7 closed questions   8 sample
  9 respondents   10 suggest
2 1 theories   2 semesters   3 project
  4 research   5 topic   6 assessed
  7 assessments   8 report   9 examination
3 1 a) Our <u>survey provides evidence</u> that attitudes towards global warming are changing.
  b) Our survey <u>proves</u> that attitudes towards global warming are changing.
  (different meanings)
  2 a) The <u>researchers</u> selected a <u>random sample</u> of volunteers for the <u>experiment</u>.
  b) Volunteers for the experiment were selected in a <u>systematic</u> way by the researchers.
  (different meanings)
  3 a) The group will carry out <u>evaluation</u> of the <u>pilot project</u> before beginning the main <u>study</u>.
  b) The pilot project will be <u>evaluated</u> by the group before they begin the main study.
  (parallel meanings)
  4 a) We found plenty of <u>anecdotal evidence</u> for the effect of weather on people's moods.
  b) We found a large amount of <u>data</u> on the effect of weather on people's moods.
  (different meanings)
  5 a) The <u>components</u> can be <u>assigned</u> to three distinct <u>classes</u>.
  b) Three distinct <u>categories</u> can be <u>identified</u> among the components.
  (parallel meanings)

5 The Language of Technology   (page 163)
1 1 utilise   2 skill   3 extract   4 bending
  5 resources   6 energy   7 manufacture
  8 machinery
2 1 base   2 connected   3 collected
  4 fan   5 forces   6 located   7 passes
  8 filter   9 leaves   10 remains
3 1 a) Hydrogen and oxygen <u>combine</u> to <u>form</u> water.
  b) Water is formed from the <u>combination</u> of oxygen and hydrogen.
  (parallel meanings)
  2 a) The experiment uses a <u>process</u> by which water is supercooled.
  b) The experiment uses a <u>device</u> which supercools water.
  (different meanings)

3 a) Roman roads had a <u>foundation layer</u> of <u>stone</u>, with a middle layer of softer <u>material</u>, and a layer of flat stones on top.
   b) Roman roads had a <u>surface</u> of flat stones under which were two layers, an upper one of softer material and a lower one of stone.
   (parallel meanings)
4 a) <u>Pumps</u> were used to bring the water up from under the ground.
   b) Water <u>was pumped</u> up to the surface of the ground.
   (parallel meanings)

6 The Language of Man and the Natural World (page 164)

1 1 industrial   2 conservation   3 unspoilt
   4 protected   5 wildlife   6 unique
   7 threat   8 survival   9 species   10 flora
2 1 environmental   2 polluted   3 contaminated
   4 toxic   5 nutrients   6 be recovered
   7 techniques   8 sustainable
3 1 a) Large areas <u>of rainforest</u> have been lost to <u>agriculture</u>.
     b) <u>Cultivation of the land</u> has helped <u>to regenerate the natural rainforest</u>.
     (different meanings)
   2 a) <u>Indigenous plants are not threatened</u> by non-native species <u>in national parks</u>.
     b) <u>Introduced species</u> are often <u>invasive in national parks</u>.
     (different meanings)
   3 a) It has been discovered that <u>some organisms</u> are able to <u>survive in extremely harsh conditions</u>.
     b) We now know that even the most <u>extreme habitats</u> can <u>sustain some life forms</u>.
     (parallel meanings)
   4 a) <u>Monoculture</u> is a <u>threat to species diversity</u>.
     b) <u>Fewer species can survive</u> in areas where <u>a single crop is grown intensively</u>.
     (parallel meanings)
   5 a) <u>Some species of insects and birds</u> are dependent on the <u>vegetation found only in tropical rainforests</u>.
     b) <u>Some plants</u> that are <u>unique to tropical rainforests support specific species of insects and birds</u>.
     (parallel meanings)

7 The Language of the Urban Environment (page 165)

1 1 urban   2 facilities   3 standard of living
   4 urbanisation   5 overcrowding
   6 public transport   7 traffic   8 infrastructure
2 1 residents   2 suburban   3 housing
   4 spacious   5 architectural   6 neighbourhoods
   7 commuting   8 communal
3 1 a) The <u>inner-city areas</u> usually have <u>lots of rubbish</u> lying around.
     b) <u>Street litter</u> is a feature of the <u>inner-city areas</u>.
     (parallel meanings)

2 a) <u>Apartments</u> that are near the <u>main urban highways</u> need to have specialised windows that <u>reduce noise levels</u>.
   b) <u>Flats</u> built next to <u>main urban highways</u> need <u>double glazing to protect them from traffic noise</u>.
   (parallel meanings)
3 a) <u>Housing</u> is less expensive in <u>under-populated areas</u>.
   b) <u>In densely-populated areas, housing</u> costs more.
   (parallel meanings)
4 a) The cities are encroaching on rural areas because of <u>urban sprawl</u>.
   b) <u>Migration to the cities</u> is depopulating rural areas.
   (different meanings)
5 a) <u>Cities grow quickly</u> when there is lots of <u>building and development</u>.
   b) <u>Rapid urban expansion</u> is a sympton of <u>increased urbanisation</u>.
   (different meanings)

8 General Academic Language   (page 166)

1 1 activities   2 works   3 fields
   4 significance   5 beliefs   6 principles
   7 relationships   8 aspects   9 phenomena
   10 organisations   11 attitudes
2 1 a) Nanotechnology has <u>applications</u> in <u>fields</u> as varied as medicine, electronics and computer science.
     b) Nanotechnology can be used in areas as <u>diverse</u> as medicine, electronics and computer science.
     (parallel meanings)
   2 a) Some historians claim that civilisation <u>has its roots</u> in trade and commerce.
     b) Civilisation <u>originated in</u> trade and commerce, claim some historians.
     (parallel meanings)
   3 a) Noise and pollution are two <u>factors</u> which must be <u>taken into account</u> when choosing a <u>site</u> for a new airport.
     b) Those choosing where to <u>locate</u> a new airport must try to avoid the effects of noise and pollution.
     (different meanings)
   4 a) The <u>role</u> of the doctor has changed considerably in recent years.
     b) There have been significant increases in the <u>demands made on</u> doctors in recent years.
     (different meanings)
3 1 developments   2 transforming   3 invention
   4 production   5 consumer   6 social
   7 impact   8 threat   9 action   10 services

TAPESCRIPTS

Mrs Blake: Hello?

Conor: Oh, hello. I'm ringing about the advertisement in yesterday's newspaper … the one for the bookcases … can you tell me if they're still available?

Mrs Blake: We've sold one, but we still have two available.

Conor: Right. Er … can you tell me a bit about them?

Mrs Blake: Sure, er … what do you want to know?

Conor: Well, I'm looking for something to fit in my study, so, well, I'm not too worried about the height, but the width's quite important. Can you tell me how wide each of them is?

Mrs Blake: They're both exactly the same size … let me see, I've got the details written down somewhere. Yes, so they're both <u>75 cm</u> wide and 180 cm high.

Conor: OK, fine, that should fit in OK. And I don't want anything that looks too severe … not made of metal, for example. I was really looking for something made of <u>wood</u>?

Mrs Blake: That's all right, they are, both of them.

Conor: So, are they both the same price as well?

Mrs Blake: No, the first bookcase is quite a bit cheaper. It's just <u>£15.00</u>. We paid £60.00 for it just five years ago, so it's very good value. It's in perfectly good condition, they're both in very good condition in fact, but the first one isn't the same quality as the other one. It's a good sturdy bookcase, it used to be in my son's room, but it could do with a fresh coat of paint …

Conor: Oh, it's painted?

Mrs Blake: Yes, it's <u>cream</u> at present, but as I say you could easily change that if you wanted … to fit in with your colour scheme.

Conor: Yes, I'd probably paint it white if I got it. Let's see, what else … how many shelves has it got?

Mrs Blake: Six – two of them are fixed, and the other four are <u>adjustable</u> so you can shift them up and down according to the sizes of your books.

Conor: Right, fine. Well that certainly sounds like a possibility.

…

Mrs Blake: But the second one's a lovely bookcase too. That's not painted, it's just the natural wood colour, a dark brown. It was my grandmother's, and I think she bought it sometime in the 1930s so I'd say it must be getting on for eighty years old, it's very good quality, they don't make them like that nowadays.

Conor: And you said it's the same dimensions as the first one?

Mrs Blake: Yes, and it's got the six shelves, but it also has a <u>cupboard</u> at the bottom that's really useful for keeping odds and ends in.

Conor: Right.

Mrs Blake: Oh, and I nearly forgot to say, the other thing about it is it's got glass <u>doors</u>, so the books are all kept out of the dust. So it's really good value for the money. I'm

really sorry to be selling it but we just don't have the room for it.

Conor: Mmm. So what are you asking for that one?

Mrs Blake: <u>£95.00</u>. It's quite a bit more, but it's a lovely piece of furniture – a real heirloom.

Conor: Yes … all the same, it's a lot more than I wanted to pay … I didn't really want to go above thirty or forty. Anyway, the first one sounds fine for what I need.

Mrs Blake: Just as you like.

Conor: So is it all right if I come round and have a look this evening, then if it's OK I can take it away with me?

Mrs Blake: Of course. So you'll be coming by car, will you?

Conor: I've got a friend with a van, so I'll get him to bring me round, if you can just give me the details of where you live.

Mrs Blake: Sure. I'm Mrs Blake, …

Conor: <u>B-L-A-K-E</u>?

Mrs Blake: That's right, and the address is 41 Oak Rise, that's in Stanton.

Conor: OK … so I'll be coming from the town centre, can you give me an idea of where you are?

Mrs Blake: Yes, you know <u>the road that goes out towards the university</u>?

Conor: Yes.

Mrs Blake: Well you take that road, and you <u>go on till you get to a roundabout, go straight on, then Oak Rise is the first road to the right</u>.

Conor: Out towards the university, past the roundabout, first left?

Mrs Blake: First *right*. And we're at the end of the road.

Conor: Got it. So I'll be round at about 7.00, if that's all right. Oh, and my name's Conor … Conor Field.

Mrs Blake: Fine. I'll see you then, Conor. Goodbye.

Conor: Goodbye.

Announcer: One of the most anticipated art events in Christchurch is the Charity Art Sale, organised this year by Neil Curtis. Neil, tell us all about it.

Neil: Well, Diane, this looks like being the biggest art sale yet, and the best thing about it is that the money raised will all go to charity. So what you probably want to know first is where it is. Well, the pictures will be on view all this week, most of them at the Star Gallery in the shopping mall, but we have so many pictures this year that we're also showing some in the <u>café</u> next door, so do drop in and see them any day between 9.00 and 5.00. Now if you're interested in buying rather than just looking – and we hope a lot of you will be – the actual sale will take place on Thursday evening, with sales starting at <u>7.30</u> – refreshments will be available before the sale, starting at 6.30. We've got about 50 works by local artists showing a huge range of styles and media, and in a minute I'll tell you about some of them. You're probably also interested in what's going to happen to your money once you've handed it over – well, all proceeds will go to support children who are <u>disabled</u>, both here in New Zealand and also in other countries, so you can find an original painting, support local talent, and help these children all at the same time.

…

Now let me tell you a bit about some of the artists who have kindly agreed to donate their pictures to the Charity Art Sale.

One of them is Don Studley, who has a special interest in the art sale because his five-year-old daughter was born with a serious back problem. After an operation earlier this year, she's now doing fine, but Don says he wants to offer something to help other less fortunate children. Don is totally self taught, and says he's passionate about painting. His paintings depict some of our New Zealand <u>birds</u> in their natural habitats.

One relative newcomer to New Zealand is James Chang, who came here from Taiwan nine years ago, at the age of 56. Mr Chang had 13 <u>exhibitions</u> in Taiwan before he came to live here in Christchurch so he's a well-established artist and art has been a lifelong passion for him. His paintings are certainly worth looking at – if you like <u>abstract</u> pictures with strong colour schemes, you'll love them.

Natalie Stevens was born in New Zealand, but has exhibited in China, Australia and Spain. As well as being an artist, she's a website <u>designer</u>. She believes art should be universal, and her paintings use soft colours and a mixture of media. Most of her pictures are <u>portraits</u> so watch out – some of them may even be friends of yours.

And then we have Christine Shin, from Korea. Christine only started to learn English <u>two years</u> ago, when she arrived in New Zealand, but she's been painting professionally for over ten years and she sure knows how to communicate strong messages through the universal language of art. She usually works from <u>photographs</u>, and paints delicate watercolours, which combine traditional Asian influences with New Zealand landscapes, giving a very special view of our local scenery.

Well, that's all I have time to tell you now, but as well as these four, there are many other artists whose work will be on sale so do come along on Thursday. We accept cheques, credit cards or cash and remember, even if you don't buy a picture you can always make a donation!

Test 1 SECTION 3   pages 12–13

Olivia: Hi, Joey. How are you doing? I heard you were sick.

Joey: Oh, hi, Olivia. Yeah, I had a virus last week, and I missed a whole pile of lectures, like the first one on the Great Books in Literature … where Dr Castle gave us all the information about the semester project.

Olivia: I can give you copies of the handouts, I've got them right here.

Joey: That's OK. I already collected the handouts but I'm not very clear about all the details … I know we each have to choose an individual author … I think I'm going to do Carlos Castenada … I'm really interested in South American literature.

Olivia: <u>Have you checked he's on the list that Dr Castle gave us? We can't just choose anyone.</u>

Joey: Yeah, I checked, it's OK. Who did you choose?

Olivia: Well, I was thinking of choosing Ernest Hemingway,

but then I thought no, I'll do a British author not an American one, so I chose Emily Brontë.

Joey: OK … and first of all it says we have to read a biography of our author – <u>I guess it's OK if we just look up information about him on the Internet?</u>

Olivia: <u>No, it's got to be a full-length book.</u> I think the minimum length's 250 pages … there's a list of biographies, didn't you get that?

Joey: Oh right. I didn't realise we had to stick with that. So what do we have to do when we've read the biography?

Olivia: Well, then we have to choose one work by the writer … again it's got to be something quite long, we can't just read a short story.

Joey: <u>But I guess a collection of short stories would be OK?</u>

Olivia: <u>Yes, or even a collection of poems</u>, they said, but I think most people are doing novels. I'm going to do *Wuthering Heights*, I've read it before but I really want to read it again now I've found out more about the writer.

Joey: And then the video … <u>we have to make a short video about our author and about the book. How long has it got to be?</u>

Olivia: <u>A minute.</u>

Joey: What? Like, sixty seconds? And we gotta give all the important information about their life *and* the book we choose …

Olivia: Well you can't do everything … I wrote it down somewhere … yes, Dr Castle said we had to 'find or write a short passage that helps to explain the author's passion for writing, why they're a writer'. <u>So, we can back this up with reference to important events in the writer's life if they're relevant, but it's up to us really.</u> The video's meant to portray the essence of the writer's life and the piece of writing we choose.

Joey: So when we read the biography, we have to think about what kind of person our writer is …

Olivia: Yes … and the historical context and so on. So for my writer, Emily Brontë, the biography gave a really strong impression of the place where she lived and the countryside around.

Joey: Right, I'm beginning to get the idea.

…

Joey: Er … can I check the other requirements with you?

Olivia: Sure.

Joey: The handout said after we'd read the biography, we had to read the work we'd chosen by our author and choose a passage that's typical in some way … that typifies the author's <u>interests and style</u>.

Olivia: Yes, but at the same time it has to relate to the biographical extract you choose … there's got to be some sort of theme linking them.

Joey: OK, I'm with you.

Olivia: And then you have to think about the video.

Joey: So are we meant to dramatise the scene we choose?

Olivia: I guess we could, but there's not a lot of time for that … I think it's more how we can use things like sound effects to create the atmosphere … the feeling we want.

Joey: And presumably <u>visuals</u> as well?

Olivia: Yeah, of course – I mean, I suppose that's the whole point of making a video – but whatever we use has to be historically in keeping with the author. We can use things like digital image processing to do it all.

Joey: So we can use any computer software we want?

Olivia: Sure. And it's important that we use a range – not just one software program. That's actually one of the things we're assessed on.

Joey: OK.

Olivia: Oh, and something else that's apparently really important is to keep track of the materials we use and to acknowledge them.

Joey: Including stuff we download off the Internet presumably?

Olivia: Yeah, so our video has to list all the material used with details of the source in a bibliography at the end.

Joey: OK. And you were talking about assessment of the project – did they give us the criteria? I couldn't find anything on the handout.

Olivia: Sure. He gave us them in the lecture. Let's see, you get 25 percent just for getting all the components done – that's both sets of reading, and the video. Then the second part is actually how successful we are at getting the essence of the work, they call that 'content' and that counts for 50 percent. Then the last 25 percent is on the video itself, the artistic and technical side.

Joey: Great. Well, that sounds a lot of work, but a whole lot better than just handing in a paper. Thanks a lot, Olivia.

Olivia: You're welcome.

Test 1 SECTION 4   pages 14–15

Hello, everybody, and welcome to the sixth of our Ecology evening classes. Nice to see you all again. As you know from the programme, today I want to talk to you about some research that is pushing back the frontiers of the whole field of ecology. And this research is being carried out in the remoter regions of our planet … places where the environment is harsh and – until recently – it was thought that the conditions couldn't sustain life of any kind. But, life forms *are* being found – and these have been grouped into what is now known as *extremophiles* – that is, organisms that can survive in the most extreme environments. And these discoveries may be setting a huge challenge for the scientists of the future, as you'll see in a minute.

Now, the particular research I want to tell you about was carried out in Antarctica – one of the coldest and driest places on Earth. But a multinational team of researchers – from the US, Canada and New Zealand – recently discovered colonies of microbes in the soil there, where no one thought it was possible. Interestingly enough, some of the colonies were identified as a type of fungus called *Beauveria Bassiana* – a fungus that lives on insects. But where are the insects in these utterly empty regions of Antarctica? The researchers concluded that this was clear evidence that these colonies were certainly not new arrivals … they might've been there for centuries, or even millennia – possibly even since the last Ice Age! Can you imagine their excitement?

Now, some types of microbes had previously been found living just a few millimetres under the surface of rocks – porous, Antarctic rocks … but this was the first time that living colonies had been found surviving – erm – relatively deeply in the soil itself, several centimetres down in fact.

…

So, the big question is: how *can* these colonies survive there? Well, we know that the organisms living very near the rock surface can still be warmed by the sun, so they can survive in their own microclimate … and this keeps them from freezing during the day. But this isn't the case for the colonies that are hidden *under* the soil.

In their research paper, this team suggested that the very high amounts of salt in the soil might be the clue – because this is what is preventing essential water from freezing. The team found that the salt concentration increased the deeper down they went in the soil. But while they had expected the number of organisms to be fewer down there, they actually found the opposite. In soil that had as much as 3000 parts of salt per million, relatively high numbers of microbes were present – which seems incredible! But the point is that at those levels of salt, the temperature could drop to minus 56 degrees before frost would cause any damage to the organisms.

This relationship between microbes and salt – at temperatures way below the normal freezing point of water – is a really significant breakthrough. As you all know, life is dependent on the availability of water in liquid form, and the role of salt at very low temperatures could be the key to survival in these kinds of conditions. Now the process at work here is called *supercooling* – and that's usually written as one word – but it isn't really understood as yet, so, there's a lot more for researchers to work on. However, the fact that this process occurs naturally in Antarctica, may suggest that it might occur in *other* places with similar conditions, including on our neighbouring planet, Mars. So, you can start to see the wider implications of this kind of research.

In short, it appears to support the growing belief that extraterrestrial life might be able to survive the dry, cold conditions on other planets after all. Not only does this research produce evidence that life *is* possible there, it's also informing scientists of the locations where it might be found. So all of this might have great significance for future unmanned space missions.

One specialist on Mars confirms the importance …

Test 2 SECTION 1   pages 38–39

Cindy: Hello, Brindall's Estate Agents here. How may I help you?

Martin: Oh, good morning, I'm ringing to see what flats you have for rent at the moment.

Cindy: Right. Can I start by just taking your name Mr em …

Martin: Hill, Martin Hill.

Cindy: Right, and are you looking for a flat for yourself or … em … a family perhaps?

Martin: Well it's for three of us: myself and two friends – we're going to share together.

Cindy: I see … erm, what about employment – are you all students?

Martin: Oh no, we've all got full-time jobs – two of us work in the Central Bank, that's Chris and me, and Phil – that's the other one – is working for Hallam cars, you know, at the factory about two miles out of town?

Cindy: I'll put you down as young professionals, then

– and I suppose you'll be looking for somewhere with three bedrooms?

Martin: Yeah – at least three. But actually, we'd rather have a fourth room as well – if we can afford it – for friends staying over and stuff.

Cindy: Is that with a living room to share? Plus kitchen and bathroom?

Martin: Yeah, that sounds good. But we must have a bathroom with a shower. We don't mind about having a bath, but the shower's crucial.

Cindy: OK, I'll just key that in … And, are you interested in any particular area?

Martin: Well, the city centre would be good for me and Chris, so that's our first preference … but we'd consider anything in the west suburbs as well really – actually for Phil that'd be better, but he knows he's outnumbered! But we aren't interested in the north or the east of the city.

Cindy: OK, I'm just getting up all the flats on our books.
…

Cindy: Just looking at this list here, I'm afraid there are only two that might interest you … do you want the details?

Martin: OK, let me just grab a pen and some paper … fire away!

Cindy: This first one I'm looking at is in Bridge Street – and very close to the bus station. It's not often that flats in that area come up for rent. This one's got three bedrooms, a bathroom and kitchen, of course … and a very big living room. That sounds a good size for you.

Martin: Mmmm … So, what about the rent? How much is it a month?

Cindy: The good news is that it's only four hundred and fifty pounds a month. Rents in that area usually reach up to six fifty a month, but the landlord obviously wants to get a tenant quickly.

Martin: Yeah, it sounds like a bit of a bargain. What about transport for Phil?

Cindy: Well, there'll be plenty of buses – so no problem for him to use public transport … er… but unfortunately there isn't a shower in the flat, and that location is likely to be noisy, of course …

Martin: OK – what about the other place?

Cindy: Let's see … oh yes, well this one is in a really nice location – on Hills Avenue. I'm sure you know it. This looks like something a bit special. It's got four big bedrooms and erm, there's a big living room and … oh, this will be good for you: a dining room. It sounds enormous, doesn't it?

Martin: Yeah, it sounds great!

Cindy: That whole area's being developed, and the flat's very modern, which I'm sure you'll like. It's got good facilities, including your shower. And of course it's going to be quiet, especially compared with the other place.

Martin: Better and better … but I'll bet it's expensive, especially if it's in that trendy area beside the park.

Cindy: Hmm, I'm afraid so. They're asking £800 a month for it.

Martin: Wow! It sounds a lot more than we can afford.

Cindy: Well, maybe you could get somebody else to move in too? I'll tell you what, give me your address and I can send you all the details and photos and you can see whether these two are worth a visit.

Martin: Thanks, that would be really helpful … my address is …

Test 2 SECTION 2 — pages 40–41

Good afternoon, ladies and gentlemen, and welcome to your very own tour of the British Library on this lovely afternoon. My name is Tony Walters and I'm your guide for today. Could I please see your tickets for the guided tour? I'd also like to remind you that any tickets bought today do not include a visit to the reading rooms. I'm afraid we don't do visits on Fridays – or any weekday during working hours, so as not to disturb the readers. But if you do want to see those rooms, the only day there are tours is on Sundays. So, I don't want anyone to be disappointed about that today. OK? Thank you.

Right. We'll start with a brief introduction. As many of you know, this is the United Kingdom's National Library and you can see that this is a magnificent modern building. It was first designed by Sir Colin St John Wilson in 1977, and inaugurated by Her Majesty the Queen more than twenty years later, in 1998.

As you can see, the size is immense and the basements alone have 300 kilometres of shelving – and that's enough to hold about 12 million books. The total floor space here is 100,000 square metres and, as I'll show you, the library houses a huge range of facilities and exhibition spaces, and it has a thousand staff members based here in the building – so, you can appreciate the scale of our operation.

In fact, this was the biggest publicly-funded building constructed in the United Kingdom last century. It is still funded by the government as a national institution, of course, and it houses one of the most important collections in the world. The different items come from every continent and span almost 3000 years.

The library isn't a public library, though – you can't just come in and join and borrow any of the books. Access to the collections is limited to those involved in carrying out research – so, it's really a huge reference library for that purpose, and anyone who wants to consult any materials that are kept here can formally apply to use the library reading rooms.

…

Right, well, here we are, standing at the Meeting Point on the lower ground floor just to the right of the Main Entrance. I've given you all a plan of the building so that we can orientate ourselves and get an idea of where we'll be going. Now, outside the Main Entrance you'll see the wide Piazza with the stunning sculpture of Newton. The sculptor was Paolozzi, but it's based on the famous image by William Blake – and it's definitely worth a closer look. On the other side of the Piazza from the statue is the Conference Centre, which is used for all kinds of international conventions – we'll take a quick look inside at the end of our tour.

Looking ahead of us now, you'll see that we're standing opposite the staircase down to the basement where you'll find the cloakroom, and to the left of that, we have the information desk where you can find out about any current exhibitions, the times of the tours and anything you need to know – if you don't have a tour guide. As you can see, on this lower ground floor we also have a <u>bookshop</u> – that's the area over to the left of the main entrance. You'll be free to browse there when we get back to the ground floor.

Now, opposite the main entrance on this floor we have the open stairs leading up to the upper ground floor. And at the top of them, in the middle of the upper ground floor, you can see a kind of glass-sided tower that rises all the way up through the ceiling and up to the first floor. This is called the <u>King's Library</u>. It's really the heart of the building. It was built to house the collection that was presented to the nation in 1823 by the King. You can see it from every floor above ground. When we go up there, you'll find the library's Treasures Gallery on the left. Can you find it on your <u>plan? That's the exciting one, so we'll be visiting that first, but we'll also take a look at the stamp display</u> situated behind it, on the way to the café – a lot of people miss that. The Cafeteria runs along the back of the floor and, in the right-hand corner you'll find the lifts and toilets … ha, always good to locate them. … The other main area on that floor is the Public Access Catalogue section and I'll show you how that operates when we get up there …

Test 2 SECTION 3 pages 42–43

Dr Green: Good afternoon, Dave, come on in and take a seat.

Dave: Hi, Dr Green … thanks.

Dr Green: Hang on a minute, I'll just find the first draft of your project paper and we can have a look at it together. Now yours is the one on Work Placement, isn't it?

Dave: Yeah, that's right.

Dr Green: So what made you choose that for your project?

Dave: Well, I suppose it was because sending students off to various companies for work experience seems to be such a typical part of educational courses these days – I mean, even school kids get to do it. <u>But, I felt everyone just kind of *assumes* it's a good thing … and I guess I wanted to find out if that's the case.</u>

Dr Green: But you don't look at schools or colleges, right? You've stuck to <u>university placement schemes</u>.

Dave: Yeah, well, I quickly found that I had to limit my research, otherwise the area was just too big. Do you think that was OK?

Dr Green: I think it's very sensible, especially as the objectives might be very different. So how many schemes did you look at?

Dave: Well, I sent out about 150 questionnaires altogether – you know, 50 of each to university authorities, students and companies, and I got responses from <u>15 educational institutions</u>, and, er, 30 students in 11 individual companies.

Dr Green: Great, that sounds like a good sample. And who did you send your company questionnaires to?

Dave: Well, the idea was to have them done by the <u>students' Line Managers</u>, but sometimes they were filled in by the Human Resources manager or even the owner of the company.

Dr Green: Right. I didn't find a full list anywhere, so I think

it's very important to provide that, really. You can put it as an appendix at the back.

Dave: Right, I've got a record of all <u>the respondents</u> so that'll be easy. I hope other things were OK. I mean, I've already put such a lot of work into this project, identifying the companies and so on.

Dr Green: Oh, I can tell … I think you've done a good job overall.

…

Dr Green: I thought your questionnaires were excellent, and you'd obviously done lots of background reading, but there were a few problems with the introduction … First of all, I think you need to make some slight changes to <u>the organisation</u> of your information there, at present it's a bit confused.

Dave: OK. What did you have in mind?

Dr Green: Well, you write quite a bit about Work Placement in general, but you never explain what you mean by the term.

Dave: So you think I should give a <u>definition</u>?

Dr Green: Exactly. And the introduction is the place to do it. And then … look, you start talking about what's been written on the topic – but it's all a bit mixed up with your own project.

Dave: So, do you think it would be better to have *two* sections there – like, a survey of the literature as the introduction … and then a separate section on <u>the aims of</u> my research?

Dr Green: I do. You can include your methods for collecting data in the second section too. It would be much clearer for your reader … you know, establish the background first, then how your work relates to it … it would flow quite nicely then.

Dave: Yes, I see what you mean.

Dr Green: Anyway, moving on … I like the way you've grouped your findings into three main topic areas.

Dave: Well, it became very obvious from the questionnaires that the preparation stage was really important for the whole scheme to work. So I had to look at that first. And I found a huge variation between the different institutions, as you saw.

Dr Green: I was wondering if you could give a summary at the end of this stage of what you consider to be the best practice you found … I think that would be very helpful …

Dave: Right, I'll just make a note of that. What did you think of my second set of findings – on <u>Key Skills</u> development? For me, this is the core of my whole project really …

Dr Green: And you've handled it very well. I wouldn't want you to make any changes – you've already got a nice final focus on good practice there.

Dave: Thanks.

Dr Green: Right, now I think the last part, which deals with the reasons why students *don't* learn …

Dave: What? The constraints on learning chapter?

Dr Green: Yes, that's the one – I think you need to refer to the <u>evidence</u> from your research a bit more closely here. You know, maybe you could illustrate it with quotations from the questionnaires, or even use any extracts from a student 'diary' if you can. And refer back to what you've written about good practice …

Test 2 SECTION 4 pages 44–45

When we look at theories of education and learning we see a constant shifting of views as established theories are questioned and refined or even replaced, and we can see this very clearly in the way that attitudes towards bilingualism have changed.

Let's start with a definition of bilingualism, and for our purposes today, we can say it's the ability to communicate with the same degree of <u>proficiency</u> in at least two languages. Now, in practical terms this might seem like a good thing – something we'd all like to be able to do. However, early research done with children in the USA in fact suggested that being bilingual interfered in some way with <u>learning</u> and with the development of their mental processes, and so in those days bilingualism was regarded as something to be avoided, and parents were encouraged to bring their children up as monolingual – just speaking one language. But this research, which took place in the early part of the twentieth century, is now regarded as unsound for various reasons, mainly because it didn't take into account other factors such as the children's <u>social and economic</u> backgrounds.

Now, in our last lecture we were looking at some of the research that's been done into the way children learn, into their cognitive development, and in fact we believe now that the relationship between bilingualism and cognitive development is actually a <u>positive</u> one – it turns out that cognitive skills such as problem solving, which don't seem at first glance to have anything to do with how many languages you speak, are better among bilingual children than monolingual ones.

And quite recently there's been some very interesting work done by Ellen Bialystok at York University in Canada, she's been doing various studies on the effects of bilingualism and her findings provide some evidence that they might apply to <u>adults</u> as well, they're not just restricted to children.

So how do you go about investigating something like this? Well, Dr Bialystok used groups of monolingual and bilingual subjects, aged from 30 right up to 88. For one experiment, she used a computer program which displayed either a red or a blue square on the screen. The coloured square could come up on either the left-hand or the right-hand side of the screen. If the square was blue, the subject had to press the left 'shift' key on the keyboard and if the square was red they had to press the right shift key. So they didn't have to react at all to the actual position of the square on the screen, <u>just to the colour they saw</u>. And she measured the subjects' reaction times by recording how long it took them to press the shift key, and how often they got it right.

What she was particularly interested in was whether it took the subject longer to react when a square lit up on one side of the screen – say the *left*, and the subject had to press the shift key on the *right*-hand side. She'd expected that it would take more processing time than if a square lit up on the left and the candidates had to press a left key.

This was because of a phenomenon known as the 'Simon effect', where, basically the brain gets a bit confused because of conflicting demands being made on it – <u>in this case seeing something on the right, and having to react on the left</u> – and this causes a person's reaction times to slow down.

The results of the experiment showed that <u>the bilingual subjects responded more quickly than the monolingual ones</u>. That was true both when the squares were on the 'correct' side of the screen, so to speak, and – even more so – when they were not. So, bilingual people were better able to deal with the Simon effect than the monolingual ones.

So, what's the explanation for this? Well, the result of the experiment suggests that bilingual people are better at <u>ignoring information which is irrelevant to the task in hand and just concentrating on what's important</u>. One suggestion given by Dr Bialystok was that it might be because someone who speaks two languages can suppress the activity of parts of the brain when it isn't needed – in particular, the part that processes whichever language isn't being used at that particular time.

Well, she then went on to investigate that with a second experiment, but again the bilingual group performed better, and what was particularly interesting, and this is I think why the experiments have received so much publicity, is that in all cases, the performance gap between monolinguals and bilinguals actually increased with age – <u>which suggests that bilingualism protects the mind against decline</u>, so in some way the life-long experience of managing two languages may prevent some of the negative effects of aging. So that's a very different story from the early research.

So what are the implications of this for education …

Test 3 SECTION 1 page 66

Ralph: Hello?
Paula: Ralph, it's Paula.
Ralph: Hi.
Paula: You know I told you we could apply to the local council for money for our drama club … I've got the application form here but we need to get it back to them by the end of the week. I could send it on to you – you really ought to fill it in as president of the club – but I don't know if it'll get to you in time.
Ralph: Well, you're the secretary, so I expect it's OK if you fill it in.
Paula: Yeah … but I'd really like to check it together.
Ralph: Right. That's fine.
Paula: Like the first part asks for the main contact person – can I put you there?
Ralph: Sure.
Paula: Right. So that's Ralph Pearson … and then I need your contact address, so that's <u>203 South Road, isn't it</u>?
Ralph: <u>No, 230</u> …
Paula: Sorry, I always get that wrong … Then it's Drayton … do you think they need a postcode?
Ralph: Better put it – it's DR6 8AB
Paula: Hmm mmm, OK … telephone number, that's 01453 586098 isn't it?

Ralph: Yes.

Paula: Right. Now, in the next part of the form I have to give information about our group … so, name of group, that's easy, we're the Community Youth Theatre Group, but then I have to describe it. So, what sort of information do you think they want?

Ralph: Well, they need to know we're amateurs, not professional actors … and how many members we've got – what's that at present – twenty?

Paula: Eighteen … and, should we put in the age range, that's 13 to 22?

Ralph: No, I don't think we need to. But we'd better put a bit about what we actually do … something like 'members take part in drama activities'.

Paula: Activities and workshops?

Ralph: OK.

Paula: Right. That's all for that section I think.

…

Paula: Now, the next bit is about the project itself – what we're applying for funding for. So first of all they need to know how much money we want. The maximum's £500.

Ralph: I think we agreed we'd ask for £250, didn't we?

Paula: OK. There's no point in asking for too much – we'll have less chance of getting it. Then, we need to say what the project … erm, the activity is.

Ralph: Right – so we could write something like 'to produce a short play for young children'.

Paula: Should we say it's interactive?

Ralph: Yes, good idea …

Paula: Right … I've got that. Then we have to say what we actually need the money for …

Ralph: Isn't that it?

Paula: No, we have to give a breakdown of details, I think.

Ralph: Well, there's the scenery.

Paula: But we're making that.

Ralph: We need to buy the materials, though.

Paula: OK. Then there's the costumes.

Ralph: Right. That's going to be at least £50.

Paula: OK. And what else … oh, I just found out we have to have insurance … I don't think it'll cost much, but we need to get it organised.

Ralph: Yes … I'd forgotten about that, and we could be breaking the law if we don't have it. Good thing we've already got curtains in the hall, at least we don't have to worry about that.

Paula: Mmm. We'll need some money for publicity – otherwise no one will know what we're doing.

Ralph: And then a bit of money for unexpected things that come up – just put 'sundries' at the end of the list.

Paula: OK, fine. Now the next thing they want to know is if they give us the grant, how they'll be credited.

Ralph: What do they mean, credited?

Paula: I think they mean how we'll let the public know that they funded us … they want people to know they've supported us, it looks good for them.

Ralph: Mmm. Well, we could say we'd announce it at the end of the play. We could make a speech or something.

Paula: Hmm, they might prefer to see something in writing … we'll be giving the audience a programme, won't we – so we could put an acknowledgement in that?

Ralph: Yeah, that's a better idea.

Paula: OK. And the last thing they want to know is if we've approached any other organisations for funding, and what the outcome was.

Ralph: Well, only National Youth Services … and they said that at present funds were not available for arts projects.

Paula: Right, I'll put that … and then I think that's it. I'll get that in the post straight away … I really hope we get the money.

Ralph: I think we've got a pretty good chance … hope so anyway. Thanks for doing all this, Paula.

Paula: That's OK … See you soon … Bye.

Ralph: Bye.

Test 3 SECTION 2   pages 67–68

Rob: Joanne?

Joanne: Hi – you must be Rob. Nice to meet you. So, I hear you're planning to visit Australia.

Rob: Yeah – and I really wanted to talk to you because I was thinking of spending some time in Darwin and my sister told me you're from there.

Joanne: That's right.

Rob: So … tell me about it.

Joanne: Well … where shall I start … well, Darwin's in what they call the 'top end' 'cause it's right up at the northern end of Australia and it's quite different from the rest of Australia in terms of cultural influences – in fact it's nearer to Jakarta in Indonesia than it is to Sydney, so you get a very strong Asian influence there. That means we get lots of tourists – people from other parts of Australia are attracted by this sort of international, cosmopolitan image. And as well as that, we've got the same laidback atmosphere you get all over Australia – probably more so if anything, because of the climate. But, what a lot of the tourists don't realise until they get there is that the city's also got a very *young* population … the average age is just 29, and this makes the whole place very buzzy. Some people think that there might not be that much going on as far as art and music and dancing and so on are concerned, because it's so remote. I mean, we don't really get things like theatre and opera in the same way as cities down in the south like Sydney for example, because of the transport expenses. But in fact what happens is that we just do it ourselves – lots of people play music, classical as well as pop, and there are things like artists groups and writers groups and dance classes – everyone does something, we don't just sit and watch other people.

Rob: You said it's very international?

Joanne: Yeah, they say there's over 70 different nationalities in Darwin. For instance, there's been a Chinese population there for over 100 years – we've even got a Chinese temple. It was built way back in 1887, but, erm, when a very bad storm – a … a cyclone in fact – hit Darwin in the 1970s it was almost completely destroyed. The only parts of the temple that survived were part of the altars and the stone lions, but after the storm they reconstructed it using modern materials … it's still used as a religious centre today, but it's open to tourists too and it's definitely worth going to see. Oh, and as far as getting around goes, you'll see places that advertise bicycles for hire, but I wouldn't recommend it. A lot of the year it's just so hot and humid. Some tourists think it'll be fine because there's not much in the way of hills, and the traffic's quite light compared with some places, but, believe me, you're better off with public transport – it's fine, and not expensive. Or you can hire a car, but it's not really worth it.

Rob: What's the swimming like?

Joanne: Well, there are some good beaches, but the trouble is that there's this nasty creature called the box jellyfish and if it stings you, you're in bad trouble. So you have to be very careful most of the year especially in the winter months … you can wear a lycra suit to cover your arms and legs, but I wouldn't like to risk it even so, personally. And there are the salt water crocodiles too … I mean, I don't want to put you off, there are protected swimming areas netted off where you'll be safe from jellyfish and crocs, or there are the public swimming pools, they're fine of course.

…

Rob: So which places would you specially recommend?

Joanne: Well, one of the most popular attractions is called 'Aquascene'. What happens is every day at high tide hundreds of fish come in from the sea – all different sorts, including some really big deep-sea fish – and some of them will even take food from your hand. It's right in the middle of town, at the end of the Esplanade. It's not free – I think you have to pay about five dollars – but it's definitely something you have to experience. Then of course Darwin has a great range of food, being such a cosmopolitan place. And if you don't have lots to spend, the best place to go is to Smith Street Mall where they have stalls selling stuff to eat, there's all sorts of different things including south-east Asian dishes, which I really like. You'd think there'd be plenty of fresh fish in Darwin as it's on the coast, but in fact because of the climate it mostly gets frozen straight away, but you can get fresh fish in the restaurants on Cullen Bay Marina – it's a nice place to go for a special meal, and they have some good shops in that area too. What else … well, there's the botanic garden; it's over a hundred years old and there's lots to see – an orchid farm, rainforest, a collection of palm trees, erm, a wetlands area … you can easily spend an afternoon there. That's at Fannie Bay, a couple of kilometres out to the north. Then, if you've got any energy left in the evening, the place to go is Mitchell Street – that's where it all happens as far as clubs and music and things are concerned – you'll bump into lots of my friends there! … Talking of friends, why don't I give you some email addresses. I'm sure they …

Test 3 SECTION 3 pages 69–70

Dr Blake: Come in. Ah yes, Stella … is Phil there too? Good. Come on in. OK, so you're here to discuss your research project. Have you decided what to focus on? You were thinking of something about the causes of mood changes, weren't you?

Stella: Yes, but the last time we saw you, you suggested we narrowed it down to either the effects of weather or urban environment, so we've decided to focus on the effects of weather.

Dr Blake: Right. That's more manageable. So, your goal is … ? Phil?

Phil: To prove the hypothesis … no, to *investigate* the hypothesis that the weather has an effect on a person's mood.

Dr Blake: Mmm. Good. And what's your thesis? Stella?

Stella: Well, our thesis is that in general, when the weather's good it has a positive effect on a person's mood and bad weather has a negative effect.

Dr Blake: Mmm. Can you define your terms here – for example, what do you mean by 'good' and 'bad'?

Phil: OK. Well, good would be sunny, warm weather and bad would be when it's cold and cloudy or raining.

Dr Blake: And how would you define an effect on a person's mood? What would you be looking to find?

Phil: An effect on the way a person feels …

Dr Blake: Mmm?

Stella: A change in the way they feel? Erm, like from feeling happy and optimistic, to sad and depressed.

Dr Blake: Right. And what sort of weather variables will you be looking at?

Phil: Oh, sunshine, temperature, cloudiness, precipitation among others. It'll depend a bit what the weather's like when we do the survey.

Dr Blake: Fine. We'll talk about that in a minute. But first, what about background reading? I gave you some suggestions – did you manage to read any of it?

Stella: Yes – we read the Ross Vickers article – the one comparing the groups of American Marines training in summer and winter. That's quite relevant to our study. It was interesting because the Marines who were training in the cold winter conditions tried to cheer themselves up by thinking of warm places, but it didn't really work.

Phil: Yes, they were trying to force themselves to have a positive mental outlook but in fact it had the opposite effect, and they ended up in a very negative state of mind.

Stella: And we found some more research by someone who wasn't on the reading list you gave us – George Whitebourne. He compared people living in three countries with very different climatic conditions. Actually he looked at several things, not just the weather, but he found some people's reactions to bad weather were much worse than others and it was linked to how stressed they were generally – the weather on its own didn't have such a significant effect on mood.

Phil: And we looked at a paper by Haver …

Stella: Haverton.

Phil: Yeah. He broke weather up into about fifteen or sixteen categories and did qualitative and quantitative research … he found that humans respond to conditions in the weather with immediate responses, such as fear or amazement, but these responses can also be linked to associations from their earlier life, such as a particular happy or sad event.

Dr Blake: Did you have a look at Stanfield's work?

Stella: Yes. It was interesting because the type of questions he asked were similar to what we were planning to use in our survey.

Dr Blake: Yes?

Stella: He asked people how they were feeling on days with good and bad weather. <u>He found the biggest factor seemed to be the humidity – moods were most negative on days with a lot of rainfall.</u> Long periods without sunshine had some effect but nothing like as much.

Dr Blake: Mmm. That could be quite a useful model for your project.

Phil: Yes, we thought so too – although we can't continue our survey for as long as he did – he did his over a six-month period.

…

Dr Blake: Right, well, you've made quite a good start. So, where are you going from here?

Phil: Well, we've already made the questionnaire we're going to use for the survey – it's quite short, just eight questions. We're aiming to survey twenty people, over a period of three months from October to December.

Stella: <u>We can't specify the actual dates yet</u>, because it depends on the weather – we want to do the survey on days with a range of different weather conditions. And we'll just be working on campus, so our data will only be statistically sound for the student population here.

Dr Blake: That's OK. Have you thought how you'll determine what will constitute each aspect of weather … and how many you're looking at?

Phil: We decided on four – the amount of sunshine, cloudiness, temperature and precipitation … we thought <u>we might use the Internet to get data on weather conditions on the days we do the survey but we haven't found the information we need, so we might have to</u> measure it ourselves. We'll see.

Stella: Then we've got to analyse the results, and we'll do that using a spreadsheet, giving numeric values to answers …. and then of course we have to present our findings to the class, and we want to make it quite an interactive session, we want to involve the class in some way in the <u>presentation … maybe by trying to create different climatic conditions in the classroom, but we're still thinking about it</u>.

Dr Blake: I see. Well, that sounds as if you're on the right lines. Now, what I'd suggest that you think about …

Test 3 SECTION 4   pages 71–72

All over the world, there are passionate arguments going on about how educational systems can be improved. And of all the ideas for improving education, few are as simple or attractive as reducing the number of pupils per teacher. It seems like common sense – but do these ideas have any theoretical basis? Today, I want to look at the situation in the USA, and at some of the research that has been done here in America on the effects of reducing class sizes.

In the last couple of decades or so, there has been considerable concern in the United States over educational standards here, following revelations <u>that the country's secondary school students perform poorly relative to many Asian and European students</u>. In addition, statistics have shown <u>that students in the nation's lower-income schools in the urban areas have achievement levels far below those of middle-class and upper-middle-class schools</u>.

So would reducing class sizes solve these problems? Well, we have to remember that it does have one obvious drawback: it's expensive. It requires more teachers and possibly more classrooms, equipment, and so on. On the other hand, if smaller classes really do work, the eventual economic benefits could be huge. <u>Better education would mean that workers did their jobs more efficiently</u>, saving the country millions of dollars. It would also mean that people were better <u>informed about their health, bringing savings in things like medical costs and days off sick</u>.

So what reliable information do we have about the effects of reducing class sizes? There's plenty of anecdotal evidence about the effect on students' behaviour. But what reliable evidence do we have for this?

Let's have a look at three research projects that have been carried out in the USA in the last couple of decades or so. The first study I'm going to look at took place in the state of Tennessee in the late 1980s. It involved some 70 schools. In its first year about 6,400 students were involved, and by the end of the study, four years later, the total number involved had grown to <u>12,000</u>. What happened was that students entering kindergarten were randomly assigned to either small classes of 13 to 17 students or regular-size classes of 22 to 26. The students remained in whatever category they had been assigned to through the third grade, and then after that they joined a regular classroom.

After the study ended in 1989, researchers conducted dozens of analyses of the data. Researchers agree that there was significant benefit for students in attending smaller classes, and it also appears that the beneficial effect was stronger for <u>minority</u> students. However, there's no agreement on the implications of this – we still don't know the answer to questions like how long students have to be in smaller classes to get a benefit and how big that benefit is, for example.

The second project was much larger and took place in California. Like the Tennessee study, it focused on students from kindergarten through to grade 3, but in this case, <u>all schools</u> throughout the state were involved. The experiment is still continuing, but results have been very inconclusive, with very little improvement noted. And the project has in fact also had several negative aspects. It meant an increased demand for <u>teachers</u> in almost all California districts, so the better-paying districts got a lot of the best teachers – including a fair number that moved over from the poorer districts. And, there were a lot of other problems with the project – for example, there weren't any effective procedures for <u>evaluation</u>. All in all, this project stands as a model of what *not* to do in a major research project.

A third initiative took place in the state of Wisconsin at around the same time as the California project began, and it's interesting to compare the two. The Wisconsin project was small – class sizes were reduced in just 14 schools – but it was noteworthy because it targeted schools at which a significant proportion of the students were from <u>poor</u> families, compared with California's one-size-fits-all approach. Analysts have found that the results are very similar to the Tennessee project, with students making gains that are statistically significant – and that are considerably larger than those calculated for the California initiative.

Now, I'd like to apply some of these ideas to …

Test 4 SECTION 1 pages 88–89

Jacinta: Hi, Lewis – it's Jacinta here.

Lewis: Oh, hi, Jacinta. I was just going to call you. I was thinking we ought to do something about accommodation for our trip to Queenstown.

Jacinta: Yeah, actually that's just why I rang you. I've been looking on the Internet – there was one place that looked OK called Travellers' Lodge, but when I checked availability for January when we're planning to go I found it was fully booked.

Lewis: Right – well, we'd better do something now I suppose.

Jacinta: I've actually got a list up here on the computer – there's one place called Bingley's that looks possible. It's 19.75 dollars a night – that's US dollars, they quote all the prices in US dollars.

Lewis: So that's about 26 or 27 New Zealand dollars. That's OK. That'll be in a dormitory, is it?

Jacinta: Yeah – they say 8-bed dorms. And the hostel's right in the town centre and they've got a café … they have theme nights every weekend, whatever that means …

Lewis: Oh, you know, like certain sorts of food and music … and people might wear special clothes like that Egyptian evening we went to last year.

Jacinta: Oh, OK. What else … they've got a sundeck area, and then all the usual things – Internet access and so on.

Lewis: Sounds good. Was there anywhere else?

Jacinta: Yeah, a couple more places. There's one called Chalet Lodge which is just 18.00 US dollars – that's for a bed in a 12-bed dorm. They do single and family rooms as well. It looks as if it's a bit out of town … says it's got an alpine setting … a 'quiet' alpine setting. What do you think?

Lewis: Mmm, not sure …

Jacinta: Oh, but actually it's not far out at all … it says 10 minutes' walk from town, so … Oh, and it says it's 'children friendly'.

Lewis: Mmm. I'm not so sure about that. What about the third place?

Jacinta: Aah. That's called Globetrotters – let's see, they do private rooms, or 5-bed dorms for 18.50 – it's in the centre, just by the lake … and that includes breakfast.

Lewis: Didn't the other two?

Jacinta: I don't think so. They didn't mention it, so probably not. Oh, and it says something about a free skydive … wow!

Lewis: Don't know if I'm all that keen on jumping out of aeroplanes …

Jacinta: Oh, actually what it says is you can win a chance to do a skydive – they give one away every day to one of the guests.

Lewis: Well, if I win it, you can do it … Anyway, do they have room?

Jacinta: Yeah, I checked the availability. Shall I go ahead and book there then?

Lewis: Fine.

…

Jacinta: I was looking at what there is to do, too … there are lots of sites offering deals for adventure sports – ah, I suppose we have to do a bungee jump.

Lewis: Why?

Jacinta: Well, it's Queenstown where they more or less started it as a sport.

Lewis: You can … if you really want to jump off the side of a bridge with an elastic rope tied round your ankles. I'll watch!

Jacinta: OK. So what do you want to do?

Lewis: As far as adventure sports go? I was talking to someone who went white-water rafting there – he said it was really awesome. They drive you up the Shotover River and then you come down on a rubber raft through the white-water rapids, where the river's really narrow and fast, and end up going through a tunnel nearly 200 metres long. I think it's quite expensive, though.

Jacinta: Oh, I'm on for that if you are.

Lewis: Cool!

Jacinta: The other thing you can do is the jet-boat ride … that sounded just a lot of noise though. It's basically just whizzing round on the river on a very fast boat, isn't it?

Lewis: My friend did that as well – he said it was a bit touristy but worth it, I'll give it a go. You go right up the river canyon. He said the drivers were really skilful. But I don't mind going on my own.

Jacinta: But there's lots to do as well as the whole commercial adventure bit … we ought to do some trekking. The scenery round there's amazing, I don't want to miss that. The place to start's Glenorchy, apparently – about 40 minutes' drive, that's where lots of the wilderness trails begin.

Lewis: OK, I'll pack my walking boots. I'd better start getting in training … I haven't done anything except sit at my desk for months. Now, is there anything else we need to decide?

Test 4 SECTION 2 pages 90–91

Announcer: There's been a great deal of interest lately in encouraging people to use bicycles instead of cars as a means of transport. But not everyone is confident about riding a bike at the best of times, let alone in the middle of a city like London. Jack Hays is a professional trainer who works for a London-based company, CitiCyclist, which provides cycle training for the public. What exactly does CitiCyclist do, Jack?

Jack: Well, our basic purpose is to promote cycling as a sustainable form of transport. We believe the best way to promote cycling is to teach people to use their bikes safely and with confidence. In European countries, people all learned from their parents, and they also learned in school, and when I tell them I teach people to ride bikes they laugh, they think it's crazy, but here in London it's completely different, you're approaching the point where a whole generation of people have grown up not being allowed by their parents to cycle, because it was considered to be getting too dangerous, and so in turn, they can't teach their children …

We believe in realistic training, so if someone wants to use a bike regularly, say to get to work or school, <u>we aim to train them by teaching them to ride on the actual roads they'll use</u>, so they can develop the basic skills they need and build up their confidence that way.

At CitiCyclist we believe cycling's for everyone, no matter what age or level of ability or mobility. We do complete beginners and also advanced courses – that's for urban cyclists who want to deal with things like riding in <u>streets with complicated intersections</u> and things like that. We *don't* promote the use of personal protective equipment for cyclists and we endorse the policy of the European Cyclists Federation that parents should be allowed to make an informed choice as to whether or not their child wears a helmet. <u>We believe the key to safe cycling is assertiveness – taking your place on the road. This has to be instilled right from the beginning. Assertive road positioning and behaviour is the key to safe cycling in congested urban environments.</u> Some people are surprised that we don't promote the segregation of cyclists from motorised traffic, but we don't think that's practical in all urban environments. Instead, we teach people to use as much road space as they need to travel safely and effectively.

…

Now as well as courses for individuals, CitiCyclist provides a number of services for organisations. For example, we can deliver fun, safe cycle-training activities at <u>schools</u>, arranging courses so that the disruption of curriculum time is kept to a minimum. As well as this, in order to promote safe cycling we have provided training courses for employees and staff of <u>local councils</u>. And we are also increasingly looking at developing training courses in <u>companies</u> in order to help employers work towards green transport plans by helping to increase the number of staff cycling to work.

Right, so that's a brief summary of what we do. If any listeners would like to find out more about the organisation, you can have a look at our website – that's citicyclist – c-i-t-i cyclist – .co.uk. And in order to book lessons, you can either phone us on <u>020 7562 4028</u>, or do it online – there's an application form on our website, and you can just download that and send it in. We charge <u>£27.50</u> per hour for one-to-one lessons plus £6.00 for each extra person – so you're looking at just £39.50 for a family of three, say. If you've never been on a bike in your life before, we reckon we can get you riding in one hour, and for most people a course of road training usually takes <u>three hours</u>. But whether you're a parent or a child, an individual or an institution, we'll be happy to discuss your special needs and make a programme just for you.

Test 4 SECTION 3   pages 92–93

Tutor: So, Sharon and Xiao Li, in your presentation last week you were talking about the digital divide – the gap between those who can effectively use communication tools such as the Internet, and those who can't. And you compared the situation here in Northern Ireland with South-East China. Right, so I asked you to do some self-evaluation, watching the video of your presentation and thinking about the three main criteria you're assessed by – content, structure and technique. What do you think was the strongest feature of the presentation, when you watched it? Sharon?

Sharon: Well, I was surprised actually, because I felt quite nervous but, when I watched the video, it didn't show as much as I expected.

Tutor: So which of the criteria would that come under?

Sharon: Er, confidence?

Tutor: That's not actually one of the criteria as such. Xiao Li?

Xiao Li: <u>Technique?</u> It's body language and eye contact, isn't it. Well, I didn't think I looked all that confident, but I think that our technique was generally good – like the way we designed and used the Powerpoint slides.

Tutor: Mmm. So you both feel happiest about that side of the presentation? OK, now on the negative side, what would you change if you could do it again?

Xiao Li: Well, at first I'd thought that the introduction was going to be the problem but actually I think that was OK. We defined our terms and identified key issues. It was more towards the end … the conclusion wasn't too bad but the problem was <u>the questions</u>, we hadn't really expected there'd *be* any so we hadn't thought about them that much.

Tutor: Uhuh. OK. Anything else?

Sharon: Well, like Xiao Li says, I thought the conclusion was OK, but when I watched us on the video I thought the section on <u>solutions</u> seemed rather weak.

Tutor: Mmm. Can you think why?

Sharon: Well, we explained what people are doing about the digital divide in China and Northern Ireland but I suppose we didn't really evaluate any of the projects or ideas, it was just a list. And that was what people were asking us about at the end, mostly.

…

Tutor: OK. Now, I also asked you to get some peer evaluation, from the other students.

Sharon: Yes, er, well, people said it was interesting, like the fact that in China the Internet was used more for shopping than in Northern Ireland. <u>They said sometimes it was a bit hard to understand because we were talking quite fast … but we didn't think so when we watched the video.</u>

Tutor: No, it's a bit different though, because you know all this information already. Mmm. If you're hearing it for the first time, you need more time to process it … that's why signposting the structure and organisation of the talk is important.

Xiao Li: That seemed OK, no one mentioned that as a problem. <u>Some people said that we could have had more on the slides … like some of the other groups had nearly everything they said written up on the visuals as well, but other people said the slides were good, they had just the key points …</u>

Tutor: Yes.

Sharon: And most people said we had quite good eye contact and body language. They all pointed out we'd over-run … they all said we were five minutes over but we timed it afterwards on the video and it was only three minutes.

Xiao Li: We were a bit unsure about the background reading at first, but I think we did as much as we could in the time … anyway, no one commented on that under content, but one thing that did come out was that they liked the fact we'd done research on both Northern Ireland and China – most other people had just based their research on one country. We managed to get quite a lot of data from the Internet, although we had to do our own analysis and we did our own surveys as well in both countries. So the class gave us best feedback for content but it was all OK.

Tutor: Right. Well, that's quite similar to the feedback I'm giving you. I was very impressed by the amount of work you'd done and by your research methodology … so, actually, I'm giving you full marks for content, five. The structure of the presentation was good, but not quite as good as the content, so, I gave that four, and the same for technique. So, well done.

Xiao Li/Sharon: Thank you.

Tutor: Now, the next stage is to write up your report. So, just a few pointers for you here. First of all, in your presentation I think your ending was rather abrupt – you suddenly just stopped talking. It wasn't a big problem but think about your closing sentences in your report – you want to round it off well. One thing I forgot to mention earlier was that I felt a very strong point was that after you'd given your results, you explained their limitations.

Xiao Li: The fact that we didn't have a very reliable sample in terms of age in China?

Tutor: Yes, that section. So don't forget to include that. And you had some excellent charts and diagrams, but maybe you could flesh out the literature review a bit – I can give you some ideas for that later on if you want. OK, is there anything else you want to ask?

Xiao Li/Sharon: No … Thank you. / Thanks.

Test 4 SECTION 4 page 94

Well, Adam's just been talking about some of the problems that have resulted from the rapid growth of cities in the last hundred years – things like housing, sanitation, crime, and so on. For my presentation, I'd like to look at some examples of what cities are doing to try to *solve* some of these problems.

As part of its healthy city programme, the World Health Organisation – the WHO – has come up with a set of criteria for a healthy city. The WHO says, that amongst other things, a healthy city must provide a clean environment which is also safe – it mustn't be dirty, or dangerous for its inhabitants. As well as that, the WHO says a healthy city has got to be able to satisfy its inhabitants' basic needs – that's *all* its inhabitants, not just the rich ones or the ones with jobs. Everyone who lives there. A third thing … a third criterion, is that it's got to have health services which can be used by all the inhabitants, and which they can access easily. The final point's to do with local government – the WHO says this is something that the whole community should be involved in, not just a few powerful politicians or businessmen. So, a healthy city's not just a matter of avoiding illness, that sort of 'healthiness', it's the way that the whole city works together for the benefit of its population.

OK. So what I'd like to do now is to look at some projects in different cities around the world where cities have tried to meet these criteria – to make their cities 'healthy' ones.

Right, the first project I'm going to discuss took place in Sri Lanka, and this project was called the 'Community Contracts System'. Its aim was to improve the places where the poorest section of the population lived – the squatter settlements. Basically, the problem was lack of infrastructure – things like drains, paths, wells for water and so on. So, a programme was set in place to construct this infrastructure, but what was different about it was that the residents did this – the people who actually lived there, not people from outside. And this meant that not only did the people end up with improved housing and infrastructure, but also because they had contracts with the community, it improved their chances from an economic point of view. So that's a way the lives of people in one urban environment were improved.

The next project I'd like to discuss took place in the capital city of Mali, in West Africa. This project involved setting up a cooperative to try to solve the problems of sanitation in the old central quarters of the city. One of the main problems was a lack of a system for garbage collection, which meant that there were a lot of insects, and this was causing disease. And again it's interesting to look at who was involved in dealing with this problem – in this case, the cooperative involved students who had graduated from secondary school in getting a system going. As well as that, the cooperative set up a campaign to educate the public about the importance of good sanitation, through showing films and setting up discussion groups among the local people, especially women and adolescents. And the outcome was an increased environmental awareness which led to changes in household behaviour as well as improved living conditions.

OK, the third project was in Egypt, just outside the capital, Cairo, which is a city that's grown very rapidly in the last few decades. This project was based in a Women's Centre in a poor area called Mokattam. The aim of the project was to support girls … young women from the area from poor families, so these were women who had no education – they'd never been to school, so they were totally illiterate, and they had no chance of getting jobs. At the Women's Centre, they were shown how to sew and how to weave, and once they'd learned these skills they were given the equipment – a sewing machine or a loom – so that they could make things to sell, and have a chance of earning their own living. And this project has meant that these young women have greater status in the community, but as well as that, they can enjoy a better quality of life.

So I don't think the problem is that cities are bad. This world and its cities have the resources to provide for the population that lives there. What it takes is a stronger will and a better distribution of resources.

Woman: Erm … I'm interested in doing some work for the library – are you the person to speak to?

Librarian: Yes. Right, well, erm, what sort of work are you interested in?

Woman: I've just come to live here in Australia … I don't want a full-time job until my children have settled down, but I really need to get out of the house a bit, and I heard you need <u>voluntary workers</u> for various projects … ?

Librarian: Right.

Woman: … but I don't know if I have the right skills.

Librarian: Well, we do provide training.

Woman: Oh.

Librarian: We always include an orientation to the library, together with emergency procedures, that's fire regulations, emergency exits, <u>first aid so you can cope with accidents or sudden illness</u>, things like that which are necessary for anyone who's working with the public. Then we give specialist training for particular projects – like using our database system.

Woman: I do have quite good computer skills, in fact.

Librarian: Umm. Great.

Woman: Is there any sort of dress requirement?

Librarian: Well, all staff have to wear a name badge – so they can be identified if they go outside the 'staff only' areas. But apart from that there aren't many regulations – <u>we ask you to sign in and sign out</u> for insurance purposes, but that's all. How about transport – do you live locally?

Woman: Not too far away. I'm at Porpoise Beach. My husband needs the car during the day but it's only about twenty minutes <u>on the bus</u>.

Librarian: <u>In fact, we can reimburse part of your travel expenses in that case.</u>

Woman: Oh. Would that be the same if I came by car?

Librarian: No, because parking is such a problem here. One thing we are looking for though is someone who can drive a minibus.

Woman: No problem. So, do the projects involve going outside the library?

Librarian: Some, yes. But not all. We've just finished one which involved working with photographs taken of the area 50 or 100 years ago – it basically involved <u>what we call encapsulation</u> …

Woman: <u>Putting them in some sort of covers to keep them safe?</u>

Librarian: Exactly. It's time-consuming work, and we were very grateful to have help with it. Then, sometime next year we're hoping to begin working on an initiative involving the sorting and labelling of objects relating to local history. We'll be needing help with the cataloguing.

Woman: I'd definitely be interested. How about at present?

Librarian: Well, we have a small team who work to support those who are unable to read.

Woman: Working with the blind?

Librarian: Yes, or other groups who have reading difficulties. <u>We provide volunteers with equipment so that they can take books home with them and read them aloud onto CDs.</u> We're gradually building up a collection that can be lent to those who need them.

Woman: Mmm. I can see it would be useful, but I'd really like to do some sort of work where I can get the chance to meet people. How about reading stories to children?

Librarian: Mmm. That's done by our regular staff. But we do have another project – it's a very long-established scheme which <u>involves helping those who are unable to have direct access to the library</u>.

Woman: <u>Oh, I noticed someone with a trolley of books when I was at the hospital</u> last week. That sort of thing?

Librarian: That would have been one of ours, yes. It's one of our most popular services – lots of people who wouldn't dream of going to the library normally, when they're at home, borrow a book when the trolley comes round the ward.

Woman: I can imagine. Yes, I'd definitely be interested in that. Right, so how do I enrol?

Librarian: Well, we do ask all volunteers to commit themselves to a regular period each week.

Woman: I could probably do five or six hours …

Librarian: Oh … be careful not to take on too much – but we do need someone for a couple of afternoons from 2 to 4 … so <u>four hours</u> altogether.

Woman: That sounds fine.

…

Librarian: Right, so here's the application form … it asks the usual questions, name and address and telephone number. <u>You also need to fill in details of who we should get in touch with in case of any accident or problem like that</u>, we do need to have that filled in, and there's a space for date of birth, but that's only if you're over 75 so, we won't worry about that.

Woman: No. Oh, it asks for qualifications – do I need to provide certificates?

Librarian: They're not necessary. We'll need <u>the names of two referees</u> – not relatives or family members, obviously. What else … signature of parent or guardian – that won't be necessary as I assume you're over 18?

Woman: Yes. What's this? It says 'civil conviction check'.

Librarian: That's a document we have to provide by law for those working on projects involving children, so we won't need it in your case. But you will need to sign this separate document – that's <u>a copy of commitment</u>; it's basically an agreement to work according to the library guidelines. So, if you'd like to fill this all in – you can do it here, or take it home, whichever you prefer.

Woman: I'll take it home if that's OK. Right, well thank you for your time …

Test 5 SECTION 2   page 111

Good morning, folks, and welcome to the Information Round-up on your own local radio station! This is Larry Knowles talking to you this morning on Tuesday 25th May … and the first item coming up is a reminder to you all out there about Canadian Clean Air Day – which is on <u>June 6th</u>.

In case you weren't around for the last one, this is a chance for Canadians everywhere to focus on the problems of air pollution and to actually try to *do* something to help reduce the problem.

How many Canadians do you think die annually because of air pollution? 2000? 3000? Well, the rate is a staggering 5000 and, it's likely to grow – unless we do something. And, it's this concern with *your* health that's the driving force behind the government campaign that is sponsoring Clean Air Day.

So what causes air pollution in the first place? Well, the transportation sector accounts for 27 percent of all greenhouse gases produced in Canada. It's also the biggest source of that thick, polluted air from traffic fumes that we call smog. And it's the tiny particles and ground-level ozone in smog that are the main causes of health problems, and even deaths, across the country. Of course, it's worse in the big cities … but researchers have only recently realised that all you need are low levels of air pollution to seriously damage your health, so we're all at risk.

…

So, what can we do to fight air pollution? Well, it should be pretty obvious by now that the way we get to and from work every day can have a big impact on the air we breathe. So the easiest action you can take on Clean Air Day is to accept what we call the 'Commuter Challenge' and get to work on foot or by cycling for a change. If you have to use your car, try 'car-pooling' and share the drive, or better still, use public transit. If everyone tries this for just one day, you'll be amazed by the difference it can make to the air in our towns and cities.

But, there's more you can do to improve air quality. For example, you can plant trees. And if you don't have a garden, then you can do your bit in other ways. For instance, did you know that modern, improved wood stoves can reduce wood smoke by as much as 80–90 percent? So you can make a big difference if you upgrade the appliances you use in your home.

The government is also working hard on your behalf to clean up our air. Its priority is to reduce the emissions that cause smog – and they have clear plans to get there. Last year, Canada and the United States agreed to reduce emissions on both sides of the border between the two countries … and they plan to reach their targets in the next few years.

The government's also taking action to get cleaner fuels. It's already reduced the sulphur contained in gasoline, and it hopes to reach the reduction target for sulphur in diesel by next year. But the measures don't just focus on the motorist – the federal government's also working to reduce emissions from power plants and factories right across the provinces.

You can find out all about government action and all the plans for Clean Air Day events …

Test 5 SECTION 3   page 112

Jack: Katy, hi. Thanks for inviting me round.
Katy: Thanks for coming … I know you're up to your neck in finals revision, but I've got to make up my mind about next year's Geography field trip and I'd really like your advice. We've got to choose between an African trip and one in Europe. They've told us a bit about both trips in the lecture but I really can't make up my mind, and I know you did the African one last year.
Jack: That's right.
Katy: So, where exactly did you go? I mean, I know it was in Kenya, in East Africa …
Jack: Yes, well, we were right up in the north-west of the country. It was beautiful. We stayed in a place called the Marich Pass Field Studies Centre.
Katy: Right. Dr Rowe said the accommodation was traditional African-style cottages … er, he had a special name for them …
Jack: Bandas. Yes, they're fine. You have to share – two or three people together. They're pretty basic but you have a mosquito net. They don't provide spray though so remember to take plenty with you – you'll need it! And there's no electricity in the Field Centre – you'll have hurricane lamps instead. They give a good light, it's no problem.
Katy: What about places to study? Dr Rowe said there was a library …
Jack: Yes, but it's quite small. There's a lecture room as well – but most of us worked out in the open air, there are plenty of places outside. And it's so beautiful – you're right in the middle of the forest clearing.
Katy: I gather it's a relatively unmodernised area?
Jack: Definitely. They actually set up the centre there because it's on the boundaries of two distinct ecological zones – the mountains, where the people are mainly agriculturalists, and the semi-arid plains lower down, where they're semi-nomadic pastoralists.
…
Katy: So, how much chance did you get to meet the local people there? Did you get the chance to do interviews?
Jack: Yes – though we had to use local interpreters. But that was OK. Then we did field observation, of course, looking at environmental and cultural conditions, and morphological mapping.
Katy: What's that?
Jack: Oh. Looking at the surface forms of the landscape, the slope elements and so on.
Katy: What about specific projects?
Jack: Yes. After the first two or three days, we spent most of our time on those. We could pretty well do what we wanted, although they all had to relate to issues concerned with development in some way. People did various things … some were based on social and cultural topics, like the effect of education on the aspirations of young people, and some did more physical process-based studies, looking at things like soil erosion. My group actually looked at issues relating to water, things like sources such as rivers and wells, and quality and so on. It was a good project to work on but, a bit frustrating – we felt we needed a lot more time really.
Katy: Right. Dr Rowe did say something about limiting project scope.
Jack: Yes, he told us that too at the beginning and I can see why now. What else … well, we had some good trips out as part of the course. We went to a market town – a place called Sigor – that was to study distribution – and to look at agricultural production we went to the Wei Wei

valley, that's an important agricultural region.

Katy: And what about animals? Did you have a chance to go to a national park?

Jack: Sure, we did a trip on the last day, on the way back to the airport at Nairobi. But actually there was lots of wildlife at the Field Centre – vervet monkeys and baboons and lizards …

Katy: Mmm. It does sound good.

Jack: It was excellent, I'd say. In terms of logistics it was very well run, but it was more than that – I mean, it's not the sort of place I'd ever have got to on my own, and it was a real eye-opener – it got me really interested in development issues and the way other people live. I did find it frustrating at the time that we couldn't get as far as we wanted on the project, but actually I'm going to follow it up in my dissertation, so it's given me some ideas and data for that as well.

Katy: So you'd say it was worth the extra money?

Jack: Definitely.

Test 5 SECTION 4 · pages 113–114

For my website design project, I decided to approach Supersave supermarkets, because I have an evening job at the supermarket, so I already have a slight insight into their organisational goals and workings.

The field research for my project was in two stages. First, I had an interview with Mr Dunne, who is in charge of Supersave's customer care department. I discussed the project with him in order to identify the supermarket's requirements. Mr Dunne said customers are often unwilling to make a face-to-face complaint when they've experienced difficulties with a product, or a member of staff, or anything related to the supermarket. So he said a website which allowed members of the public to get in touch with the organisation and bring the problem to their attention in a private manner might be very useful, and we agreed that I'd work on this.

For the second stage of my research, I devised a questionnaire to put to Supersave customers. I needed to find out about the customers' experiences of problems, together with their attitudes towards making complaints, both directly and indirectly. I used a mixture of closed questions such as 'Have you ever experienced a problem at any Supersave store?' and open questions such as 'What would you find helpful about a customer complaint website?'

I decided to do interviews rather than rely on distribution of the questionnaire, as I felt this was likely to lead to a higher take-up rate. I visited four Supersave stores, two in the city centre and two in the outskirts and altogether I interviewed 101 respondents. Then finally, I analysed the results.

I found the results of the questionnaires to be very informative. I found that out of the total number of customers investigated, 64 percent had at some stage encountered a problem in a Supersave store. Out of these people, the vast majority said that they hadn't reported the problem to any member of staff – they'd just kept it to themselves. The next thing I tried to find out was why they hadn't complained. Well, about 25 percent of the people I interviewed said the reason was that they couldn't be bothered, and a slightly smaller percentage said they didn't have enough time, but 55 percent said the reason was that they felt intimidated. I finally asked if they would be more likely to complain if they didn't have to do it face-to-face, and nearly everyone I asked said that they would – 95 percent, to be exact.

I then set about designing the website to meet these needs. Once I'd completed the website, I made another appointment with Mr Dunne, to find out what he thought of it.

Mr Dunne said he felt that the pages would benefit his organisation by giving customers a new way of expressing their complaints, and by making it easier to collect complaints, identify specific places where service and customer care were not as good as they should be, and act upon them accordingly. Supersave is already a highly customer-orientated organisation and he thought our website would be an excellent addition to their customer care effort.

This is all well and good but there still remains the general problem with websites, that there's a lack of access to on-line computers. Surprisingly, in my survey I found that 88 percent of those interviewed had access to the Internet, which I felt was quite high. But this access wasn't always direct – for some people it was through their children and grandchildren and neighbours and so on, rather than being readily available in their own homes. This could prove to be a major drawback to the site, but it is still better to have it now to get the edge over competitors, however slight, and in the very near future it is expected that almost everyone will have direct access to the Internet.

Another thing to consider is that at the moment I can only base our conclusions on data gathered from a tiny fraction of the supermarket's customer base. In order to get a better idea of how the site is doing and to see how well I have met my objectives, the site will need to have been up and running for at least a few months. After this time, it'll be possible to see whether or not people are actually using the site, and if it's helping to make improvements to their customer service.

It would also be interesting to study the effect of the site on staff at the supermarket. Morale could be dented, as more complaints come in. Staff may feel they are being unfairly criticised and that there is no need for another way for customers to complain. But also, the site could boost morale by making staff come together to overcome the constructive criticism, and they may gain more job satisfaction by knowing that they are making a difference to the customer.

So, overall, I feel my website has met my objectives, but there is scope for improvement and expansion. Are there any questions?

Test 6 SECTION 1 · page 128

Council Officer: Environmental Health Department, Paul speaking.

Mrs Shefford: Oh, hello. Erm, I wanted to report a vehicle that's been left parked near where I live – I think it's been abandoned. I wondered if the council could arrange to get it towed away. Have I got through to the right department?

Council Officer: Yes, you have. If I could just take a few details … your name, please?

Mrs Shefford: Mrs Shefford.

Council Officer: Thank you.

Mrs Shefford: It's not my vehicle, though … I just thought someone ought to report it.

Council Officer: No, that's fine. What I need to do is take some details first, then we can decide what to do about the problem.

Mrs Shefford: Oh, I see.

Council Officer: So the next thing I need to know is your address.

Mrs Shefford: Right. It's 41, Lower Green Street.

Council Officer: Yes …

Mrs Shefford: Barrowdale. And the post code's WH4 5JP.

Council Officer: Fine. And if I could just ask for a telephone number?

Mrs Shefford: It's 01778 552387. I'm out quite a lot, but you can just leave a message on the answerphone if you need to. Or I could give you my mobile number?

Council Officer: That's all right, don't worry. Now, could you tell me a little more about this vehicle. You say it's been abandoned?

Mrs Shefford: Well, it certainly looks like it.

Council Officer: Can you give me an idea of where it is?

Mrs Shefford: Yes. It's near the main road that goes through Barrowdale.

Council Officer: Is that the A69?

Mrs Shefford: Yes. That's right. Now, there's the primary school just towards the end of the village, and then next to that, next to the children's playground, there's a field, and it's in there.

Council Officer: Aah … I wonder how it got in there?

Mrs Shefford: There's a gate to allow farm machinery in and out. I thought something ought to be done about it – the children from the school might start playing in the vehicle and lock themselves in or something.

Council Officer: Yes, you were quite right to report it. And what type of vehicle are we talking about here?

Mrs Shefford: It's a van actually. You know, the sort with just a couple of little windows at the back.

Council Officer: Right. You don't happen to know the make and model, do you?

Mrs Shefford: Oh, yes. I went and had a look and got all the details. I thought you might need them. I'm surprised the school hasn't contacted you about it. Anyway, I wrote the details down … Er, right, it's a Catala, and the model's a Flyer 2000.

Council Officer: Is that F-L-Y-E-R?

Mrs Shefford: That's right.

Council Officer: Very good. And the colour?

Mrs Shefford: Well, it's not all that easy to see because it's absolutely filthy. And actually, it looks as if it's had a paint job at some stage … it's blue, but you can just see white underneath where it's been scratched.

Council Officer: Right. Well, I'll just make a note of the present colour. And if you could just tell me the vehicle number. Did you make a note of that?

Mrs Shefford: Oh, yes. It's S 322 GEC.

Council Officer: OK. … And it sounds as if the general condition of the vehicle isn't too good, from what you say.

Mrs Shefford: No, it's pretty poor. It wouldn't be drivable. It's got a flat tyre, and there's a crack in the windscreen. I reckon someone just wanted to get rid of it.

Council Officer: That's usually the way.

Mrs Shefford: It's been there for nearly a week … no, it must be eight days, I remember it was a Sunday morning when I noticed it. It wasn't there the day before. I walk past it most days on the way to the shops. I'd have thought the school would have reported it.

Council Officer: Does the field actually belong to the school?

Mrs Shefford: No, it's part of Hill Farm Estate.

Council Officer: Right. I'll just make a note of that. And I don't suppose you have any information about who might own the vehicle?

Mrs Shefford: No, I've no idea. So what will you do now?

Council Officer: Well, we'll come and have a look, and see if we can trace the owner. And if we can't, the vehicle will be removed as rapidly as the law permits. It could be anything up to 20 days.

Mrs Shefford: One thing I should say, I'm quite sure this doesn't belong to anyone round here. I'd definitely recognise it if it was from someone who lived here.

Council Officer: So you don't think it was anyone local. Right. I'd say at a guess we're looking at a stolen vehicle here.

Mrs Shefford: I did wonder if it might have been. You hear such a lot about car thieves nowadays.

Council Officer: Well, we certainly will be looking into that possibility. Anyway, thank you for contacting us, Mrs Shefford, and we'll keep you informed of what happens.

Mrs Shefford: Right. Thank you very much.

Council Officer: Goodbye.

Mrs Shefford: Goodbye.

Test 6 SECTION 2 page 129

Right, so here we are in Fairhaven, and we have a couple of hours to spend in this historic centre before we carry on to our motel. And as you'll know from the itinerary of our trip, we're visiting Fairhaven because of its historical links with a man called Manjiro Nakahama. So I'll begin by giving you a brief overview of his life, and then you can explore the town at your leisure.

Well, Manjiro Nakahama, as he was then known, was born in 1827 in a village by the sea in what is now Tosashimizu in Japan. And like many people in that town, he became a fisherman when he was just a youngster. One day in 1841, when he was just 14 years old, he and some others were fishing far off the coast of Japan when they were caught in a storm and shipwrecked on a small deserted island. They had to wait for six months before they were rescued by an American whale ship that had stopped at the island by chance. Four of the five Japanese were put ashore in Hawaii, but Manjiro had become friends with the captain, William Whitfield, who came from the town of Fairhaven, where we are now, and he chose to remain aboard, and to return with the boat to the USA. So Manjiro unwittingly became the first Japanese ever to set foot on American soil. He came back right here to Fairhaven with Whitfield, and stayed with the Whitfield family who paid for his education here in the town. He studied Mathematics and Geography as well as shipbuilding and navigation. But he missed his mother, and his own country, and eventually he went back to Japan where he had a responsible position as a university teacher and also served an invaluable role as interpreter during the initiation of relations between Japan and the United States in the middle of the nineteenth century.

But the most interesting thing is that the links between Tosashimizu and Fairhaven have remained and grown stronger over the years, in spite of the distance between them, and in fact the two places now have the official status of sister cities. Both places are ports, so in fact the inhabitants have a lot in common. There have been a number of visits by the inhabitants of Tosashimizu, in particular at the time of the Festival, which is held every two years here in Fairhaven to celebrate the life and achievements of John Manjiro. It takes place in the fall, and there's an ever-growing programme including drumming, singing, martial arts, and stalls selling Japanese and American food. So if you're going to be in the region around then, it's really worth a visit.

…

Now, many of the buildings that Manjiro Nakahama knew in Fairhaven are still standing today, and so if you'd just like to hand round some copies of this map I'll suggest the best route to follow to see them. OK, so if you look at the bottom of the map you can see the Millicent Library, and that's where we are now. Now to follow the John Manjiro trail, you go out of here along Center Street, and then head up Main Street until you get to Pilgrim Avenue. Go down there and turn right at the end, go straight on and just on the corner with Oxford Street you'll see a two-storey house. This is the Whitfield family house, and this is where Manjiro first stayed when he came to Fairhaven. It's still a private residence, so please respect the owner's privacy. OK. Now, if you carry on along Oxford Street, then turn left at the end, you'll come to North Street, and about half-way down there is what's known as Old Oxford School. This was the very same school that Manjiro attended when he lived here. It was considered to be the best school in town because of the quality of the building – unusually, it was built of stone – and the quality of the teaching. Nowadays it's usually closed, except on special occasions. Go on to the end of North Street and turn the corner onto Adams Street. If you follow the road down, back towards the library, you go round a couple of sharp bends and on the second of these, you can see the School of Navigation which Manjiro also attended. And if you follow the road on, you'll soon find yourself back here at the library, and I'd suggest you spend some time looking round that too, if you have any time left.

Right, now, does anyone have any questions …

Test 6 SECTION 3   pages 130–131

Dr Hilsden: Right Julia, so from your CV and portfolio, and what you've already told me, you seem to be very much the sort of person we're looking for on the postgraduate course. So tell me, you finished your Fashion Design course in London four years ago – did you think of carrying straight on and doing a higher degree at the time?

Julia: Yes – but there were financial pressures. So I ended up working in the retail industry, as you can see from my CV. And actually it was a very useful experience.

Dr Hilsden: Mmm. In what way?

Julia: Well, I was lucky to get the job with FashionNow – they're a big store, and, one of my priorities was to get as much experience as possible in different areas, so that was good because I had the chance to work in lots of different departments. And having direct contact with the customers meant I was able to see how they reacted to innovation – to new fashion ideas, because with FashionNow, a designer might show something in New York or Milan and there'll be something similar in the shop within weeks. So, that was probably the most useful thing for me.

Dr Hilsden: Right. And so what's made you decide to do a postgraduate course now?

Julia: Erm … Well, while I enjoyed working at FashionNow, and I learned a lot there, I felt … well, the way forward would have been to develop my managerial skills rather than my skills in fashion design, and I'm not sure that's what I want to do.

Dr Hilsden: Mmm, yes.

Julia: When I was doing my degree in London I'd been interested in women's wear. But I know that there's been a lot of work done in areas like new fabric construction – and, though I'm not intending to go too deeply into the technology – I'd be very interested in looking at how new fabrics could be used in children's wear, so I'd like the chance to pursue that line.

Dr Hilsden: Yes. Good. And are you at all concerned about what it's going to be like coming back into an academic context after being away from it for several years?

Julia: No, I'm looking forward to it. But I'm basically more interested in the application than the theory – or at least that's what I've found so far, and I'm hoping the course will give me the contacts and skills I need eventually to set up my own enterprise. I'm particularly interested by the overseas links that the department has.

Dr Hilsden: Yes, many of our students look overseas or to international companies for sponsorship of their projects.

…

Julia: And the facilities here look excellent. I just went to look at the library – it's really impressive. There's so much room compared with the one at my old university.

Dr Hilsden: Yes, most students find it's a good place to study. And there are linkups to other universities, of course, and all the usual electronic sources – the staff run an Information Skills Programme which we recommend all postgraduates do in the first week or two. Design students find the Special Collections particularly useful.

Julia: Yes.

Dr Hilsden: Then we have a separate Computer Centre, which has its own academic coordinator, Tim Spender – he's got a background in art design, and the ethos of the centre is that it's a studio for innovation and creativity, rather than a computer laboratory.

Julia: Oh, right. I liked the study spaces where students can sit and discuss work together – very useful for joint projects. We always had to do that sort of thing in the cafeteria when I was an undergraduate. And I read in the brochure that there's a separate resource for photography.

Dr Hilsden: Yes, it's called Photomedia. It's not just for photography, but things like digital imaging and new media. It's a resource for all our students, not just fashion design, and we encourage students to work there producing work that crosses disciplinary boundaries. It's well used – in fact, it's doubled in size since it was set up three years ago. And we also have an offshoot from that which is called Time Based Media – this is for students who want to develop their ideas in the area of the moving image or sound. That's in a new building that was specially built for it just last year, but there are plans to expand it as the present facilities are overstretched already.

Julia: Right.

Dr Hilsden: Now, is there anything you'd like to ask about the course itself?

Julia: Erm, … I know it's a combination of taught modules and a specialist project, but how does assessment fit in?

Dr Hilsden: Well, as you'd expect on a course of this nature, it's an ongoing process. The degree course has four stages, and there are what we call progress reviews at the end of each of the first three. Then the final assessment is based on your project. You have to produce a report which is a critical reflection on your work.

Julia: And is there some sort of fashion show?

Dr Hilsden: There's an exhibition. The projects aren't all focused on clothes as such, some are more experimental, so that seems more appropriate. We ask representatives of fashion companies along, and it's usually well attended.

Julia: Right. And another thing I wanted to ask …

Test 6 SECTION 4   page 131

Good afternoon, everybody … and in our second talk on social psychology I want to look at the role of laughter in our lives – something that usually gets everyone smiling from the start.

So, first of all, I'll start by looking at the actual nature of laughter. Well, when someone laughs you've got movement of the muscles of the face and the chest, and you've got sound formed when the air's forced out of the body as part of this process, so we're talking about a *physical* activity. But obviously other things are involved as well – and this is where it gets more complicated. Laughing isn't something that you normally *decide* to do, so it's not voluntary behaviour, like ordinary speech. Instead it's regulated by our instincts – rather like the singing of a bird, or the roaring of a lion. And once you start to laugh, it can be quite hard to stop – that's not always under your conscious control either.

But why *do* we laugh? Because we find something funny, most of us would say. But in fact it appears that laughter has little to do with jokes or funny stories – only about 10 percent of laughter is caused by things like that. One suggestion is that human laughter may have originally started out as a shared response to signal *relief* at the passing of danger. And it's true that even these days,

laughter's rarely an activity carried out by an individual on his or her own. In fact, people are 30 times more likely to laugh when they're with other people than when they're completely alone. Laughter still seems to be a kind of social signal, it occurs when people are in a group and they're comfortable with one another. And it seems likely that laughter can result in the creation of bonds between the people in the group.

And it's precisely because of this social aspect of laughter that people like public speakers and politicians often try to get their audience to laugh – it encourages their listeners to trust them and to connect with them. But this kind of thing – controlling the laughter of a group, that is – indicates that there's a link between laughter and power, and this is supported by several studies that indicate that bosses use humour more than their employees. And research has also shown that female listeners are likely to laugh much more if the speaker is male, so it appears that there are *gender* issues associated with how much we laugh.

I should also point out that laughter can be used as a negative signal as well as a positive one. I think we've all probably seen evidence of a group using laughter to exclude someone … to emphasise that they are not accepted. So it's not always a positive type of behaviour, either. So what all this goes to show is that laughter is a very, very complex issue.

It does appear however that laughter has definite benefits. If we look first at the psychological aspects, we know that people often tend to store negative emotions, such as anger, sadness and fear, rather than expressing them, and it seems that laughter provides a harmless way for the release of these emotions. But there are also clear *physical* effects that have been monitored too. For example, laughter is good aerobic exercise – it speeds up heart rate and respiration, and raises blood pressure; one researcher suggests that 100 laughs a day is the equivalent of 10 minutes' jogging.

Laughter also helps prevent the stress that so many people suffer from today, which results from the faster pace of life and all that goes with it. It does this by reducing the levels of hormones in the blood which are caused by stress. And, in addition, it is known to *increase* the levels of chemicals that protect the body from infection or pain and so it helps to boost the immune system. One interesting study showed that people who had had surgical operations asked for fewer pain killers if they'd been viewing comic films. In fact, research has even shown that the quality of dreams can be positively affected by laughter – a good laugh 10 minutes before going to sleep can prevent you from having bad dreams and give a much more pleasant and restorative night's sleep. So, there's now little argument that finding things funny and enjoying a good laugh is extremely beneficial to us all.

What we need to consider now are the ways in which laughter can be used as a treatment for people who …

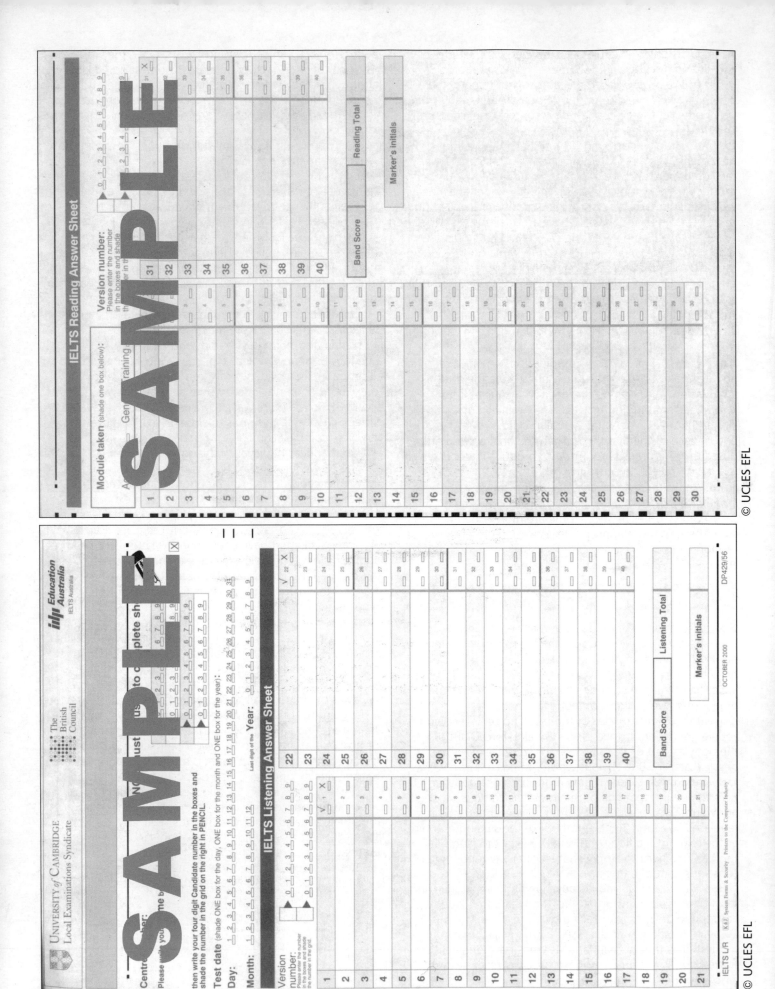